Children Act 1989 – A

Children Act 1989 - A Procedural Handbook

P M Harris,
Barrister, of the Lord Chancellor's Department

D E Scanlan,
LLB, Solicitor, Principal Clerk, Manchester City Magistrates' Court

Butterworths
London, Dublin, Edinburgh
1991

United Kingdom   Butterworth & Co (Publishers) Ltd, 88 Kingsway, LONDON WC2B 6AB and 4 Hill Street, EDINBURGH EH2 3LZ

Australia   Butterworths Pty Ltd, SYDNEY, MELBOURNE, BRISBANE, ADELAIDE, PERTH, CANBERRA and HOBART

Canada   Butterworths Canada Ltd, TORONTO and VANCOUVER

Ireland   Butterworth (Ireland) Ltd, DUBLIN

Malaysia   Malayan Law Journal Sdn Bhd, KUALA LUMPUR

New Zealand   Butterworths of New Zealand Ltd, WELLINGTON and AUCKLAND

Puerto Rico   Equity de Puerto Rico, Inc, HATO REY

Singapore   Malayan Law Journal Pte Ltd, SINGAPORE

USA   Butterworth Legal Publishers, AUSTIN, Texas; BOSTON, Massachusetts; CLEARWATER, Florida (D & S Publishers); ORFORD, New Hampshire, (Equity Publishing); ST PAUL, Minnesota, and SEATTLE, Washington.

A CIP Catalogue record for this book is available from the British Library.

ISBN 0 406 00140 5

Typeset by Kerrypress Ltd, Luton, Beds.
Printed and bound in Great Britain by Mackays of Chatham PLC.

Foreword

It is with great pleasure that I agreed to write a foreword to this book, *The Children Act 1989: A Procedural Handbook.* The Children Act 1989 is one of the most important pieces of legislation to become part of the Statute Book in recent years. The Children Act 1989 has been described by some as revolutionary. In the sense that it sets out a new philosophy and attempts to change attitudes I would endorse that description. The Act emphasises the importance of responsibilities in respect of children: the responsibility of parents for the upbringing and welfare of their children, the responsibility of local authorities to ensure that families are given such support as necessary to assist them in exercising these responsibilities and the responsibility of all of those concerned with the welfare of children to listen to what children want. The Act provides a framework for judges, lawyers, and other professional people involved in the welfare and care of children. But it does not give detailed guidance to cover every situation that might be encountered. That is why a book such as this will, I am sure, prove invaluable in assisting lawyers and other people involved in civil court proceedings concerning children to understand and follow the correct procedures. I doubt that any other piece of legislation has generated so much training and guidance material as the Children Act, but I am sure this book will soon come to be regarded as an indispensable support.

Mackay of Clashfern
C

Lord Chancellor

Preface

On 14 October 1991 the Children Act 1991 came into force creating a virtually uniform substantive and jurisdictional framework for matters relating to the care and upbringing of children. The associated rules established, with very minor variations, a uniform procedure for children cases in the High Court, county courts and magistrates' courts.

This book is a guide for lawyers and those whose work relates to civil court proceedings concerning children. It deals essentially with Parts I to V of the Children Act 1989, the procedural rules for the High Court and county courts contained in the Family Proceedings Rules 1991, Part IV (Proceedings under the Children Act) and the rules for magistrates' courts proceedings contained in the Family Proceedings Courts (Children Act 1989) Rules 1991. The purpose of the book is to provide a handy practice guide with an outline of the relevant statutory provisions and highlighting the changes which the Children Act 1989 has made to the remedies available, and procedures to be followed, in children cases.

We have sought to give a comprehensive explanation of the procedural rules, and how they apply in practice. Our aim has been to provide a step-by-step guide to what is required at each stage of the proceedings, with checklists which we hope will prove helpful. Some 69 forms are prescribed for Children Act proceedings, but even so we thought it desirable to offer precedents for written applications and requests for which no form has been prescribed by the rules. These adopt the general style and format of the prescribed forms, the objective of which is clearly intended to be to set before the relevant tribunal a comprehensive statement of information germane to the matter under consideration, which is why a questionnaire format has been adopted.

We have endeavoured to set our account of the procedure in the context of the duties of the parties, and the responsibilities of local authorities in respect of family support. With this book we hope that the practitioner will be able to ascertain quickly what he or she has to do to make progress with a client's case. Such matters as the appropriate form of application, how time limits operate and how evidential statements should be prepared, are dealt with in detail. The procedure in children cases is common to the three tiers of court (though expressed in two sets of rules), and the High Court, the county courts and the occasional necessary distinction being made for the sake of clarity. magistrates' courts are dealt with together, subject to the The book also explains local authority powers and duties where these may have a direct effect on the way in which the child and his or her family may be dealt with in the course of family proceedings.

On 14 October 1991 Parliament brought into effect a body of law and procedure which codified the law relating to the care and upbringing of children, with new remedies and new rules which had been devised after lengthy discussion and debate over a period of about 7 years. Within a few months, in about April 1992, the Child Support Act 1991 will come into force and supplant the provisions in the Children Act 1989 relating to the maintenance of children. In due course, in the large majority of cases, it will also remove this aspect of the upbringing of children from the courts and place it in the hands of the Child Support Agency. It remains to be seen whether this fragmentation of the law will enhance the welfare of the child – it seems unlikely to make the task of the courts, or lawyers and others involved in children cases, easier. In the meantime we hope this will prove to be a useful guide to every feature of proceedings under the Children Act 1989.

Peter Harris
David Scanlan
11 September 1991

Contents

Contents

Contents

Contents

Table of statutes

References in this Table to *Statutes* are to Halsbury's Statutes of England (Fourth Edition) showing the volume and page at which the annotated text of an Act may be found.

Table of statutes

Table of statutes

Table of cases

INTRODUCTION

How the Children Act 1989 came about

The origin of the Children Act 1989 is to be found in two reports, the first was concerned with relations between the child, the family and the State and the other with the upbringing of the child within the family.

In 1984 the Parliamentary Select Committee on the Social Services recommended in its report Children in Care (HC Paper (1983–84) no 360) that the government should put in hand a review of the law of child care. In July 1984 a government interdepartmental committee was set up including, unusually, a Law Commissioner and officials from the Law Commission as members. That committee (known as the Child Care Law Review) published its final report 'Review of Child Care Law', as a consultative document in September 1985. The Department of Health and Social Security carried out a review of the law relating to child care, both by public bodies and by private individuals, contemporaneously with the Child Care Law Review, and made recommendations about children's homes, fostering and child-minding.

Most of the recommendations were accepted and incorporated in the government White Paper 'The Law on Child Care and Family Services' (Cm 62). In due course these proposals were brought before Parliament as part of the Children Bill. The majority of the private law provisions of the Bill were based upon the other report, the Law Commission's Report on 'Guardianship and Custody' (Law Com no 172), part of its second programme of law reform, upon which work was begun in 1984 and completed with the publication of the report in July 1988.

The new law

The Children Act therefore represents a major overhaul of the law relating to the care and upbringing of children, save for

1

adoption (which is currently under consideration), and child abduction. Its provisions deal with the principles upon which courts are to make their decisions relating to children, orders with respect to children in family proceedings, care and supervision proceedings, the use of secure accommodation, the protection of children, community, voluntary and registered children's homes, fostering, child-minding and day care. This book, however, does not concern itself with the parts of the Act which deal with children's homes, fostering and child-minding.

The family court is a concept which has found favour in many jurisdictions, and such courts have been established in other common law jurisdictions – in recent years most notably in Australia and New Zealand. A family court was first raised as a serious proposition in the United Kingdom in the Finer Report ('Report on One Parent Families') (Cmnd 5629) in 1974. The idea has been much debated since then, and has been the subject of an interdepartmental working party which reported to Ministers in 1986. Whatever form a family court might take it would be a major undertaking for any government, and one which would not be undertaken lightly.

The Children Act 1989, while reforming the substantive law relating to children does not overturn all that has gone before, but it will pave the way for at least a unified family jurisdiction. It confers upon all three tiers of civil courts of first instance, that is the High Court, the county courts and the magistrates' family proceedings courts, a uniform jurisdiction in respect of children, subject to a few minor exceptions. Most importantly, it allows the transfer of cases between all three tiers in accordance with rules of court. The reform of the substantive law has been complemented by a reform of procedure, the underlying purpose of which is to provide, so far as possible, a uniform procedure in which the court is to take a more directive and inquisitorial role.

On 14 October 1991, therefore, a major package of reform came into effect which aims to not only improve the lot of children unfortunate enough to have become involved in the forensic process, but which may also be the precursor of a new direction in the whole of family proceedings. In an address to the Professional Associations Parliamentary Support Group on 12 June 1991 the Lord Chancellor, Lord Mackay of Clashfern, said:

'The Children Act is in many ways the test bed for the review of the family justice system. It should teach us lessons for the future and help guarantee the longer term success of the review as a whole. The principle that the welfare of the child or of children generally should be at the centre of the review is reflected in the opening statement of the Act that in decisions relating to a child's upbringing his welfare should be paramount. Indeed, it was because of the government's clear conviction that children are entitled to be treated as of the highest priority that we were led to begin the review of the family justice system.'

CHAPTER 1

An outline of the Act

Scope of the book

1.1 This book is a guide for lawyers and those whose work relates to civil court proceedings concerning children. It does not attempt to provide information for those who are concerned with community homes, voluntary homes and registered children's homes, fostering or child-minding. The outline of the Act which follows accordingly describes Parts I to V and the relevant Schedules, that is those Parts which are concerned with family proceedings. From the point of view of the legal practitioner, at whom this book is primarily (though not exclusively) aimed, perhaps the most important feature of the Act is the way in which it confers powers upon 'the court', coupled with section 92(7) which provides that: *'For the purposes of this Act 'the court' means the High Court, a county court or a magistrates' court.'* Although subsection (4) of that section prohibits a magistrates' court from dealing with property belonging to, or held in trust for, a child, or the income from it, for most practical purposes the Act confers a uniform jurisdiction throughout the court system. It therefore creates a coherent and consistent jurisdictional structure in which matters concerning children may be dealt with, and it also provides a rational and consistent set of principles and remedies to be applied in proceedings relating to the care and upbringing of a child.

PART I - GENERAL AND GUIDING PRINCIPLES

Three cardinal principles

1.2 Three cardinal principles are expressed in section 1 of the Act, and underpin the policy which it implements. Firstly, that the *child's welfare shall be the court's paramount consideration.* Secondly that *the court shall have regard to the general principle that any delay is likely to prejudice the welfare of the child* when an issue relating to the upbringing of the child has to be determined. Thirdly that the court shall not make an order under the Act in respect of a child *unless it considers that doing so would be better for the child than making no order at all*. Section 1 also requires the court, when making an opposed order relating to the care of the child to have regard to a checklist of items, most importantly the wishes and feelings of the child. It would seem to be good practice for the court to have regard to that checklist when making an unopposed or consent order, to the extent that it may be appropriate to do so in the individual case (see para **3.4**).

Parental responsibility – the concept

1.3 The statutory concept of parental responsibility is introduced in section 3, which provides a definition of 'parental responsibility', meaning – *all the rights, duties, powers, responsibilities and authority which by law a parent of a child has in relation to the child and his property*. This Part of the Act also deals with the equality of parental responsibility of a mother and a father who are married to each other, or who have been married to each other. It confers parental responsibility solely on the mother of an illegitimate child. It goes on to give the court power to confer parental responsibility on the father of an illegitimate child; alternatively the unmarried parents of a child can make a 'parental responsibility agreement' giving the father joint parental responsibility with the mother.

1.4 Provision is also made in this part for the appointment and removal, or disclaimer, of guardians, and for the making of welfare reports in proceedings under the Act, the evidence in such reports being exempted from the hearsay rule of evidence. The general principles are dealt with in greater detail in chapter 3 (see paras **3.7** to **3.9**).

PART II – ORDERS WITH RESPECT TO CHILDREN IN FAMILY PROCEEDINGS

Guardians and guardianship

1.5 The law relating to guardians has been simplified and clarified in Part I of the Children Act 1989; the appointment of a guardian is now governed solely by the provisions of section 5 of the Act and revocation or disclaimer of an appointment by section 6. A guardian is an individual who stands in place of a parent with parental responsibility for the child, and may consent, or withhold consent, to adoption. He may be appointed by a parent who has parental responsibility for the child, a guardian of the child or the court. An appointment by a parent or guardian of the child must be made in writing, dated and signed by the appointer, may appoint an individual or two or more persons jointly, and takes effect after the death of the appointer. The written appointment will often be incorporated in a will. Such an appointment will take effect immediately on the death of the appointer if there is then no parent with parental responsibility for the child, or if the appointer had a residence order in respect of the child in force at the time of his death unless the residence order was also made in favour of a surviving parent. Otherwise the appointment will take effect when the child no longer has a parent with parental responsibility for him. The court may appoint an individual to be a child's guardian if the child has no parent with parental responsibility for him, or the child was the subject of a residence order in favour of a parent or guardian who has died while that order was in force, unless the residence order was also made in favour of a surviving parent of a child. Where the application for the appointment of a guardian is made by an individual the court may appoint that individual, but the court may also appoint a guardian of its own motion in any family proceedings.

1.6 A later appointment revokes an earlier appointment (whether by unrevoked will, codicil or otherwise), unless it is clear from the terms of the appointment, or by necessary implication, that the later appointment is in addition to the earlier. An appointment may be revoked by a written, signed and dated instrument, or by destroying the appointing instrument with the intention of revoking it. A person who is appointed may disclaim the appointment by an instrument in writing, provided he does so within a reasonable time of learning of the appointment. An appointment may also be terminated by the court on the application of a person with parental responsibility for the child or the child, with the leave of the court, or by the court of its own motion.

Section 8 orders – what they are

1.7 A number of concepts, such as legal custody, care and control and access, are superseded by the orders which the court may make under section 8 of the Act (referred to generically as 'section 8 Orders'). The four types of section 8 order are:

- a residence order – which provides with whom the child is to live
- a contact order – which allows a child to visit, stay with or have other contact (eg telephone conversations) with a named person
- a prohibited steps order – which empowers the court to order that no step of a specified nature may be taken in respect of the child and
- a specific issue order – which enables the court to give directions as to how any specific question arising about the child is to be determined.

Certain restrictions are placed on the making of section 8 orders. For example, only a residence order may be made in respect of a child in care (and if made, discharges the care order), and a local authority is prohibited from seeking a contact or a residence order. Where a child is being provided with accommodation by a local authority (in the exercise of any of its functions which stand referred to its social services committee),[1] the local authority may apply for a prohibited steps order or a specific issue order. However, this may require a local authority to make a difficult choice in a case where, for example, it is considered that an urgent but controversial medical procedure, such as abortion, sterilisation or a blood transfusion, should be carried out on a child and it becomes necessary to consider whether the authority of the court should be obtained (see para **2.36**).

[1] The functions referred to are those which arise under the Local Authority Social Services Act 1970, and in particular the duty imposed by s 20(1) of the Children Act 1989.

Timetable for section 8 orders

1.8 In accordance with rules of court, where a section 8 order may be in issue, the court is required to *draw up a timetable with a view to determining the question without delay*, and the court must give directions to ensure that the timetable is adhered to. Part II also deals with such diverse matters as change of name, and removal from the United Kingdom, of a child, enforcement of residence orders, orders for child maintenance (detailed provisions in Schedule 1 and Part III of Schedule 2) and Family Assistance Orders (FAO) – another new form of order (see para **2.26**).

PART III – LOCAL AUTHORITY SUPPORT FOR CHILDREN AND FAMILIES

1.9 This Part sets out the duties and functions of local authorities with regard to children and their families. It identifies a particular class of children, namely those 'in need', and lays a duty upon each local authority to promote and safeguard the welfare of such children within its area, and so far as possible to promote the upbringing of these children within their families. Local authorities are also required to provide day care for under-fives and other pre-school children, as is appropriate within their area, and accommodation for any child in need who appears to require accommodation. In addition they must provide accommodation for children in 'police protection' (see para **1.14**), in detention, or on remand or in care. A further important local authority duty is to make reasonable provision of services to prevent children in the area suffering neglect or ill-treatment, to seek to reduce the need to bring proceedings to take children into care or to bring criminal proceedings against children.

1.10 Family support is another requirement which this Part of the Act lays upon the local authorities, by way of advice, counselling and guidance services, as well as activities, home help and assistance with travel to make use of family services. As part of these services local authorities must provide family centres where such services as advice, counselling and activities can be provided. Where a child in need is living away from home, his local authority must take steps to enable him to live with his family, or to promote contact between him and his family. Assistance to families may be given in kind or, exceptionally, by cash payments, and this may include contributions to the maintenance of a child who is living with a person by virtue of a residence order, provided that person is not a parent or stepparent.

PART IV – CARE AND SUPERVISION

1.11 This Part of the Act is essentially concerned with the powers of the court to make orders for the care or supervision of a child by a local authority social services department, and the initiation of care and related proceedings for the protection of a child who is thought to be at risk. Proceedings for a care or supervision order may only be taken by a local authority, or authorised person (only the NSPCC). This is the *only* route by which a child may now enter into care. Subject to certain conditions a local authority is required to promote contact between a child and his parents, guardian or the person with whom the child was living before being taken into care. The court also has power to make an education supervision order in favour of a designated local education authority if it is satisfied that a child of school age is not being properly educated. The court may also, in the course of any family proceedings, direct a local authority to investigate the circumstances of a child whom it believes may be at risk, and the local authority must report back to the court within eight weeks if they decide not to initiate care proceedings, with their reasons for so deciding. If a court asks a local authority to investigate, it is empowered to make an interim care or interim supervision order in respect of the child. Provision is also made for the variation and discharge of orders and for interim care orders to continue pending an appeal.

Appointment of guardian ad litem

1.12 A very important feature of this Part is the appointment of a guardian ad litem to represent a child. This must be done by the court for every child, unless it is satisfied that such an appointment is not necessary in order to safeguard his interests. It is likely that a guardian ad litem will be necessary in most cases, and the guardian ad litem will have a critical role since she, or he, will be akin to an officer of the court whose reports to the court will have great weight. The guardian ad litem will instruct a solicitor for the child, if necessary, where the child is incapable of instructing a solicitor himself. If the child is not represented by a solicitor and has no guardian ad litem, but is capable of giving instructions to a solicitor himself, the court may appoint a solicitor to represent him if it thinks that it would be in his best interests to do so. A guardian ad litem is given the right to inspect and copy local authority or NSPCC records relating to the application, and social services or NSPCC records relating to the child. The Act does not, however require records of other bodies, such as the police, probation service, Crown Prosecution Service or health authorities, to be disclosed to a guardian ad litem.

PART V - PROTECTION OF CHILDREN

1.13 This Part deals with orders designed to provide a means of protecting children who may be at risk of harm. The court may make various orders which may be tailored to meet the requirements of the particular circumstances. Those orders are Child Assessment Orders (CAO), Emergency Protection Orders (EPO), Recovery Orders (RO) and warrants authorising a police constable to take action for the protection of children, and orders to search for and take care of a child who may be at risk. The two most significant orders are the CAO and EPO. The purpose of the CAO is to allow a child to be examined, eg by a paediatrician or child psychiatrist, to establish whether the child's health or development indicates that he is suffering, or is likely to suffer, harm because of the way in which he is being treated. The EPO allows the applicant (usually a social worker or NSPCC officer) to remove the child from the custody of the person with whom he is living, and place him in safe accommodation, where there is reasonable cause to believe that the child is likely to suffer significant harm if he is allowed to remain with that person. An assessment order has effect for a maximum of seven days, and an emergency protection order has effect for not more than eight days. If a child is of sufficient understanding to make an informed decision he may refuse to submit to any examination or assessment under a CAO.

Police protection

1.14 The power under section 46 of the Act to take a child into 'police protection' replaces the powers conferred on a police constable by section 28 of the Children and Young Persons Act 1969 to detain a child, and on the authority of a senior officer keep him in a place of safety for up to eight days. A child may only be kept in police protection for up to 72 hours, and the police must inform the local authority in whose area the child was found as soon as is reasonably practicable. The child must be placed in local authority accommodation, or a children's refuge, and the local authority may ask an officer specially designated by the Chief Constable to apply on the local authority's behalf for an EPO. A local authority which is informed that a child is in police protection must investigate the circumstances to enable it to decide whether it should take action to promote or safeguard the child's welfare.

Requirement to give information

1.15 As an aid to the protection of children, a court making an emergency protection order may order any person whom it believes can give information as to the whereabouts of a child to disclose that information to the applicant, if the information is not available to the applicant. It may also authorise the applicant to enter specified premises and search for the child, and if that person is, or is likely to be, prevented from doing so it may issue a warrant to a constable to assist the applicant, using force to enter premises if necessary.

Abduction from care

1.16 By virtue of section 49, a person who abducts a child from care, keeps the child from a responsible person or encourages the child to run, or stay, away from a responsible person commits a criminal offence. A responsible person in this context is one who has care of him under a care order, or while he is in police protection or subject to an emergency protection order. The court may also make a Recovery Order (RO) under section 50 which, inter alia, requires any person who is in a position to do so to produce the child or to give information as to his whereabouts.

1.17 An EPO, CAO or RO will almost always be made in a magistrates' court. It is only in exceptional cases where care-related proceedings are pending in the High Court or a county court, that one of the child protection orders may be sought there, or where the High Court or a county court has directed an investigation under section 37.

Children's refuges

1.18 This Part also addresses the issue of children's refuges by enabling the Secretary of State for Health to certify a voluntary home or registered children's home, or a nominated foster parent, as a refuge for children at risk. A certified children's refuge (such as certain Church of England Children's Society houses) is exempt from criminal offences in relation to harbouring children in care or subject to police protection etc. The certification of refuges is provided for in the Refuges (Children's Homes and Foster Placements) Regulations 1991 (SI 1991 No 1507).

PART XII – MISCELLANEOUS AND GENERAL

1.19 Part XII includes provisions amongst other things relating to:

- Jurisdiction of courts (s 92)
- Attendance of children at hearings (s 95)
- Evidence by or with respect to children (s 96)

- Privacy for children in magistrates' courts proceedings (s 97)
- Self-incrimination (s 98)
- Search warrants (s 102)

Section 92 changes the nomenclature of domestic proceedings and domestic courts to family proceedings and family proceedings courts, prohibits a magistrates' court from dealing with property belonging to or held in trust for a child and defines the meaning of 'the court' as being the High Court, a county court or a magistrates' court for the purposes of the Act. A court is empowered by section 95 to secure the attendance of a child at any stage of the proceedings, if necessary by authorising a constable to take charge of the child and bring him to court. The unsworn evidence of a child is made admissible by section 96, provided that the court is satisfied that he understands that it is his duty to tell the truth and he has sufficient understanding to justify his evidence being heard. Hearsay evidence is made admissible in civil proceedings in the High Court and county courts and in family proceedings in magistrates' courts, when given in connection with the upbringing, maintenance or welfare of a child by the Children (Admissibility of Hearsay Evidence) Order 1991 (SI 1991 No 1115), made under section 96. The Family Proceedings Courts (Children Act 1989) Rules 1991 (SI 1991 No 1395) provide for the family proceedings courts to sit in private when hearing cases involving children, and section 97(2) prohibits the publication of material which is intended, or likely, to identify a child as being involved in proceedings in which any power under the Children Act 1989 may be exercised. A further evidential provision is made in section 98, whereby a person giving evidence in a hearing for an order under Parts IV or V may be required to give evidence, or answer a question, even though doing so might incriminate him or his spouse of an offence; but any statement or admission made may not be used against the person in evidence in proceedings for an offence other than perjury. Various powers are conferred by the Children Act 1989 in respect of children in residential and foster care, with child-minders or who are under supervision orders, and by the Adoption Act 1976 in respect of protected children, to visit children and inspect accommodation. In order to assist persons who are seeking to exercise those powers but who are being prevented from doing so, section 102 provides that the court may issue a search warrant to a constable to assist the person, using reasonable force if necessary.

SCHEDULE 1 - FINANCIAL PROVISION FOR CHILDREN

1.20 This Schedule deals with the making, duration and variation or discharge of orders for financial relief in respect of children. The court may make orders, for the benefit of a child, for the payment of periodical payments (maintenance), lump sums and the transfer of property against either or both parents of a child, on the application of a parent, guardian or a person with whom the child is living by virtue of a residence order. A magistrates' court is restricted to making unsecured maintenance orders and lump sum orders. Provision is made for maintenance orders to be made, or to continue to be paid, in favour of a child who has attained the age of 18 where the child is, or is likely to be, receiving further education or vocational training beyond his eighteenth birthday, and in 'special circumstances'. Such circumstances are likely to exist when the child is so disabled that he is incapable of supporting himself. Otherwise orders for maintenance come to an end on the child's seventeenth birthday, unless the court thinks it right that the order should continue; but an order comes to an end on the child's eighteenth birthday at the latest, save in the circumstances described above.

The checklist

1.21 There is a checklist of matters to which the court is required to have regard when considering whether to make an order for financial provision, which broadly speaking seeks to balance the needs and circumstances of the potential payer/donor against the needs and circumstances of the potential child recipient. Lump sums may be paid, in particular, in respect of expenses incurred to meet the reasonable needs of a child before the order was made and to meet expenses in connection with the birth. Magistrates' courts are restricted to making orders of £1,000, or less, per child per occasion. A lump sum may also be ordered when a court varies or discharges a maintenance order. The Schedule also confers power on the court to make interim orders, vary maintenance agreements, to make an order in favour of a child living outside England and Wales, and on a local authority to make a contribution to the maintenance of a child living with a person other than a parent or stepparent by virtue of a residence order. Orders under earlier legislation may be revoked, varied or altered by virtue of paragraph 8 of the Schedule.

1.22   The provisions relating to child maintenance will require to be read carefully with the provisions of the Child Support Act 1991 when this is brought into force.

SCHEDULE 2 – LOCAL AUTHORITY SUPPORT FOR CHILDREN AND FAMILIES

1.23   Every local authority is required to take reasonable steps to establish the extent to which there are children in need in their area, and publish information about the services which they provide under sections 17 (services for children in need, their families and others), 18 (day care for pre-school and other children), 20 (provision of accommodation for children) and 24 (advice and assistance for certain children). They are also required to take all reasonably practicable steps to ensure that the prospective beneficiaries of such services learn about them. Local authorities must also maintain registers of disabled children within their areas. A child who appears to be in need within a local authority's area may have his needs assessed for the purposes of the Act when they are being assessed under the Chronically Sick and Disabled Persons Act 1970, the Education Act 1981, the Disabled Persons (Services, Consultation and Representation) Act 1986 or any other statute.

1.24   Duties are laid upon local authorities by Part I of Schedule 2 to take reasonable steps to prevent children within their areas suffering ill-treatment or neglect, to enable disabled children to lead lives which are as normal as possible and to reduce the need to bring care, criminal or family or other proceedings which might bring a child into local authority care. A useful new feature, incorporated in paragraph 5, enables a local authority to help a suspected perpetrator of ill-treatment to move out of the house in which the child lives, by giving him assistance to find alternative accommodation, including cash assistance. Local authorities are also required to provide advice and counselling services, activities and home help in respect of children in need, and to provide family centres to an extent which they consider appropriate for their areas.

Children being looked after by a local authority

1.25   Part II of this Schedule is concerned with children being looked after by a local authority. Various regulation-making powers are conferred on the Secretary of State in respect of placing children with foster parents, arrangements for the accommodation of children and conditions under which a child in care is allowed to live with a parent or other guardian. Where a child is being looked after by a local authority, contact between him and his parents and relatives must be promoted by the local authority; the authority may make payments to a parent or other relative, or to the child, to enable the parent etc to visit the child, or vice versa. Where a child is not visited, or is visited only infrequently, a local authority must appoint a suitable person to visit him (if satisfied that to do so would be in the child's best interests). They also have power to guarantee apprenticeship deeds or articles of clerkship, and to assist a child to live abroad, with the approval of the court.

1.26 Part II deals with contributions towards the maintenance of a child looked after by a local authority. If a local authority thinks it reasonable to do so they may seek contributions towards the maintenance of any child they are looking after from his parents if he is under 16, and from him if he is not. Contributions may be sought by way of an agreement with the contributor or, failing agreement, by a court order.

SCHEDULE 3 – SUPERVISION ORDERS

1.27 The Schedule confers power upon a person supervising a child under a supervision order made under section 31(1)(b), 'the supervisor', to give directions to the child as to where he is to live, or stay for a period, which persons he must see at specified places and when, and what activities he must participate in. It excludes from the supervisor's powers the right to give directions about undergoing medical or psychiatric examination or treatment. However, the court may include in a supervision order a requirement that the child submit to a medical or psychiatric examination, or from time to time submit to such an examination when directed to do so by the supervisor. The medical practitioner by, or under whose direction, the examination is to be made must be specified in the order if the child is treated as an out-patient, as must the place where the child is to attend. Where the child has been, or is to be, admitted to a health service hospital, mental hospital or mental nursing home, the court may order the examination to be carried out there (but only if this is necessary for the treatment of the child or for the purposes of the examination itself). A court may also include in a supervision order, if satisfied on the evidence of a doctor that the child needs medical treatment, a requirement that the child submits to treatment. In the case of psychiatric treatment the doctor must be approved for the purposes of section 12 of the Mental Health Act 1983. The court must be satisfied that, if the child has the capacity to make an informed decision, he consents to the examination or treatment.

1.28 With the consent of the 'responsible person', ie the person who has parental responsibility for the child and any other person with whom the child may be living, a supervision order may require him to take reasonable steps to ensure that the child complies with the supervisor's directions and submits to any medical examination or treatment specified in the order. The responsible person may also be required to take part in activities at specified times by the supervisor, with or without the child (eg attendance at a family centre established under paragraph 9 of Schedule 2).

1.29 Part II of the Schedule imposes requirements on a supervised child, and any associated responsible person, to keep the supervisor informed of the child's address and to allow the supervisor to visit him. Limitations are placed upon the appointment of supervisors so that only a consenting local authority within whose area the child lives, or will live, may be appointed; and a probation officer may not be appointed save at the request of the local authority concerned where the probation officer is exercising, or has exercised, probation duties in relation to another member of the child's household. The making of a fresh supervision order brings to an end any earlier care or supervision order made in respect of the child which would otherwise have remained in force.

1.30 Part III deals with education supervision orders. Under such orders the supervisor must advise, assist and befriend, and may give directions to, a child *and his parents* with a view to seeing that the child is properly educated, taking into account the wishes and feelings of both the parents and the child. An education supervision order brings to an end any school attendance order, and disapplies enactments relating to such orders, parental wishes concerning education and parental preference and appeals against admission decisions. Where a supervision order is in force contemporaneously with an education supervision order, directions given under the former take precedence over those of the latter. Like a supervision order, an education supervision order expires after a maximum of 12 months, but may be extended for up to three years.

1.31   The child and his parent must inform the supervisor of any change of address and allow the supervisor to visit him. The order may be discharged on the application of the child, a parent or the local education authority, and on discharge the court may require the local authority of the area within which the child lives, or will live, to investigate the child's circumstances (eg where the supervision order has been ineffective and consideration may have to be given to taking the child into care). A *parent* who persistently fails to comply with a direction given under the order will be guilty of an offence, unless he took all reasonable steps to comply, or the direction was unreasonable, or it was not reasonably practicable to comply both with the direction and the directions or requirements under a supervision order made in respect of the child. If a child persistently fails to comply with directions the appropriate local authority must be informed and thereupon investigate the child's circumstances.

SCHEDULE 11 - JURISDICTION

1.32   The Lord Chancellor is given power to make certain statutory instruments. By means of this power he may specify proceedings under the Act and the Adoption Act 1976 which must be commenced in a specified level of court, or a court within a specified class, or a particular court determined in accordance with, or specified in, the order. He may also specify circumstances in which specified proceedings under those Acts must be commenced in one of those courts. Where proceedings involving a child under either of those Acts, or under the inherent jurisdiction of the High Court (ie wardship), have been commenced in, or have been transferred to, any court, the Lord Chancellor by order may also require other proceedings affecting or otherwise connected with the child to be commenced in that court. Furthermore, he is given the power to allow the whole or part of specified proceedings to be transferred to another court. If the proceedings are not under the Act or the Adoption Act 1976 then transfer may only be made for the purposes of consolidating them with proceedings under either of those two Acts, or wardship proceedings; the transfer for consolidation provision does not allow proceedings under the inherent jurisdiction of the High Court to be transferred. He has exercised these powers in part in the Children (Allocation of Proceedings)

Order 1991 (SI 1991 No 1677), in respect of proceedings under the Children Act 1989 and the Adoption Act 1976.

1.33   The Lord Chancellor also has power under the Schedule to specify by order that a single justice may make an emergency protection order in specified circumstances. This power includes conferring jurisdiction on a single justice to decide questions relating to the exercise of the transfer provision mentioned above, to or from a magistrates' court. The power has been exercised in the Family Proceedings Courts (Children Act 1989) Rules (SI 1991 No 1895), r 2b (see paras **7.7–7.11**).

SCHEDULE 14 – TRANSITIONALS AND SAVINGS

1.34   This Schedule (as amended by Schedule 20 to the Courts and Legal Services Act 1990, and the Children Act 1989 (Commencement and Transitional Provisions) Order 1991 (SI 1991 No 828) as itself amended by SI 1991 No 1990) is concerned with the effects of the new regimes introduced by the Act, and deals with orders having effect, or proceedings which are continuing, when various provisions of the Act are brought into force. Broadly speaking, the policy is to leave untouched proceedings under the pre-existing law started before the Act came into force, and which have not been concluded, and to preserve the effect of existing orders for a limited period or to modify them so that they deemed to be, or are akin to, equivalent orders under the Act.

Pending proceedings

1.35   In the case of pending proceedings, nothing in the Act (apart from two repeals) is to affect *any proceedings pending* immediately before the relevant provision came into force. Furthermore, any order made in proceedings pending when the Act comes into force is treated as if it were an order made before the Act came into force. Thus all 'old', that is to say pre-1989 Act, orders are treated in the same way, including any made *after* the Act comes into force. This includes any interim care order made in wardship, which will continue in effect until 13 October 1992 unless a final order is made before that date.[1] A declaration under section 42(3) of the Matrimonial Causes Act 1973, which empowers a divorce court to declare that a party to a marriage is unfit to have custody of a child, and an order under section 38 of the Sexual Offences Act 1956, which empowers the court to divest a person of authority over a child in cases

19

of incest, by virture of the repeal of those enactments ceased to have effect on 14 October 1991.

1 Schedule to the Children Act 1989 (Commencement No 2 – Amendment and Transitional Provisions) Order 1991 (SI 1991 No 1990).

'Old' parental rights and duties orders

1.36 An order made under section 4(1) of the Family Law Reform Act 1987, giving a father parental rights and duties in respect of his children is deemed to be an order under section 4 of the Act, giving parental responsibility to the father.

Private law orders

1.37 Detailed provisions are made in respect of particular types of order in force immediately before the coming into force of Parts I and II, which were made under certain Acts ('existing orders'). The types of order in question are those which determine any matter with respect to a child's education or upbringing, or who is to have custody (including legal custody and joint custody) or care and control, or access. The Acts in question are:

- the Domestic Proceedings and Magistrates' Courts Act 1978,
- the Children Act 1975,
- the Matrimonial Causes Act 1973,
- the Guardianship of Minors Acts 1971 and 1973,
- the Matrimonial Causes Act 1965, and
- the Matrimonial Proceedings (Magistrates' Courts) Act 1960.

The general effect is to do four things. The first is to apply the provisions of section 2 of the Act regarding parental responsibility to the parent of a child subject to an order, with necessary modifications. The second is to give parental responsibility to a person who is not the parent of a child, but who has custody or care and control of him, while an existing order is still in force. The third is to enable a parent, guardian or other person who has custody, or care and control of a child to apply for a section 8 order, and one with an access order to apply for a contact order. The fourth is to provide that the making of a residence order or a care order discharges any existing order, and that existing orders continue subject to any other section 8 orders. A parent or guardian of the child or any person named in the order may apply for an existing order to be discharged, as may a child with the leave of the court.

Guardianship

1.38 Existing guardianships are also assimilated to the provisions of section 5 of the Act. Any appointment which was made under:

- sections 3 to 5 of the Guardianship of Minors Act 1971
- section 38(3) of the Sexual Offences Act 1956

and was in effect when Part I came into force is deemed to have been made under section 5, and any appointment which takes effect afterwards does so in accordance with section 5 of the Act (as modified by paragraph 8 of this Schedule). Any disposition by will of the custody and tuition of a child is deemed to be an appointment by will of a guardian of the child.

Care and supervision orders etc, and wardship

1.39 Every child in care, whether by an order of a court or by the resolution of a local authority, is deemed to be in care by virtue of a care order made under the Act on the day Part IV came into force. Various necessary modifications are made to align the operation of such orders and the Act. These include the continuation in force of any directions given by a court under section 4(4)(a) of the Guardianship Act 1973 and section 43(5) of the Matrimonial Causes Act 1973, or in the exercise of the High Court's inherent jurisdiction with respect to children, until varied or discharged by a court (subject to section 25 and any regulations made under that section). A child who was a ward of court in care ceased to be a ward on the coming into force of the Act (but see para **1.35** with regard to interim orders made in pending proceedings). The effects of certain ancillary orders, or local authority actions, relating to a person who is caring for a child and access to a child in care are assimilated to the equivalent orders or situations provided for by the Act. Similarly children subject to supervision orders made under the Children and Young Persons Act 1969 are deemed to be subject to an order made under section 31 of the Act, but the duration of such orders is limited to a maximum of 12 months, unless the court otherwise directs. Other supervision orders continue in force for a year after Part IV came into effect, unless they would have ceased to have effect earlier by virtue of the provisions under which they were made - or the court directs that such an order shall cease to have effect.

Place of safety orders

1.40   An order or warrant authorising a child to be moved to a place of safety is unaffected by the Act, but it is not possible to make interim orders under the relevant repealed enactment to retain in care a child who has been taken into care in this way. Likewise, a summons or warrant for the recovery of a child taken from care is unaffected by the coming into force of Part IV.

Voluntary organisations

1.41   A parental rights resolution made under section 64 of the Child Care Act 1980 in favour of a voluntary organisation will continue in effect for a period of up to six months after Part IV is brought into force. The Act treats a foster child who was not being privately fostered when Parts VII and IX came into force as a child being provided with accommodation in a children's home, and otherwise as a foster child for the purposes of Part IX. So far as child-minding and nurseries are concerned, the Act does not apply to persons or premises registered when Part X came into force during a transitional period of a year, or until the premises or the person concerned are registered under Part X by the relevant local authority.

Criminal care orders

1.42   Care orders made under sections 7(7)(a) or 15(1) of the Children and Young Persons Act 1969 remain in force for six months after the Act takes effect, unless brought to an end sooner, and the relevant provisions of the 1969 Act and the Child Care Act 1980 continue to have effect with respect to it.

UNIFORMITY OF JURISDICTION

1.43   One of the most important features of the Children Act 1989 is that it provides for the same remedies, by way of the orders the court may make, in whichever court proceedings relating to child may be taking place, subject to a few minor exceptions. These include the restriction on the exercise of the inherent jurisdiction of the High Court to appoint a guardian of the estate of a child imposed by section 5(11)[1] (subject to rules of court), and the exclusion of a magistrates' court from the power to make orders for secured periodical payments and the settlement or transfer of property, to or for the benefit of a child (paragraph

1(1)(b) of Schedule 1). In making orders the courts will be guided by the same set of principles and the same guidelines. For example, in considering the welfare of the child, whether in 'private law' or 'public law' proceedings, they must have regard to section 1; furthermore all section 8 orders (residence, contact, prohibited steps and specific issues orders) are governed by the general principles in section 11 and when making orders for financial provision for children every court must have regard to the matters set out in paragraph 4 of Schedule 1.

[1] Coming into effect on 1 February 1992 by virtue of the Children Act 1989 (Commencement and Transitional Provisions) Order 1991 (SI 1991 No 828) as amended by SI 1991 No 1990.

1.44 This is not to say that any proceedings relating to a child may be brought in any court. Provision is made in Schedule 11 (jurisdiction) for the Lord Chancellor, by order, to direct that proceedings must start in specific courts or levels of court. In general, proceedings under Parts IV and V must commence in a magistrates' court. Proceedings under the inherent jurisdiction of the High Court must take place, of course, in the High Court. The Children (Allocation of Proceedings) Order 1991 (SI 1991 No 1677) requires applications for:

- use of secure accommodation (s 25)
- care and supervision orders (s 31)
- child in care – leave to change name or remove from UK (s 33)
- parental contact orders (s 34)
- education supervision orders (s 36)
- child assessment orders (CAO) (s 43)
- emergency protection orders (EPO) (s 44)
- duration of EPOs etc (s 45)
- application for EPO by police officer (s 46)
- powers to assist recovery of children etc (s 48)
- recovery orders (RO) (s 50)
- protection of children in emergency (child-minding etc) (s 75)
- appeal against refusals etc. (child-minding etc) (s 77)
- warrant authorising constable to assist (s 102)
- approval for child to live abroad (Sch 2, para 19)
- contribution orders (Sch 2, para 23)
- appeals on fostering of children (Sch 8, para 8)
- substitution of adoption agencies (Adoption Act 1976, s 21)

to be made in a magistrates' court, with two exceptions. The order (article 2(2)) provides that the court which gives a direction to a local authority to investigate a child's circumstances under section 37(1) shall be the court in which any consequent application is to be made under sections 31, 36, 43, 44, 46(7) or 48, where that court is the High Court or a care centre,[1] or to such care centre as that court directs. It also provides (article 2(3)) that where proceedings under section 25 (use of secure accommodation), Parts IV and V, section 102 (power of constable to assist) or Schedule 2, paragraph 19 (arrangements to assist a child to live abroad) are pending in a county court or the High Court, an application under those provisions shall be made to the court in which the proceedings are pending.

[1] Care centre means a court listed in Schedule 2 to the Children (Allocation Proceedings) Order 1991.

1.45 There are no restrictions on where, that is to say in which level of court, 'private law' proceedings (eg for an order under sections 4, 5 or 8) may be commenced.

TRANSFER

Transfer of public law cases

1.46 The Children (Allocation of Proceedings) Order 1991 makes provision for the applications for most of the orders mentioned in para **1.43**, which must normally be commenced in a magistrates' court, to be transferred to a county court. A county court may transfer such proceedings (and any other proceedings under the Children Act 1989 and the Adoption Act 1976), to the High Court where it considers that the exceptional nature of the proceedings makes them appropriate for determination in the High Court, and that it would be in the interests of the child to do so. An application for an EPO, and other emergency orders under sections 75 and 77, may not be transferred because the delay could be prejudicial to the child, nor may an application for contribution order (Schedule 2, paragraph 23) or appeals relating to privately fostered children (Schedule 8, paragraph 8). Applications under section 25 (secure accommodation) and section 102 (assistance by constable) may only be transferred for the purpose of consolidation with other family proceedings arising out of the same circumstances, and a section 25 application may not be transferred for this purpose from a magistrates' court which is not a family proceedings court. In considering whether to transfer any proceedings the court must have regard to the general principle in section 1(2) of the Act that delay is likely to prejudice the welfare of a child. A case may only be transferred from a magistrates' court if the court believes transfer to be in the interests of the child having considered that principle, and it meets one or more of three criteria for transfer. They are:

- the issues are exceptionally grave, important or complex
- it would be appropriate to hear the case at the same time as other family proceedings pending in another court
- delay would seriously prejudice the interests of the child and the receiving court can deal with the case more quickly than the transferring court or another magistrates' court.

The first criterion (gravity, importance or complexity) must be satisfied because of:

- complicated or conflicting evidence about the risks involved to the child's physical, moral well-being or other matters relating to the child's welfare
- the number of parties
- conflict with the law of another jurisdiction
- some novel or difficult point of law
- some question of general public interest.

The second criterion is largely self-explanatory, and is likely to arise where proceedings involving the child's family are under active consideration by another court, particularly where common issues may arise in each case. The urgency criterion will depend upon the circumstances of the court, as well as on the circumstances of the child. Children cases will have to be given a high degree of priority in any court, by virtue of section 1(2) of the Act. It will only be in exceptional circumstances that a court will be unable to order its other priorities to avoid delay to a child case which would prejudice the welfare of the child. Before a case which is otherwise suitable for hearing by a family proceedings court is transferred to a county court, transfer to another family proceedings court should be attempted. It is axiomatic that a case transferred under this criterion would be heard with significantly less delay by the receiving court. Transfer from a county court to the High Court will take place where the proceedings are in the nature of a test case, or the result is likely to have an important impact beyond the instant case. The High Court may transfer public law proceedings to a care centre if it considers that the county court is the appropriate venue and that transfer would be in the interests of the child.

A care centre may transfer public law proceedings which have been transferred to it under Article 7 of the Children (Allocation of Proceedings) Order 1991 where the reason for transfer was the exceptional gravity, importance or complexity of the case and it is satisfied that the reason does not apply (article 11). It may also transfer down where the reason for transfer up was to consolidate, and the proceedings with which the transferred proceedings were to be heard have been determined, or where the case was transferred up because this would be likely significantly to accelerate their determination and that is no longer the case.

Transfer of private law cases

1.47 There are powers under sections 38 and 39 of the Matrimonial and Family Proceedings Act 1984 to transfer family proceedings between the High Court and a county court, and vice versa. However, those powers are disapplied by article 5 of the Children (Allocation of Proceedings) Order 1991 in respect of proceedings under the Children Act 1989 or the Adoption Act 1976. A magistrates' court may transfer private law proceedings (that is proceedings under Parts I and II) up to a county court whenever it considers they can be more appropriately dealt with there in the interests of the child (article 8). A county court may transfer any proceedings under the Children Act 1989 or the Adoption Act 1976 to the High Court if it considers that the proceedings are appropriate for determination in the High Court, and it would be in the interests of the child to do so (article 12). Similarly, the Order (article 13) enables the High Court to transfer such proceedings down to a county court on corresponding grounds, the proceedings being appropriate for determination in a county court. Private law proceedings may not be transferred from the High Court or a county court to a magistrates' court.

CHAPTER 2

The new children law

Policy of the legislation in general terms

2.1 The policy of the Act is to reform the law relating to children by collating in a single statute the new law regulating the care, upbringing and protection of children, in a rational, coherent and consistent way. The Act has radically changed the law in a large number of ways, not least of which is to import common principles to the 'private law' concerning children and the 'public law' of child care. Underlying this is the proposition that it is best for a child if he can be brought up within his family, with both parents playing a full part in his upbringing, and that legal proceedings should be avoided unless they are the best way, in all the circumstances, to safeguard his welfare. To give effect to this proposition the Act incorporates new concepts and imposes new duties upon local authorities and the courts. While the 'welfare principle' is merely restated in slightly different terms ('... *the child's welfare shall be the court's paramount consideration.*'), the court must now have regard, in any proceedings in which any question with respect to the upbringing of a child arises, to the general principle that any delay in determining the question is likely to prejudice the welfare of the child. This principle is backed up by a requirement to draw up a timetable with a view to determining issues without delay, and to ensure that so far as reasonably practicable the timetable is adhered to. The court must also refuse to make any order under the Act with respect to a child unless it is satisfied that to make the order would be better for the child than making no order at all.

2.2 The Act introduces the statutory concept of 'parental responsibility', and in so doing places the emphasis on the responsibilities of parents for their children, rather than on parental rights over them. It also provides the facility for the unmarried parents of a child to agree to share parental

27

responsibility, and to have this formally recognised without the need for one parent to take uncontested proceedings against the other in order to obtain a consent order from the court. 'Parental responsibility' is the sum of the duties, rights and authority which a parent exercises with regard to his child. Parents who were married to each other when the child was born share parental responsibility, the mother has it in any event and the father of an illegitimate child may acquire it by agreement with the mother or by order of a court. An order of the court may limit the extent of parental responsibility in private law proceedings, but it cannot remove it altogether and a parent may continue to exercise it subject to any order of the court. A care order has the effect of giving parental responsibility to the local authority designated in the order. It does not deprive a parent or guardian of the child of parental responsibility, but makes his or her exercise of parental responsibility subject to the discretion of the local authority, to the extent that it is necessary to do so in order to safeguard or promote the welfare of the child.

2.3 *The policy expressed in these provisions is to support each parent's relationship with the child and to maintain it to the greatest possible extent compatible with the child's interests.*

2.4 Duties are imposed upon the local authorities which are intended to have the effect of assisting in the policy of bringing a child up within his family unless this would be detrimental to his welfare. These include a duty to give support to children in need and their families, and it subsumes the duty to reduce the need for children to be brought before the courts or to be in care. They also include a duty to return a child to his family, where the child has been looked after by the local authority, unless this is contrary to the child's interest. Where the child is looked after away from home the local authority has a duty to ensure contact with his parents whenever possible.

MAJOR CHANGES AND INNOVATIONS

2.5 A great deal of pre-existing law is repealed and swept away by the Children Act 1989. The whole of the following Acts have been made redundant and are accordingly repealed:

- The Custody of Children Act 1891
- The Nurseries and Child-Minders Regulation Act 1948
- The Guardianship of Minors Act 1971

- The Guardianship Act 1973
- The Children Act 1975
- The Child Care Act 1980
- The Foster Children Act 1980
- The Children's Homes Act 1982
- The Children and Young Persons (Amendment) Act 1986

The substantive law which was contained in these enactments has been replaced by the relevant parts of the Children Act 1989, and to that extent the Children Act has codified the law relating to children.

2.6 The 1989 Act also makes amendments to a large number of Acts, perhaps the most important of which are:

- The Education Act 1944
- The Children and Young Persons Acts 1963 and 1969
- The Family Law Reform Act 1969
- The Matrimonial Causes Act 1973
- The Adoption Act 1976
- The Domestic Proceedings and Magistrates' Courts Act 1978
- The Child Abduction Act 1984
- The Family Law Act 1986
- The Family Law Reform Act 1987
- The Legal Aid Act 1988

These amendments have been made mainly to accommodate the new regime of orders and remedies which are created by the Children Act 1989; but they also provide for a consistent fit with the principles embodied in the Act. On the one hand, in the 'private law' sphere, the divorce courts and the family proceedings courts (exercising jurisdiction respectively under the Matrimonial Causes Act 1973 and the Domestic Proceedings and Magistrates' Courts Act 1978) now look exclusively to the Children Act 1989 for their powers in relation to children. (However, issues relating to the maintenance of children will be governed by the Child Support Act 1991, when it is brought into force.) On the other hand, in the 'public law' sphere, the power to place a child in the care of a local authority is removed from the ambit of the Education Act 1944 and the Children and Young Persons Act 1969. In the following paragraphs the more significant changes and innovations are described in summary form.

Welfare of the child

2.7 The fundamental consideration which any court must take into account when determining the upbringing of a child, or the administration of a child's property or the application of any income arising from it, has been changed from the formulation used in section 1 of the Guardianship of Minors Act 1971 (repealed). That enactment required the court to have regard to the welfare of the child as *the first and paramount consideration*. Section 1 of the Children Act 1989 requires the child's welfare to be simply the *paramount consideration*. The word 'first' has caused confusion in the past, which was resolved in *J v C* [1970] AC 668, [1969] 1 All ER, but the Act removes any uncertainty which might have remained by omitting 'first' from the requirement. This does not go as far as the Law Commission recommended in their Review of Child Law, Guardianship and Custody (Law Com no 172), in which they proposed that the welfare of the child should be the court's *only* concern.

Parental responsibility – who has it

2.8 The new statutory concept of parental responsibility has superseded the concept of 'parental rights and duties' expressed in section 85 of the Children Act 1975, and also used in section 12 of the Adoption Act 1976 and section 3 of the Child Care Act 1980, and the reference to 'powers and duties' in the latter and to 'rights and authority' in section 1 of the Guardianship Act 1973. The Law Commission in their report (Law Com no 172) thought that this would make little difference in substance, but that 'parental responsibility' would better reflect the everyday reality and would emphasise the responsibilities of all who are in the position of parents (including local authorities). The Act makes clear, in section 2(5) and (6), that more than one person may have parental responsibility for a child simultaneously, and that parental responsibility does not cease solely because some other person acquires it. Furthermore, where a local authority has parental responsibility for a child it must allow a parent or guardian to exercise his parental responsibility, unless satisfied that it is necessary to limit it in order to safeguard or promote the welfare of the child.

2.9 The starting point for considering who has parental responsibility is section 2(1) of the Children Act 1989, which provides that where a child's father and mother were married to each other at the time of his birth they shall each have parental responsibility for the child. This must be construed in accordance with section 1 of the Family Law Reform Act 1987, subsection (1) of which enacted the general principle that relationships shall be construed without regard to whether the parents of any individual were, or had been, married to each other at any time. Subsection (2) of that section goes on to require a reference to a person whose father and mother were married at the time of his birth to be construed as including a person treated as legitimate by virtue of section 1 of the Legitimacy Act 1976, a person legitimated within the meaning of section 10 of that Act, an adopted child or a person who is otherwise treated in law as legitimate.

Section 4 agreements

2.10 By virtue of section 2(2) of the Family Law Reform Act 1987 the mother of an illegitimate child was given the parental rights and duties in respect of her child to the exclusion of the father, unless a court ordered otherwise. That position is, in effect, perpetuated by section 2(2) of the Act, subject to an important addition. Section 4 of the Act not only provides for the father to acquire parental responsibility by way of an order of the court, it also enables the mother and father to make a 'parental responsibility agreement' providing for the father to have parental responsibility for the child. Such an agreement will only take effect if it is made in the form prescribed by the Parental Responsibility Agreement Regulations (SI 1991 No 1478), and recorded in the manner required by the regulations (see Appendix 5).

Delay and timetables

2.11 A new general principle is enacted in section 1(2) that any delay is likely to prejudice the welfare of a child. This principle is supported in procedural terms by the requirement in sections 11 and 32 for the court, when hearing an application under section 8 and Part IV respectively, to draw up a timetable with a view to disposing of the application without delay, and to give directions to ensure, so far as practicable, that the timetable is adhered to.

Time limits on interim care and Part V orders

2.12 If the court in care proceedings was not in a position to decide what order it ought to make under the Children and Young Persons Act 1969, it could make an interim care order, which lasted for 28 days. It could also make such an order while a child was detained in a place of safety. It was common for courts to make successive interim care orders and in extreme cases more than ten might be made, each lasting 28 days, and in those circumstances it was almost inevitable that a full order would be made eventually. The Act imposes strict (but more realistic) time limits. An interim order may be made for a maximum of eight weeks, and may be extended for up to *four more weeks*, or if the initial order lasted less than four weeks the extension may be continued until eight weeks have elapsed from the day the initial order was made. An interim order under the Act may be made on an application for a care or supervision order, and where the court directs the local authority to carry out an investigation under section 37. It may also include directions for the medical or psychiatric examination, or other assessment, of the child. Time limits are also placed on the duration of CAOs (seven days), EPOs (eight days) and police protection (72 hours). A local authority must report back to a court which directs it to investigate a child's circumstances under section 37 within 8 weeks, unless the court directs otherwise.

No order unless in child's interest

2.13 Section 1(5) introduces a presumption that an order under the Children Act 1989 will not be made unless the court considers that making an order would be better for the child than making no order at all. Accordingly, the court should only make an order where the effect on the welfare of the child of doing so will be better than the effect of not making an order, whether in private or public law proceedings. This gives statutory recognition to the fact that the court may be faced with the choice of the lesser of two evils, or an application which is made more in the interests of an adult party than the child.

Section 8 orders – how they work

2.14 These orders are designed to sit comfortably with the concept of parental responsibility, which continues throughout childhood unless terminated by an order of the court, and to recognise that the day-to-day incidents of parental responsibility can only effectively be discharged by the person with whom the child is living. The residence order is significantly different from an order for legal custody or care and control, in that it is a good deal more flexible and can, for example, be made in favour of separated parents specifying when the child is to live in each household. The contact order is much more specific than the access order which it replaces, since it may direct visits to a named person, and that the child should be allowed to stay with him, or for that person and the child to have contact in other ways, such as by telephone or letters. Specific issue orders replace the (rarely made) orders under section 1(3) of the Guardianship Act 1973, and enable either parent to submit a particular dispute to the court for resolution. The prohibited steps order is modelled on the wardship jurisdiction whereby the court can require that no important step in the child's life be taken without the consent of the court. The steps which are prohibited, however, must be identified in the order.

The checklist – section 1(3)

2.15 This is a means of bringing greater consistency and a more systematic approach to decisions concerning the making, variation or discharge of section 8 orders and care and supervision orders. It helps to ensure that the same basic factors are borne in mind by those considering implementing the welfare criterion. It also assists both parents and children to understand how judicial decisions about such orders are made. This may in some cases be instrumental in focusing the minds of the parties to litigation on the real issues and thereby promoting a settlement. While it is not exhaustive, it does provide a clear indication of what the most important factors in the welfare of a child are considered to be; and prominent among these is the ascertainable wishes and feelings of the child concerned.

Financial provision and checklist

2.16 The provisions regarding child maintenance in other Acts, eg the Matrimonial Causes Act 1973; section 23(1) and the Domestic Proceedings and Magistrates' Courts Act 1978, section 2(1), remain in force, but the Children Act 1989 contains equivalent provisions, which govern all applications for child maintenance under the Act, in Schedule 1. A checklist of considerations to be taken into account when the court is considering whether to make an order for child maintenance, and if so for how much, is contained in paragraph 4. This is substantially the same as those contained in the two above mentioned statutes. The powers conferred in Schedule 1 replace those conferred in the Guardianship of Minors Acts 1971–1973, the Children Act 1975 and the Family Law Reform Act 1987. But see section 8 of the Child Support Act 1991, when it is brought into force.

One route into care

2.17 One of the important routes into care was by way of the Matrimonial Causes Act 1973, section 43 of which empowered the court of its own motion to make an order committing a child to the care of a local authority, or to make a supervision order, when considering the arrangements for the child, or when considering an application for the custody of the child in matrimonial proceedings. It was similarly possible for a care or supervision order to be made under section 10 of the Domestic Proceedings in Magistrates' Courts Act 1978 on an application for custody in the course of domestic proceedings, or under section 2 of the Guardianship Act 1973 on an application under section 9 of the Guardianship of Minors Act, or under section 26 of the Adoption Act 1976 on the refusal of an adoption order. All these provisions have been repealed and the only way in which a child may be taken into the care, or placed under the supervision, of a local authority is by virtue of an order under section 31 of the Children Act 1989. Such an application may only be made by the relevant local authority or the NSPCC. All of the other powers to make care orders, eg under the Children and Young Persons Act 1969 or the Child Care Act 1980 have been repealed. Any child who was subject to a care under any of those powers (listed in paragraph 15(1) of Schedule 14) when the Act came into force is deemed to be subject to a section 31 care order. A court, however, may require the local authority to investigate the circumstances of a child under section 37 of the Children Act 1989 where in any family proceedings it appears to the court that it may be appropriate for a care or supervision order to be made. The decision whether to initiate proceedings for a care or supervision order remains with the local authority, and after having referred the matter to the local authority for investigation the court has no further role unless its jurisdiction is invoked. The local authority must report back to the court within eight weeks if it decides not to institute proceedings, giving its reasons and explaining what action, if any, it has taken, or proposes to take, with respect to the child.

Guardians ad litem

2.18   The role of the guardian ad litem is not changed in its essentials by the Act, but the appointment of guardians ad litem will be much more frequent since in proceedings specified in section 41(6) and rules of court (see paras **8.53–8.57**), the court must appoint a guardian ad litem unless it is satisfied that it is not necessary to do so to safeguard the child's interests. The court is freed from the ordinary rules of evidence so far as the guardian ad litem's report is concerned, since it may take into account any statement or evidence in the report which in the opinion of the court is relevant. The guardian ad litem is given extensive powers to examine local authority and NSPCC records relating to the child, and she may refer to any copy which she takes in her report, or in giving evidence, regardless of any evidential rule which might otherwise make the copy inadmissible.

Emergency Protection Order (EPO)

2.19   The former place of safety order has been replaced by the emergency protection order (section 44). The EPO enables a successful applicant not only to remove a child from his home, or keep him in a safe place (eg a hospital), but if the court so directs to arrange for medical, psychiatric or other assessment of the child. The EPO may have effect for no more than eight days, but it may be extended once for no more than a further seven days. An application may be made to discharge an EPO by the child, a parent or someone who has parental responsibility for him or with whom he was living, but not until 72 hours have elapsed. The court may add to an EPO a provision for a named person to give information to the applicant as to the child's whereabouts. It may also authorise the applicant to enter specified premises to search for a child, and if the court is satisfied that there may be another child on the premises who ought to be subject to an EPO it may authorise the applicant to search for that child too. These powers replace the power to issue a search warrant under section 40 of the Children and Young Persons Act 1933. In addition, where a person has been prevented, or is likely to be prevented, from exercising powers conferred by an EPO the court may issue a 'warrant of assistance' authorising a constable to assist a person acting under an EPO, using reasonable force if necessary (section 48(9)).

Child assessment order (CAO) – section 43

2.20 This is an entirely new feature of the court's armoury of child protection measures, and its introduction into the Bill was controversial. A local authority or the NSPCC may apply for a child assessment order if it suspects that a child is suffering, or is likely to suffer, significant harm and that an order for the assessment of the child is needed to establish whether this is the case. The order is intended to assist where the applicant is not sure that there are grounds for seeking an EPO, and needs to establish whether there is some risk to a child's health or development, or whether he is being ill-treated. In order to avoid the possibility of a CAO being treated as a 'soft option', when the circumstances demand that in order to protect the child from harm an EPO is required, the court may not make a CAO if it is satisfied that there are grounds for making an EPO and that it ought to make an EPO rather than a CAO.

Recovery order (RO) – section 50

2.21 These orders allow a child in care, or subject to an EPO, or in police protection, who has been abducted to be recovered by the person who has care of him. An RO requires *any person* who is in a position to do so to produce the child, or to give information as to the child's whereabouts, and it authorises the removal of the child and a constable to enter specified premises to search for the child, using reasonable force if necessary.

Police protection – section 46

2.22 The police are given power to take care of a child, or prevent him being removed from hospital or other place, if a constable has reasonable cause to believe that the child may otherwise suffer significant harm. The Act introduces a new legal concept of a child being in 'police protection'. It gives the police new powers to take into their protection, at their discretion, a child whom they perceive to be at risk of harm. No child may be retained in police protection for more than 72 hours. The police must inform the local authority for the area that the child has been taken into police protection as soon as is reasonably practical, as well as the child's parents, anyone who may have parental responsibility for him or with whom the child was living. The local authority is under a duty to investigate the circumstances of the child with a view to deciding whether they should take any action to safeguard his welfare. The same duty applies when they are informed that an emergency protection order has been made in respect of a child.

Refuges

2.23 When a child runs away from home, whether this be from a parent, foster parent or a local authority care, he may seek to avoid the police and 'authority' and remain at risk of harm while he is homeless. Certain voluntary organisations provide safe house, or refuges, for such children. The organisation and its responsible officers may be at risk of committing an offence by harbouring a child in these circumstances because the child may only use the refuge if he is sure that the person from whom he has run away is not told of his whereabouts. However, under section 51(4) the Secretary of State has made the Refuges (Children's Homes and Foster Placements) Regulations 1991 (SI 1991 No 1507) which provide for him to issue a certificate to a local authority or voluntary organisation to provide a refuge for children who appear to be at risk of harm. Such a certificate enables those responsible for the refuge (which may be provided by a foster parent) to be free of the risk of prosecution.

Children in detention

2.24 Section 21 of the Children Act 1989 imposes upon local authorities a duty to receive and accommodate children received under section 38(6) of the Police and Criminal Evidence Act, or who are on remand under sections 16(3A)(b) or 23(1) of the Children and Young Persons Act 1969. Section 23(3) of the latter authorises the detention of a child or young person remanded to local authority accommodation. Otherwise, the keeping of a child in secure accommodation, that is accommodation restricting liberty, is not lawful unless he has a history of absconding and is likely to abscond and if he does so is likely to suffer significant harm, or is likely to injure himself or another person if not kept in secure accommodation. Placing and keeping a child in secure accommodation is governed by regulations made by the Secretary of State – the Children (Secure Accommodation) Regulations 1991 (SI 1991 No 1505).

Juvenile offenders

2.25 A local authority may apply for a care or supervision order in respect of a juvenile offender if the fact, and circumstances, of the offence or offences give rise to concern that his social or behavioural development may be impaired. A court sentencing a juvenile offender, however, cannot make a care order in respect of him since the Children Act 1989 has repealed section 7(7)(a) of the Children and Young Persons Act 1969, thereby abolishing the power of a juvenile court to make a 'criminal' care order. A supervision order may still be made under the Act of 1969, but it is of a different nature to that which may be made under section 31(1)(b) of the Children Act 1989. A supervision order under section 12AA of the Children and Young Persons Act 1969 may contain a requirement that the child (or young person) must live in accommodation provided by, or on behalf of, the local authority for up to six months, and it may also require the child not to live with a named person during that time.

Family assistance order (FAO) – what it does

2.26 These orders, made under section 16 of the Children Act 1989, are short-term orders lasting no more than six months; the purpose of which is to enable expert help to be given to a family. Such an order may be made where the court has the power to make an order under Part II (orders with respect to children in family proceedings) whether or not it makes a Part II order. It may require a probation or local authority officer to be made available to advise, assist and where appropriate befriend any person named in the order. This may be any parent or guardian of the child, any person with whom the child is living or in whose favour there is a contact order in force with respect to the child, and the child himself. The local authority must agree if the child concerned lives, or will live, within their area. There are two restrictions on making an FAO. The court must be satisfied that the circumstances are exceptional and an order may only be made with the consent of every person named in it, other than the child. The order is intended to provide the family with assistance, and an element of compulsion would be inconsistent with this. While a party may not apply for such an order, a court might be prepared to exercise its discretion to make an order at the request of a party. However, the order may specify that a person, or persons, named in the order must keep the assisting officer informed of the address of a person named in the order and allow him to visit any such person.

Education supervision orders – no care

2.27   The power to place a child in the care of a local authority is removed from the ambit of the Education Act 1944. The court may only place a child in care by virtue of an application made by a local authority (in effect the social services committee) or the NSPCC under the Children Act 1989. The local education authority no longer has the power to seek an educational care order. The court does have the power to make an education supervision order under section 36 of the Children Act 1989 if it is satisfied that the child is of compulsory school age and is not being properly educated. That is to say that he is not receiving efficient full-time education suitable to his age, ability and aptitude and any special educational needs he may have (if, for example, he is disabled).

Uniform jurisdiction

2.28   By virtue of section 92 of the Act the High Court, the county courts and the magistrates' courts (ie the family proceedings courts) may make any of the orders which the Act empowers a court to make, save that a magistrates' court may not make any order involving the property of, or held in trust for, a child or any income from such property. Further restrictions are placed on magistrates' courts in the making of financial provision for children; they are limited by paragraph 1 of Schedule 1 to making orders for periodical payments (ie maintenance) and lump sums (not exceeding £1000 per child per occasion). The High Court and county courts may in addition make secured orders, and orders for settlements and transfers of property. Provision is made by rule for certain ancillary orders, eg contribution orders under paragraph 23 of Schedule 2, and orders relating to day care under section 75, to be made exclusively by magistrates. In the High Court and county courts the powers of judges to make certain orders is subject to directions by the Lord Chancellor under section 9 of the Courts and Legal Services Act 1990 – the Family Proceedings (Allocation to Judiciary Directions 1991).

Transfer – magistrates' courts/county courts/High Court

2.29   The Act confers power on the Lord Chancellor to provide by order for proceedings to be transferred from one level of court to another, or to a court in a specified class or to a particular court. For the purpose of the order there are three levels of court, namely the High Court, county courts and magistrates' courts. The Lord Chancellor has exercised his powers by making the Children (Allocation of Proceedings) Order 1991 (SI 1991 No 1677). Thus for the first time in civil proceedings a case may be transferred between a magistrates' court and a county court or the High Court, on one or more of three basic ground of transfer:

- complexity, importance or gravity
- consolidation with other proceedings
- urgency.

HOW THE CHILDREN ACT 1989 FITS INTO FAMILY PROCEEDINGS

Divorce, judicial separation and nullity

2.30   Paragraph 31 of Schedule 12 to the Children Act 1989 substituted a new section for section 41 of the Matrimonial Causes Act 1973, so that the divorce court's duty to be satisfied with the arrangements for each child of the family before granting a decree nisi has been modified. The court's duty now is to consider whether, in the light of any arrangements which have been made for the child's upbringing and welfare, or which it is proposed to make, it should exercise any of its powers under the Children Act 1989. The court must first consider whether the circumstances require it, or are likely to require it, to exercise any of those powers. If that question is answered affirmatively and it is not in a position to exercise its powers without giving further consideration to the case, *and* it appears to the court that there are exceptional circumstances which, in the interest of the child, make it desirable for the court to do so, it may give a direction that the decree of divorce or nullity is not to be made absolute (or in the case of judicial separation that a decree is not to be granted), until the court orders otherwise. Where there are children of the family the court will have before it the Statement of Arrangements for Children – Form M4. It is upon this statement (or its incompleteness or absence) that the court will decide whether it appears that it should, or is likely to have to, exercise any of its powers under the Act.

2.31 The court must also have in mind, of course, section 1(5) of the Children Act 1989 which prohibits the court from making any order under the Act unless it considers that doing so would be better for the child than making no order at all. If the court does consider that it may be necessary to exercise any of its powers under the Children Act 1989, then it will almost certainly include in any direction which it gives under section 41 a requirement for a welfare officer to report on any matter which gives rise to concern, or it may direct the appropriate local authority to undertake an investigation in accordance with section 37 of the Children Act 1989.

2.32 The combined effect of section 41 of the 1973 Act and section 1(5) is to deter the parties to divorce etc from seeking section 8, or other orders, as a matter of course, while ensuring that the welfare of the children in every case is addressed by both the parties and the court. The parents continue to have parental responsibility for each of their children, by virtue of section 2(1) of the Children Act 1989, and it is only where there is a dispute which cannot be resolved otherwise that the court will make an order. The court is enabled to carry out its duty under section 41 of the Act by the Statement of Arrangements for Children which the parties must file in each case.

2.33 The attendance of the parties at court at what was known as a 'Section 41 Appointment' will no longer be required in the very large majority of cases. The arrangements for the children will be considered by a district judge, on the Statement of Arrangements for Children, generally without the need for a hearing.

Domestic violence and the matrimonial home

2.34 Since proceedings under the Domestic Violence and Matrimonial Proceedings Act 1976 and sections 1 and 9 of the Matrimonial Homes Act 1983 are family proceedings for the purposes of the Children Act 1989, by virtue of section 8 (3)

2.34 *The new children law*

and (4), the court dealing with proceedings under those enactments has power to make orders under the Children Act 1989 in respect of any child affected by those proceedings. The court may also transfer proceedings under the Children Act 1989 to any court which may be dealing with proceedings under the Acts of 1976 and 1983, if it considers that to do so would be in the interests of any child concerned.

Adoption

2.35 The Children Act 1989 makes a number of amendments to the Adoption Act 1976 in order not only to take account of the terminology and concepts of the 1989 Act, but also to align the operation of the two Acts. By virtue of section 8 (3)(b) and (4)(d) adoption proceedings are 'family proceedings', and accordingly any order under the Children Act 1989 may be made by the court at any stage during the course of adoption proceedings. The restrictive conditions of section 37 of the Children Act 1975, which were designed to encourage the making of a custodianship order instead of an adoption order, have been repealed; they added little to the court's duty to give paramount consideration to promoting the welfare of a child when considering any question relating to its upbringing. So also has section 26 of the Adoption Act 1976, and the court's power to make a supervision or care order 'in exceptional circumstances'. The court may instead direct a local authority to investigate the child's circumstances under section 37 of the Children Act 1989. The addition of a subsection (2A) to sections 18 and 27 of the Adoption Act 1976 means that no application to free a child for adoption may be made without the consent of a parent or guardian unless the child is in the care of a local authority; and a parent or guardian may not remove a child who is the subject of an adoption application from his home, against the will of the person with whom he has his home, if the child is in the care of a local authority. The position of a putative father is also safeguarded by the provisions of subsections (7) and (8) which have been added to section 18 of the 1976 Act. The court, by virtue of those provisions, must satisfy itself that a father who does not have parental responsibility for a child does not intend to apply for a parental responsibility order under section 4(1) of the Children Act 1989, or a residence order under section 10; or that if he did so; it would be likely to refuse the application.

Wardship

2.36 So far as the private law use of wardship is concerned, where proceedings are brought by an individual, the inherent jurisdiction of the High Court is left largely undisturbed. The Children Act 1989 prevents the use by a local authority of wardship as a means of taking a child into care, by repealing section 7 of the Family Law Reform Act 1969, and in section 100(2) by enacting that the High Court's inherent jurisdiction may not be invoked to place a child under the care or supervision of a local authority. It also prohibits that jurisdiction being exercised so as to require a child to be accommodated by or on behalf of a local authority, to be made a ward while the subject of a care order or to enable a local authority to decide how parental responsibility shall be discharged. Thus, for example, in the classic case of the child of parents who refuse for religious reasons to allow a child to be given a life-saving blood transfusion or to undergo an abortion, a local authority will not be able to have recourse to making the child a ward so that the court may order the transfusion to be carried out.[1] In those circumstances the local authority would have to seek the leave of the court to apply for a specific issue order under section 8. Its locus standi for doing so would be, of course, in pursuance of its duty under section 17(2) and paragraph 4(1) of Schedule 2 to take reasonable steps, through the provision of services under Part III of the Act (ie social services provision), to prevent the child suffering ill-treatment or neglect; and its duty under section 47(1) and (8) to investigate and take action to safeguard or promote the child's welfare where it has reasonable cause to suspect that the child is suffering, or is likely to suffer, significant harm. It would appear that because the local authority could obtain a section 8 order it would be prevented from seeking to invoke the inherent jurisdiction of the High Court by section 100(4) of the Children Act 1989.

[1] *Re B (a minor)* (1991) Guardian, 21 May.

Marriage

2.37 In the Marriage Act 1949 the law concerning consent to marry has been modified by the Children Act 1989 and now provides a simpler set of rules. Who may give consent to the marriage of a minor depends upon whether there is, or was immediately before the child attained the age of 16, a residence order in force, or a care order in force. If not, each parent who has parental responsibility for the child and each guardian may give consent. If a residence order is in force, then the consent of the person, or persons, with whom the child lives (or is to live) as a result of the order may be given. If a care order is in force then the local authority designated in the order and each parent who has parental responsibility, and each guardian, must consent. If the child is over 16 and a residence order was in force immediately before he attained that age, then the person or persons with whom he lived (or was to live) as a result of the order may consent.

Conflict of laws and the Family Law Act 1986

2.38 The conflict of laws issues which the Family Law Act 1986 seeks to resolve are, by and large, unaffected by the Children Act 1989 save that the 1986 Act is modified to take account of the terminology and concepts of the 1989 Act. The provisions of Part I of the 1986 Act have been amended to refer, inter alia, to section 8 orders and any order made under the inherent jurisdiction of the High Court. Chapter VI of Part I of the 1986 Act consequently applies to proceedings relating to such orders, and empowers the court to order the disclosure of a child's whereabouts and to order recovery of the child. It also contains provisions (in section 33(2)) requiring a person to make disclosure even if doing so might incriminate him or his spouse of an offence, but a statement or admission made in compliance with such an order is not admissible in evidence against either, save in proceedings for perjury.

LEGAL AID

2.39 Civil legal aid, the grant of which is the responsibility of the Legal Aid Board, is available to the parties in all courts in proceedings under the Children Act 1989. Criminal legal aid will no longer be granted by magistrates' courts in respect of care proceedings. Separate forms for Children Act cases have been introduced by the Legal Aid Board to distinguish them from other applications for civil legal aid. There are, in effect, three ways of obtaining legal aid for Children Act proceedings, described in the following paragraphs.

2.40 In most private law cases and in some public law cases applications for legal aid will be made in the normal way, through a solicitor in writing to a legal aid area office. The decision whether to grant legal aid will be made in accordance with the rules of financial eligibility and the reasonableness of the case, including the prospects of success.[1] The second mode of application will be where there is genuine urgency which does not allow time for a full application to be considered before legal aid can commence. In these cases an emergency application may be made, either in writing or by telephone to the local legal aid area office. A decision on such an application will be made the same day. Where it seems likely that a full application would be successful an emergency legal aid certificate will be issued to provide temporary cover while a full application is considered. This follows the normal procedure for emergency legal aid and the temporary certificate will only last until a decision has been taken on the full legal aid application.

[1] Free-standing Children Act, adoption or wardship proceedings are made on Form CLA5, with the appropriate means form (and Form CLA3 if an emergency certificate is sought); applications in matrimonial and other family proceedings made on Form CLA2A. Where ABWOR is available Form ABWOR1A should be used.

2.41 The third route has been specially introduced for children, parents and those with parental responsibility in care and emergency protection proceedings under sections 31 and 44 respectively. The usual legal aid means and merits tests will be waived so that legal representation is available as of right for parents and children, and there is no possibility of delay in providing legal aid in these particular cases where children and parents are at risk of separation. In these circumstances a solicitor will be able to act immediately if he is satisfied that the child or parent falls into the relevant category. The Legal Aid Act 1988 (Children Act 1989) Order 1991 (SI 1991 No 1924) amends the Legal Aid Act 1988 to this effect, but the solicitor will have to make a formal application to notify the local legal aid area office that he is acting[1] so as to enable the office to issue a legal aid certificate. In respect of an emergency legal aid application, as well as under these arrangements, cover will be given for necessary work done by a solicitor should proceedings start over a weekend or overnight, provided that:

- the solicitor submits a legal aid form setting out full details within three working days – special procedure
- the legal aid area office approves an emergency application on the next working day – emergency application.

There will be no legal aid merits test for persons who apply to be, or have been, joined as parties in proceedings under sections 31 or 44 of the Children Act 1989.[2] However, apart from children, parents and those with parental responsibility, other persons will have to qualify under the usual financial eligibility rules for legal aid.

[1] Form CLA5A alone should be used.
[2] Form CLA5 with the appropriate means form (and Form CLA3 if an emergency certificate is sought).

2.42 The special dispensation for children and parents in emergency protection and care proceedings will continue until the proceedings are concluded and will cover all directly related issues, eg consideration by the court of an interim care order under section 38 of the Children Act 1989 or where care proceedings conclude with a court making section 8 order. On the other hand, a separate legal aid application would have to be made to cover proceedings between parents such as an injunction or maintenance. Where care or emergency protection proceedings start while other proceedings are pending the special dispensation will apply from that point, eg if a court treats an application under section 43(3) (CAO) as an application for an EPO. The waiver of the legal aid means test will continue in respect of an appeal, but a merits test will apply. An application for the discharge of an EPO under section 45(8) will be covered by the special dispensation, but not an application to discharge or vary a care order under section 39(1). The latter will require a full legal aid application, using the emergency procedure where necessary.

2.43 By virtue of section 15(3B) of the Legal Aid Act 1988 (as amended by section 99(2) of the Children Act 1989), civil legal aid must be granted to any child who is the subject of an application under section 25 of the Children Act 1989 to place him in secure accommodation, and who is not represented but wishes to be legally represented.

CHAPTER 3

General principles

PRINCIPLES RELATING TO THE WELFARE OF THE CHILD

3.1 The 'welfare' principle that has existed in statutory form for many years in the Guardianship of Minors Acts is perpetuated in a slightly modified form in section 1(1) of the Children Act 1989. But whereas the Guardianship of Minors Acts provided that in any question relating to the upbringing of a child, or the administration of his property, *the first and paramount consideration* shall be the welfare of the child, in the Children Act 1989 the child's welfare is required simply to be the court's *paramount consideration*. This reflects in statutory form the old principle of the Court of Chancery that in proceedings relating to children the welfare of the child is the paramount consideration and is not to be overridden by the claim of either parent. The approach of the courts to such questions is unlikely to be significantly different from the situation which has been reached in this respect through the development of the law over the years, and it is reasonable to expect the courts to have regard to the existing case law when reaching decisions about the welfare of the child. The court is required to come to a decision that will best promote the interests of the child and his welfare.[1] However, such decisions will be informed invariably by other factors, because although the welfare of the child must be the court's paramount consideration, it will not be the court's sole consideration. All the relevant facts, relationships, claims and wishes of the parents, risks, choices and other circumstances must be taken into account and weighed to arrive at the course which is most in the interests of the child.[2] The Children Act 1989 assists the court, and those having to interpret the welfare principle, by providing a checklist in section 1(3) (see para **3.4**).

[1] *J v C* [1970] 668 AC, [1969] 1 All ER 788, HL.
[2] *W v P (custody application)* [1988] FCR 349, CA.

3.2 General principles

Avoidance of delay

3.2 A principle of the widest possible application is that *in any proceedings* in which *any* question of the upbringing of a child arises, the court must have regard to the general principle that any delay in determining the question is likely to prejudice the welfare of the child – section 1(2). This question does not simply apply to proceedings under the Act, and it would include for example proceedings under the Matrimonial Causes Act 1973, the Adoption Act 1976, the Domestic Violence and Matrimonial Proceedings Act 1976, and the Domestic Proceedings and Magistrates' Courts Act 1978. During the course of any litigation the parties are inevitably under some degree of stress, and the sense of time of a child, particularly a small child, is generally much more acute than that of an adult so that delay may be especially damaging to a child. Delay also tends to narrow the court's options for finding the best outcome for a child because it is liable to reinforce the status quo. The prolongation of an unsatisfactory situation in which a child is placed, eg with one parent or in the interim care of a local authority, may mean that it has become more prejudicial to the child's welfare to change that situation than to allow it to continue. It is in order to reduce the likelihood of undue delay that the Act requires the court, in both public law and private law cases, to establish a timetable for the proceedings; the rules also require a date to be fixed for the next stage in the proceedings on the completion of each interlocutory hearing so that the pace of the litigation is maintained by the court, rather than being left in the hands of the parties.

3.3 It has become the practice, where there is a child of the family, to include in a divorce petition a prayer for custody of the child, and while this may have been desirable when a mother required a court order to acquire parental powers, in the large majority of cases there is no issue between the parents about whom the child is to live with. Even where this is the case seeking an order can be seen as a hostile step in the emotionally charged circumstances of family proceedings. It is generally accepted that it is in the child's interest to maintain his relationship with both parents, and that this will not be promoted by an order which may be a formality but which nevertheless appears to favour one parent over the other. Anything which will tend to assist the parties to keep separate the issues of being a spouse in conflict and being a parent will better enable a child's relationships with his parents to flourish. It is also better to maintain and support those relationships rather than allow the state to intervene through the agency of a local authority, unless that is the best way of safeguarding the child's welfare.

USE OF CHECKLIST

3.4 The court must have regard to the section 1(3) checklist in the circumstances set out in section 1(4), that is to say where the court is considering whether to make, vary or discharge a section 8 order, and the application is opposed, or where it is considering whether to make, vary or discharge any of the orders under Part IV (relating to care and supervision) – opposed or unopposed. In other cases the court is likely to find it helpful to have regard to the checklist even though it is not bound to do so, and as a consequence anyone who is considering a question concerning the upbringing of a child, or the administration of its property, will need to take account of the matters contained in the checklist. These are:

- the ascertainable wishes and feelings of the child concerned (considered in the light of his age and understanding)
- his physical, emotional and educational needs
- the likely effect on him of any change in his circumstances
- his age, sex and background and any characteristics of his which the court considers relevant
- any harm which he has suffered or is at risk of suffering
- how capable each of his parents, and any other person in relation to whom the court considers the question to be relevant, is of meeting his needs
- the range of powers available to the court under this Act in the proceedings in question.

The first and last considerations on this list are indicative of important matters which underpin the policy which Parliament has approved in this legislation. The Act requires the child's voice to be heard because he is the focus, and not an incident, of the proceedings. The court is required to play an active role in finding the best solution for promoting the child's welfare by having regard to the range of powers available to it, and going beyond whatever proposals may be put before it by the parties where necessary. However, where urgent action may be called for, eg the making of an emergency protection order under Part V, the checklist is not mandatory because the court may not be in a position to have regard to all the matters listed above, and it may also only hear evidence from one side.

3.5 The checklist is by no means exhaustive, and the parties may well wish to put other considerations before the court. The court itself may require a report by a welfare officer or guardian ad litem to deal with other matters which it will specify. Nevertheless it provides a means of encouraging consistency of approach, and should be of assistance in ensuring that the same basic factors are being used to implement the welfare criterion. It is also a helpful tool for advisers in the task of explaining what the court is likely to think is best for the child in particular circumstances, and thereby promoting the settlement of disputes over children.

Non-intervention

3.6 No court has the power to make any order under the Children Act 1989 in respect of a child in any proceedings unless the court is satisfied that it would be better for the child to make the order than to make no order at all. This focuses the minds of the adult parties and the court on the needs of the child, as opposed to the perceived needs of the adult parties. It has become a matter of form for a petition for dissolution or judicial separation, for example, to include in the prayer for relief at the end of the petition an application for the custody of the children of the marriage. This on occasion served more as a bargaining point for the spouses than as a requirement for the protection of the interests of the children, about whom there was frequently no substantial dispute. Indeed, the inclusion of a request for the custody of a child in the petition could add unnecessarily to the tensions and conflicts which inevitably exist between the parties, and create an issue which would not otherwise arise. In public law proceedings the conditions for making a care, supervision or emergency protection order may exist, but the court is still required to consider whether such an order would be better for the child than making no order at all. Thus the court in every case should address the question whether the harm which a child may suffer from the making of an order, eg the sudden removal of the child from his home, his parents and brothers and sisters, is as great or greater then the harm which he is likely to suffer if the order is not made.

PARENTAL RESPONSIBILITY

Parental responsibility – the principles

3.7 Prior to the implementation of the Children Act 1989 the statutory concept of parental responsibility did not exist, and in various enactments terms such as 'parental rights and duties'[1] or 'powers and duties'[2] or 'rights and authority'[3] were used to describe a parent's legal relationship with a child. The judges, and in particular the House of Lords,[4] took the view that the powers which parents exercise over their children are no more than a necessary concomitant of their parental duties. After extensive consultation, and a general consensus in favour, the Law Commission recommended that 'parental responsibility' should '. . .replace the ambiguous and confusing terms that are used at present'.[5] The term 'parental responsibility' has now been defined in section 3(1) of the Children Act 1989, and means:

'. . .all the rights, duties, powers, responsibilities and authority which by law a parent of a child has in relation to a child and his property.';

Subsections 3(2) and (3) go on to provide that it includes:

'. . .the rights, powers and duties which a guardian of the child's estate . . . would have had in relation to the child and his property.';

and

'. . .in particular, the right of the guardian to receive or recover in his own name, for the benefit of the child, property of whatever description and wherever situated which the child is entitled to recover.'

The definition thus also clarifies the position of a parent with regard to his or her right to receive property on behalf of a child, by equating that right with the right vested in a guardian.

[1] Children Act 1975, s 85; Adoption Act 1976, s 12; Child Care Act 1980, s 3.
[2] Child Care Act 1980, s 10.
[3] Guardianship Act 1973, s 1.
[4] *Gillick v West Norfolk and Wisbech Area Health Authority* [1986] AC 112.
[5] Review of Child Law Guardianship and Custody (Law Com No 172).

3.8 It would be superficially attractive to list all those 'rights, powers, duties, responsibilities and authority' referred to in section 3(1), but it would be impracticable to do so. In order to meet differing needs and circumstances such a list would have to change from time to time, and as the House of Lords recognised in the Gillick case,[1] the list must vary with the age and maturity of the child in question and the particular circumstances before the court. However, whether or not a person has parental responsibility for a child does not affect any obligation which he may have in relation to the child (eg a duty to maintain), nor does it affect his (or any other person's) right to succeed, on the child's death, to the child's property.[2]

[1] *Gillick v West Norfolk and Wisbech Area Health Authority* [1986] AC 112.
[2] Children Act 1989, s 3(4).

3.9   Parental responsibility is conferred by operation of law on the mother and the father, if married to the mother, of the child. It may be acquired by the father of a child who is not married to the mother, by virtue of section 4(1)(b) of the Children Act 1989, by agreement with the mother. It may be given to the father of a child who is not married to the mother, or any other person, by order of the court. It may also be conferred on a person by appointing him or her, in writing (or by will), to be the child's guardian on the death of a parent or guardian. A local authority, or the NSPCC, acquires parental responsibility for a child when a care order is made placing the child in their care. While parental responsibility may be exercised by more than one person, each person who has parental responsibility in relation to a child may exercise it independently of any other. It is not lost simply because some other person acquires parental responsibility for the child, and it cannot be surrendered or transferred, but it may be delegated in whole or in part to one or more other persons to act on behalf of a person with parental responsibility (eg a school). Shared parental responsibility could include not only married parents, but unmarried parents if it is conferred upon the father under the Act, one or more parents and a local authority when a child is in care, or a parent and a non-parent where the latter has acquired it under the Act. However, it would be lost for instance on the making of an adoption order because the Adoption Act 1976 transfers parental responsibility wholly to the adoptive parents.

Children of unmarried parents

3.10   By virtue of section 2(2)(a) of the Children Act 1989 the mother of a child who was not married to the father at the time of the child's birth has parental responsibility for the child. The father of the child does not, unless he acquires it in accordance with the Act. He can acquire it in four ways. Two ways apply only to the father of a child, and these are provided by section 4 of the Act; the other two ways are of general application.

3.11 Where there is no dispute that a man is the father of the child, and the mother agrees with the father that he should also have parental responsibility for the child, mother and father may make a *parental responsibility agreement.* To have effect in law the agreement must be made in the form prescribed by the Lord Chancellor in the Parental Responsibility Agreement Regulations 1991, and recorded in the manner prescribed in the regulations (see Appendix 5). This provides a simple way for an unmarried couple to share parental responsibility for a child without having to resort to court proceedings.

3.12 If the parents cannot agree, or there is a dispute about paternity, the man may seek an order that he shall have parental responsibility. Before it may grant such an order the court must be satisfied that the man is the father of the child and this is the means by which a man may establish his paternity. An order under section 4 of the Act does not affect the child's residence or compel the mother to allow the father to have contact with the child. If these matters remain in dispute, the father must obtain a section 8 residence or contact order. The putative father may apply to the court for a residence order in his favour, and if the court decides to make such an order it must also make a parental responsibility order (section 12(1)). A father may also acquire parental responsibility by being appointed a guardian under section 5(1) where the child has no parent with parental responsibility for him.

REPRESENTATION OF THE CHILD'S VIEWS

3.13 A different approach is taken in the Act to the manner of representing the views and wishes of the child according to whether the proceedings are 'public law' proceedings (ie under section 25 or as defined in section 41(6)), or 'private law' proceedings. In the case of the latter, the approach taken in the Children Act 1989 is to recognise that the child is entitled to be treated as an independent person, and not merely as an adjunct of his parents or an incidental factor in family proceedings. This is achieved by several provisions which, respectively require the court to:

- have regard to the ascertainable wishes and feelings of the child (section 1(3)(a))
- consider an application by a child for leave to apply for an order (section 4(3)(b), section 6(7)(b), section 10(1)(a)(ii) and (2)(b))

- allow a child who has reached the age of eighteen to apply for an order for maintenance against his parents in certain circumstances (Schedule 1, paragraph 2)
- appoint an individual to be a guardian of its own motion in any family proceedings (section 5(1) and (2)).

Where a child seeks leave to apply for an order the court must be satisfied that the child has sufficient understanding to make the proposed application. Even where a child is not a party to the proceedings the court may order a welfare report, and direct that the welfare officer shall consult the child about his wishes and feelings and include a statement in that regard in her report.

3.14   Where a child is being looked after by a local authority and the local authority considers that it is necessary to place the child in secure accommodation, to prevent him from absconding or from doing harm to himself or others, it must apply to the court under section 25 and the Children (Secure Accommodation) Regulations 1991 (S.I. 1991 No 1505)[1] if the child is to be kept in secure accommodation for more than an aggregate of 72 hours in any period of 28 consecutive days. The court may not exercise its powers to order the child to remain in secure accommodation unless the child is legally represented, or has refused or failed to apply for legal aid having been informed of his right, and given the opportunity, to do so.

[1] Extended by the Children (Secure Accommodation) (No 2) Regulations 1991 (SI 1991 No 2034).

3.15   In any proceedings under Part IV or V the child will be joined as a party to the proceedings. The court must appoint a guardian ad litem for the child in accordance with section 41, unless it is satisfied that it is not necessary to do so in order to safeguard her interests. If the child is not represented and no guardian ad litem has been appointed for the child, the court may appoint a solicitor to represent her, if the child has sufficient understanding to instruct a solicitor, and wishes to do so, and it appears in the child's best interests that she should have a solicitor. On appointment a guardian ad litem must instruct a solicitor to act on behalf of the child, unless the child has already instructed a solicitor. If the child is instructing a solicitor direct, or intends to conduct the proceedings on her own behalf (and is capable of doing so), the guardian ad litem must inform the court. The guardian ad litem will carry out her duties (save for instructing a solicitor) in accordance with the rules, and may seek the leave of the court to have legal representation. A solicitor appointed by a guardian ad litem will represent the child in accordance with the instructions of the guardian ad litem, unless the solicitor considers that the child wishes to give instructions which conflict with those of the guardian ad litem and that she is capable of doing so; the solicitor must then conduct the proceedings according to the child's instructions. If no guardian ad litem has been appointed the solicitor of course follows the child's instructions – but if the solicitor receives no instructions from either guardian ad litem or child she must represent the child in furtherance of the child's best interests (see chapter 10).

Attendance of the child

3.16 The court may order the attendance of a child in proceedings under Parts IV and V when it is hearing an application for an order, or is considering making an order, under those Parts at any stage of the proceedings. If the order is not complied with, or the court has reasonable cause to believe that it will not be complied with, the court may order:

- any person who is in a position to do so to bring the child to court
- a constable or other specified person to bring the child to court, and to enter and search any premises in which there is reasonable cause to believe that the child may be found
- any person whom the court has reason to believe has information as to the child's whereabouts to disclose it.

In any proceedings under the Children Act 1989 the court may direct that the proceedings, or any part of them, shall take place in the absence of the child if the court considers that it is in the interests of the child to do so, having regard to the matters to be discussed or the evidence likely to be given, provided that the child is represented by a guardian ad litem or a solicitor. Before it does so the court must give the guardian ad litem, the solicitor for the child (if either has been appointed) and, if she is of sufficient understanding, the child an opportunity to make representations.

3.17 There is a rule (rule 9.5 of the Family Proceedings Rules 1991) of general application to all family proceedings (that is business of any description which in the High Court is dealt with in the Family Division)[1] which allows the court to appoint either the Official Solicitor or any other person to be the guardian ad litem of a child who the court thinks ought to be separately represented. Such an appointment may only be made with the consent of the person who it is proposed should be appointed. It enables, for example, a guardian ad litem to be appointed in the High Court or a county court for the mother of a child who is the subject of proceedings under Parts IV or V of the Children Act 1989, where the mother is under the age of 18.

[1] Section 32 of the Matrimonial and Family Proceedings Act 1984.

Change of child's surname and removal from the United Kingdom

3.18 When spouses or unmarried partners separate, and the person with whom the child is living forms a new relationship, or remarries, the new couple (and indeed the child) may wish the child to be known by a new surname. Similarly, the foster parents of a child in care may wish the child to be known by their surname, or the local authority may have other reasons for wishing to give the child a new name. If a residence order is in force with respect to a child, or if a child is in care, sections 13(1) and 33(7) respectively require the leave of the court to be given before the child's surname may be changed, unless the written consent of every person who has parental responsibility for the child is obtained. This is necessary even where the change of name is effected informally, as well as when a formal change is intended, for example by deed poll.

3.19 The same procedure must be followed where a child who is the subject of a residence order, or who is in care, is to be removed from the United Kingdom for a month or more. If the period during which the child is to remain outside the United Kingdom is less than one month, then the person in whose favour the residence order is made, or the authority in whose care he is, may take the child, or arrange for him to be taken, abroad. When making a residence order the court may grant leave for the child to be removed from the United Kingdom either generally or for specified purposes. It may also make it a condition of the residence order that the child shall not be removed even for one month, and a specific issue or prohibited steps order could be made to the same effect.

EVIDENCE

3.20 The evidence of children in any civil proceedings (not only family proceedings) is governed generally by section 96 of the Children Act 1989. This enables a court, when it is of the opinion that the child does not understand the nature of the oath, to receive a child's unsworn evidence. The court must be satisfied, however, that the child understands that it is his duty to speak the truth and that he has sufficient understanding to justify his evidence being heard. In addition that section empowers the Lord Chancellor, by order, to make admissible hearsay evidence. He has made the Children (Admissibility of Hearsay Evidence) Order 1991 (SI 1991 No 1115) which makes the evidence given in connection with the upbringing, maintenance or welfare of a child admissible notwithstanding any rule of law relating to hearsay. The order applies to civil proceedings in the High Court, a county court and to family proceedings in a magistrates' court.

3.21 In both public law and private law proceedings affidavits are not used, but written statements of the substance of the oral evidence which a party intends to adduce must be filed, and served on the parties and any welfare officer or guardian ad litem. Copies of documents, including experts' reports, must similarly be filed and served. A party may not adduce evidence or rely upon documents without the leave of the court, unless he has complied with the requirement to file and serve statements and documents (see paras **5.11** to **5.14**).

3.22 A child may not be examined, medically or psychiatrically, or otherwise assessed, by an expert for the purpose of preparing a report for proceedings without the leave of the court. If the leave of the court is not obtained, no evidence arising out of such an examination or assessment may be adduced without the leave of the court (see para **5.14**).

Self-incrimination

3.23 A witness in any proceedings under Parts IV or V may not be excused from giving any evidence, or from answering any question put to him on the ground that he might incriminate himself, or his spouse, by doing so (section 96(1)). But any such statement or answer is not admissible in evidence against the person who made the statement, or gave the answer, or his spouse save in proceedings for perjury. This provision is similar to the provision in section 33(2) of the Family Law Act 1986 in relation to the requirement to disclose information as to where a child is, in proceedings for a section 8 order or for an order of any court exercising the inherent jurisdiction of the High Court.

KEEPING CHILDREN WITH THEIR FAMILIES

3.24 An important element in the underlying policy of the Act is to foster the family and to provide support so that, so far as possible, a child may remain with, or at least in contact with, the members of his family. This is achieved in a number of ways. The concept of parental responsibility, for example, means that a parent living apart from a child nevertheless retains parental responsibility for the child, that is all those rights, duties, powers, responsibilities and the authority which by law a parent has in relation to a child and his property. The exercise of those powers, duties etc may be circumscribed by orders of the court such as a residence order or a care order. Nevertheless they continue in existence only subject to the limitations which a court may impose.

Family assistance order – purpose

3.25 In any family proceedings where the court has power to make a section 8 order it may make a Family Assistance Order (FAO) under section 16, whether or not it makes a section 8 order (see para. **2.26**). The court must, however be satisfied that the circumstances of the case are exceptional and that every person to be named in the order consents. The purpose of an FAO is to require a probation officer or officer of the local authority (ie a social worker) to advise, assist and where appropriate befriend any person named in the order. That may include a parent or guardian of the child, a person in whose favour a contact order has been made or with whom the child is living, and the child. An FAO may not last for more than six months. It may be made when the child, and his family, require expert help to deal with problems arising out of the family situation, for example a traumatic separation or divorce in which the child, or his parents, are having difficulty in coming to terms with the breakdown in relationships. The assistance given would be aimed at preserving or promoting the child's relationship with his parents, or other members of his family from whom he might otherwise become alienated, and perhaps to resolve behavioural problems which might eventually culminate in a care or supervision order being made.

General local authority duties

3.26 More generally, under Part III of, and Schedule 2 to, the Children Act 1989 local authorities are under a duty to provide support for children and their families. They must, amongst other things, promote the upbringing by their families of children within their area who are in need by providing a range and level of services appropriate to the needs of those children. The services which they must make available are:

- advice, guidance and counselling
- occupational, social, cultural and recreational activities
- home help, including laundry facilities
- assistance with, or facilities for, travelling to make use of services, and
- assistance to enable a child and her family to have a holiday.

In relation to a child in need, 'family' includes any person who has parental responsibility for the child and any other person with whom she has been living.

Family centres

3.27 A further general duty of a local authority, which will assist in keeping a family together and to function effectively as such, is the requirement to provide family centres. A family centre is defined as a centre at which a child, his parents or anyone who may have parental responsibility for him and any other person who is looking after him, may attend for activities as defined above, advice, guidance and counselling.

Provision of accommodation to protect a child

3.28 Where a child has suffered, or is likely to suffer, abuse by another member of his household, whether sexual, physical or emotional, the local authority may be faced with the dilemma that to leave the child where he is will expose him to the risk of further harm, but to remove him from his home may itself damage the child. The best solution from the child's point of view might be for the suspected or actual abuser to leave the home; but that person may have no alternative accommodation readily available which he can afford. Assistance to find alternative accommodation may be given by the local authority under paragraph 5 of Schedule 2, including assistance in cash.

In this way the child may be able to stay in his home, and the need for the local authority to seek an emergency protection order, for example, is diminished. This may be coupled with the duty which is laid upon the local authority by paragraph 7 of Schedule 2, which requires them to take reasonable steps to reduce the need to bring proceedings for care and supervision orders, or any family proceedings which might lead to a child being taken placed in care, or wardship proceedings. A local authority must also take reasonably practicable steps to enable a child to live with his family, or to promote contact between him and his family, where the child is living apart from his family. This duty only applies in respect of a child who is in need and who is not being looked after by the local authority.

CHAPTER 4

Procedure up to directions or other hearing

PROCEDURE GENERALLY

4.1 Procedure in the High Court and in county courts is governed by the Family Proceedings Rules 1991 (SI 1991 No 1247), Part IV of which is concerned with proceedings under the Children Act 1989. Part IV, together with other relevant extracts from the rules, is reproduced in Appendix 1. The Rules are made by the Lord Chancellor under section 40(1) of the Matrimonial and Family Proceedings Act 1984 in respect of all family proceedings, save adoption (see Adoption Rules 1984 (SI 1984 No. 265)). In the magistrates' courts procedure under the Children Act 1989 is governed by the Family Proceedings Courts (Children Act 1989) Rules (SI 1991 No 1395), also made by the Lord Chancellor - under section 144 of the Magistrates' Courts Act 1980. References to rules in those instruments are indicated by the abbreviations *FPR* for the Family Proceedings Rules 1991, and *FPC* for the Family Proceedings Courts (Children Act 1989) Rules 1991. Transfer of proceedings between courts is governed by The Children (Allocation of Proceedings) Order 1991 (SI 1991 No 1677), article 5 of which specifically disapplies the transfer provisions of sections 38 and 39 of the Matrimonial Proceedings Act 1984 to proceedings under the Children Act 1989 or the Adoption Act 1976. In respect of proceedings under those Acts that order also regulates the commencement of proceedings in, and allocation to, particular county courts. There are three classes of county court for family work:

- divorce county courts,[1] some of which only have interlocutory hearings before a district judge
- family hearing centres[2] where family jurisdiction is exercised in private law cases by circuit judges and district judges
- care centres[3] where circuit judges and district judges exercise jurisdiction in public law as well as private law cases.

4.1 *Procedure up to directions or other hearing*

A map showing the locations of these courts appears in Appendix 4. The Principal Registry of the Family Division is treated as if it were a divorce county court, a family hearing centre and a care centre, and where any magistrates' court refuses to transfer a case under article 7 of the Children (Allocation of Proceedings) Order 1991, an application under article 9 of the order may be made to the Principal Registry of the Family Division.

¹ Divorce county courts are those courts designated under s 33 of the Matrimonial and Family Proceedings Act 1984 (see Appendix to the County Court Practice).
² Family hearing centre means a court listed in Schedule 1 to the Children (Allocation of Proceedings) Order 1991.
³ Care centre means a court listed in Schedule 2 to the Children (Allocation of Proceedings) Order 1991.

4.2 Part IV of the Family Proceedings Rules is very similar to the Family Proceedings Courts (Children Act 1989) Rules 1991: rules 1 to 21 in each set correspond to each other, and several of the remaining rules also correspond although they are not numbered identically. Most of the prescribed forms are common to the High Court, county courts and magistrates courts. Whereas the Family Proceedings Courts (Children Act 1989) Rules 1991 are self-contained, Part IV of the Family Proceedings Rules 1991 must be read, of course, with Part I which contains:

- definitions (rule 1.2)
- the application of the Rules of the Supreme Court 1965 and the County Court Rules 1984 to family proceedings (rule 1.3)
- the application of the rules to the Principal Registry of the Family Division (rule 1.4)
- the computation of time under the rules (rule 1.5).

Reference may also need to be made to rules in Parts VIII (appeals), IX (disability) and X (procedure – general). The Children (Admissibility of Hearsay Evidence) Order 1991 (SI 1991 No 1115) makes hearsay evidence, when given in connection with the upbringing, maintenance or welfare of a child, admissible in any civil proceedings in the High Court, a county court (which, of course, encompasses family proceedings under the Children Act 1989 and other enactments and wardship) and 'family proceedings' in a magistrates' court. Since proceedings under Part V of the Children Act 1989 are not included in the definition set out in section 8, the order has no effect in relation to proceedings for emergency protection. Family proceedings are defined in subsections (3) and (4) of section 8 as any proceedings under the inherent jurisdiction of the High Court in relation to children, and any proceedings under the following enactments:

- Parts I, II and IV of the Children Act 1989
- Matrimonial Causes Act 1973
- Domestic Violence and Matrimonial Proceedings Act 1976
- Adoption Act 1976
- Domestic Proceedings and Magistrates' Courts Act 1978
- Sections 1 and 9 of the Matrimonial Homes Act 1983
- Part III of the Matrimonial and Family Proceedings Act 1984.

Privacy (FPR 4.16(7)/FPC 16(7))

4.3 In the High Court and county courts, unless the court directs otherwise, all hearings of applications under the Children Act 1989, including directions appointments, are held in chambers. It is therefore a matter for the court whom it will allow to observe the proceedings in chambers, other then the parties, and their legal representatives. Where it is desirable for the judgment, or part of it, to be reported the court may adjourn into open court, or it may decide that the whole of the proceedings will be held in court rather than chambers. It will only take that course exceptionally since it will rarely be in the interests of a child for the press and public to have access to the hearing. The publication of information relating to proceedings before any court sitting in private where the proceedings are concerned with the care of a child is a contempt of court by virtue of section 12 of the Administration of Justice Act 1960. The judge has power to allow disclosure of information given in proceedings if it is in the public interest and would not prejudice any legitimate interest of the child.[1] The publication of the text, or a summary of, the whole or any part of an order made by the court sitting in chambers is not of itself a contempt, unless the court (if it has the power to do so) expressly prohibits the publication (section 12(2) of the Act of 1960).

[1] *Re R (MJ) (a minor)* [1975] Fam 89, [1975] 2 All ER 749.

4.4 In the magistrates' courts the privacy of proceedings is governed by FPC 16(7), section 97 of the Children Act 1989 and sections 69 and 71 of the Magistrates' Courts Act 1980. FPC 16(7) allows the court, where it considers it expedient in the interests of the child, to hear in private any proceedings under:

- the Children Act 1989
- any statutory instrument made under it

- any amendment made by the Children Act 1989 in any other enactment.

The media are prohibited from publishing (which includes broadcasting by television or radio) any material which is intended, or likely, to identify any child as being involved in any proceedings in a magistrates' court, in which any power under the Children Act 1989 may be exercised with respect to the child, or any other child. Nor may they identify the address or school of such a child. To do so is an offence by virtue of section 97(6). In addition, under sections 69 and 71 of the Magistrates' Courts Act 1980, newspapers or periodicals may only publish the grounds of the application, submissions on points of law and the court's decision, including its reasons. It is a defence under section 97 for the accused to prove that he did not know, and had no reason to suspect, that the published material was intended, or likely, to identify the child.

Timing of proceedings (FPR 4.15/FPC 15)

4.5 It is, of course, one of the basic principles of the Children Act 1989 that any delay in determining a question with respect to the upbringing of a child is likely to prejudice its welfare. FPR 4.15/FPC 15 has been devised to exert a discipline upon the court and the parties to proceedings by requiring the date of the next hearing to be fixed upon, or as soon as practicable after:

- the transfer of a case
- the adjournment or completion of any hearing in the proceedings which does not bring them to a conclusion.

The fixing of the date upon which the proceedings will come before the court again is a function of the court or, in the High Court or a county court 'the proper officer' – ie the listing officer, and in a magistrates' court the justices' clerk. Upon fixing the date the proper officer will send a notice of the date to the parties, and the welfare officer and/or the guardian ad litem if one has been appointed.

APPLICATIONS

Where applications may be made (FPR 4.3/FPC 3)

4.6 Every application must be made in the appropriate form in Appendix 1 to the Family Proceedings Rules 1991 (High Court or a county court) or in Schedule 1 to the Family Proceedings

Courts (Children Act 1989) Rules 1991 (magistrates' court). If there is no such form in Appendix 1/Schedule 1 the application must be made in writing. If it is being made to a county court the application must be filed in a divorce county court in accordance with article 14 of the Children (Allocation of Proceedings) Order 1991. Special arrangements exist for London, where the Principal Registry of the Family Division (in Somerset House) is treated for the purposes of the Children (Allocation of Proceedings) Order 1991 as a divorce centre and a family hearing centre by virtue of article 19; an application for a section 8 order or under the Adoption Act 1976 may be commenced and tried in Lambeth or Woolwich County Courts by virtue of article 20 of the order. If the application is to be made to the High Court it must be filed in a District Registry or the Principal Registry of the Family Division. Where the rules require a document to be 'filed' this is done by delivering it to the court staff for it to be entered in the records of the court, either by handing it in at, or by posting it to, the appropriate court office.

Filing the application (FPR 4.4/FPC 4)

4.7 When an application is filed, the proper officer of the court or the justices' clerk, ie the court official dealing with the application, must fix a date for a hearing or directions appointment (whichever is appropriate) and endorse the date on the copies of the application filed by the applicant. The applicant is then required to serve upon each respondent (see paras **4.15** and **4.16**) a copy of the application. He must do this in the case of a section 8 order within 21 days, and in the case of any other application under Part I or II of the Children Act 1989 within 14 days, prior to the date fixed for the hearing or directions appointment (but see para **4.8** for ex parte orders and chapter 10 for applications under Parts IV or V). Where an application is made under Schedule 1 to the Children Act 1989 (Financial Provision for Children) the application must be accompanied by a statement setting out the financial details which the applicant believes to be relevant to the application, and containing a declaration that the statement is true to the best of the applicant's knowledge and belief. Sufficient copies of the statement must be filed for one to be served on each respondent. In summary, the steps to be taken are:

- Select and complete the appropriate form in Appendix 1/ Schedule 1 to the rules, or if there is no such form type the application

4.7 *Procedure up to directions or other hearing*

- If a financial provision is being sought make a statement setting out relevant financial details
- Make a copy for each respondent
- File the copies in the appropriate court office
- Check column (ii) of Appendix 3/Schedule 2 to the Rules for the number of days to allow for service prior to the date fixed for the hearing/directions
- Serve a copy of the application, endorsed with the date of the hearing or directions appointment, on each respondent within the time allowed.

Where no form is provided for the application in Appendix 1 to the rules the format opposite is suggested for the written application.

APPLICATION FOR A ＿＿＿＿＿ ORDER

Section ＿＿＿ of the Children Act 1989

To The ＿＿＿＿＿＿＿＿＿ [High][County][Magistrates'] Court

Case No ＿＿＿＿＿

I apply for ＿＿＿＿＿＿＿＿＿＿＿＿＿＿＿＿＿＿＿

＿＿＿＿＿＿＿＿＿＿＿＿＿＿＿＿＿＿＿＿

[I am making this application within other family proceedings, the case number of which is ＿＿＿＿＿.]

The name of the child is ＿＿＿＿＿; [s]he is a [boy] [girl] born on ＿＿＿＿＿ 19 ＿, now aged ＿＿.

The child lives at ＿＿＿＿＿＿＿＿＿＿＿＿＿＿

＿＿＿＿＿＿＿＿＿＿＿＿＿＿＿＿＿＿＿＿

＿＿＿＿＿＿＿＿＿＿＿＿＿＿＿＿＿＿＿＿

The applicant is [a parent] [a person with parental responsibility]

[another party to the proceedings ＿＿＿＿＿]

[a person seeking leave to make this application]

[the child]

My title is ＿＿＿＿＿ Mr[ ] Mrs[ ] Miss[ ] Ms[ ] Other ＿＿＿＿

My full name is ＿＿＿＿＿＿＿＿＿＿＿＿＿＿＿

My full address is ＿＿＿＿＿＿＿＿＿＿＿＿＿＿

＿＿＿＿＿＿＿＿＿＿＿＿＿＿＿＿＿＿＿＿

＿＿＿＿＿＿＿＿＿＿＿＿＿＿＿＿＿＿＿＿

My telephone no is ＿＿＿＿＿＿＿＿

My solicitor is ＿＿＿＿＿＿＿＿＿＿＿＿＿＿＿

＿＿＿＿＿＿＿＿＿＿＿＿＿＿＿＿＿＿＿＿

＿＿＿＿＿＿＿＿＿＿＿＿＿＿＿＿＿＿＿＿

Tel: ＿＿＿＿＿ Fax ＿＿＿＿＿ Ref ＿＿

The grounds of my application are:

＿＿＿＿＿＿＿＿＿＿＿＿＿＿＿＿＿＿＿＿

＿＿＿＿＿＿＿＿＿＿＿＿＿＿＿＿＿＿＿＿

＿＿＿＿＿＿＿＿＿＿＿＿＿＿＿＿＿＿＿＿

＿＿＿＿＿＿＿＿＿＿＿＿＿＿＿＿＿＿＿＿

I declare that the information I have given is correct and complete to the best of my knowledge ＿＿＿＿＿＿ date ＿＿＿＿

4.7 *Procedure up to directions or other hearing*

A Notice of Hearing must be completed in respect of each respondent upon whom the application is to be served, and filed with the application. A practice form, CHA70 or CHA71, is available in district registrars, county courts and the Principal Registry of the Family Division, which may be used; the CHA71 is for an addressee who is not a respondent. A proforma example of each form was included in Appendix 9 to the 'Special Issue – Chidren Act 1989' of Court Business distributed to those offices in October 1991.

Urgent applications (FPR 4.4(4)/FPC 4(4))

4.8 Certain applications may be made ex parte (that is to say without any other party affected by the application being present) in circumstances of urgency, in order to safeguard a child's welfare. These include a prohibited steps order or a specific issue order under section 8, and three kinds of public law applications and a Warrant of Assistance under section 102 (see chapter 10). The rules provide for such an application to be made by telephone, in which case the applicant must file an application in respect of each child, in the appropriate form in Appendix 1/Schedule 1 to the rules, within 24 hours of the telephone application. Otherwise the appropriate form for each child must be filed at the time the application is made. If the court grants the order sought ex parte a copy of the application must be served by the applicant on each respondent within 48 hours after the making of the order. If the court refuses to make an order ex parte it may direct that the application should be made inter partes, and the procedure set out at para **4.7** will apply.

Withdrawing an application (FPR 4.5/FPC 5)

4.9 Once an application has been made it can only be withdrawn by leave of the court. This may be done by filing in the court office a written request which sets out the reasons why the applicant wishes to withdraw the application. Alternatively, such a request may be made orally to the court (that is to say, to a judge or one or more justices) if the parties and the welfare officer are present. If made in writing, a copy of the request must be served on all the parties to the application. If the other parties consent to the request in writing, and the court sees fit, the court will grant the request. There will be no hearing, and the proper officer or justices' clerk will notify the parties, the welfare officer and the guardian ad litem (if either has been appointed) that the request has been granted. If the other parties do not consent, or the court does not see fit to grant the application without a hearing, the proper officer or justices' clerk will give the parties, and the welfare officer and guardian ad litem, at least seven days of the date he has fixed for the hearing of the request to withdraw the application.

Leave to make an application (FPR 4.3/FPC 3)

4.10 Certain persons require the leave of the court (which may in a magistrates' court be a single justice) to bring proceedings under the Children Act 1989. When made by a child an application to terminate a parental responsibility order, or to end the appointment of a guardian, requires the leave of the court under section 4(3)(b) (parental responsibility order) and section 6(7)(b) (guardian) respectively. Similarly, leave is required to apply for a section 8 order in family proceedings by a person who is not entitled to apply for a section 8 order by virtue of section 10(4)-(7) (see section 10(1)(a)(ii)). A free-standing application for a section 8 order, under section 10(2), requires leave by virtue of subsection (2)(b)) if the applicant is not entitled to apply for such an order by subsections (4)-(7) of that section. The persons entitled to apply for any section 8 order without leave are:

- any parent or guardian of the child
- any person in whose favour a residence order is in force with respect to the child.

And those who are entitled to apply only for a residence or contact order without leave are:

- any party to a marriage (whether subsisting or not) in relation to whom the child is a child of the family
- a person with whom the child has lived for three years or more
- a person who has the consent of each of the persons in favour of whom a residence order is in force
- a person who has the consent of the local authority where the child is in the care of that local authority
- a person who has the consent of each of those who have parental responsibility for the child.

In addition, a person who is, or was at any time within the last six months, a local authority foster parent of a child may only seek leave to apply for a section 8 order if one of the following applies:

- he has the consent of the authority
- he is a relative of the child
- the child has lived with him for at least three years preceding the application.

Where a person wishes to be allowed contact with a child in care under section 34(3) he must obtain the leave of the court unless he is:

- a parent
- a guardian
- a person in whose favour there was a residence order in force immediately before the care order was made
- a person who had care of the child as a ward immediately before the care order was made.

A person seeking the leave of the court to bring proceedings under the Children Act 1989 must file a request for leave setting out the reasons for the application. The request must be accompanied by a draft of the application (in the prescribed form in Appendix 1/Schedule 1 to the rules or if there is no such form, in writing – see para **4.6**) and sufficient copies of it for one to be served on each respondent. The court may either grant the request, in which case the court staff will inform the person making the request, or it will direct that a date be fixed for hearing the request and the notice which those concerned are to be given of that date. In the latter case, the person making the request, and the other persons concerned, will be given notice by the court staff of the date which has been fixed. A suggested form of request is shown opposite.

REQUEST FOR LEAVE TO [BRING PROCEEDINGS] [WITHDRAW APPLICATION] CHILDREN ACT 1989

To The _____ [High][County][Magistrates'] Court

Case No _____

Section _____[4(3)(b)] [6(7)(b)] [10(1)(a)(ii)] [10(2)(b)] of the Children Act 1989.

[I seek leave to [withdraw my application] [bring proceedings] under the above section.]

The name of the child is _____; [s]he is a [boy] [girl] born on _____ 19 ____, now aged _____.

The child lives at _____

_____

_____

The applicant is [the child] [a person connected with the child]

My title is _____ Mr[ ] Mrs[ ] Miss[ ] Ms[ ] Other _____

My full name is   _____

My full address is   _____

_____

_____

My telephone no is _____

My solicitor is   _____

_____

_____

Tel: _____ Fax _____ Ref _____

My reasons for [withdrawing] [making] the application [attached] are:

_____

_____

_____

_____

I declare that the information I have given is correct and complete

to the best of my knowledge _____ date _____

71

APPLICATIONS UNDER PARTS I AND II IN MATRIMONIAL AND DOMESTIC PROCEEDINGS

4.11 The Children Act 1989 defines family proceedings in section 8(3) and (4) as proceedings under the inherent jurisdiction of the High Court and under:

- Children Act 1989, Parts I, II and IV
- Matrimonial Causes Act 1973
- Domestic Violence and Matrimonial Proceedings Act 1976
- Adoption Act 1976
- Domestic Proceedings and Magistrates' Courts Act 1978
- Matrimonial Homes Act 1983, sections 1 and 9
- Matrimonial and Family Proceedings Act 1984, Part III.

All the above enactments, save the Children Act 1989, are primarily to do with disputes between adults but are nevertheless proceedings in which the upbringing of a child may be relevant. While leaving these enactments in place the Children Act 1989 provides for the same remedies in respect of children to be available in proceedings brought under them as are available under Parts I and II as 'free-standing' applications. Thus a common set of powers in relation to children is available in all courts whenever decisions have to be made by a court in respect of a child. Before the commencement of the Children Act 1989, most applications in respect of children were made in divorce proceedings. It is likely that applications made in divorce proceedings will continue to predominate, despite the fact that fewer applications will be made because the court may not make an order in respect of a child unless it considers that doing so would be better for the child than making no order at all. By virtue of FPR 2.40(1), where a matrimonial cause (that is an action for divorce, nullity or judicial separation) is pending, any application in respect of a child of the family[2] must be made 'in the cause', that is to say as an application in those proceedings. The large majority of applications will be for a section 8 order, and must be made in form CHA10D (FPR Appendix 1). It will be possible, although unusual, to make an application under section 5 in form CHA3 (appointment of guardian), or under section 6(7) in form CHA5 (termination of appointment of a guardian). More frequently, applications may be made under section 13 to change a child's surname, in form CHA11, or to remove a child from the United Kingdom, in form CHA11A. It is possible for an application to be made for an order under section 5 or under section 10 by a person who is not a party to the cause, provided that he has obtained leave under rule 4.3 to make the application (see para. **4.10**). If leave has been obtained in this way by a third party, it is not necessary for her to ask for leave to intervene in the matrimonial cause. If proceedings relating to any child of the family are begun in one court while a matrimonial cause is pending in another, the person making the application is required, by FPR 2.40(2), to file in the matrimonial cause a concise statement of the nature of the proceedings relating to the child. If that person is not a party then the petitioner in the matrimonial cause must file the concise statement. It is also possible in family proceedings for a court to make an FAO (see para. **2.26**) under section 16, whether or not it decides to make any other order under Part II of the Children Act 1989.

[1] A child of the family is a child of both parties to the marriage or any other child who has been treated by both of them as a member of their family (Matrimonial Causes Act 1973, s 52(1)).

PARTIES

Respondents (FPR 4.7/FPC 7)

4.12 The parties to applications are the applicant and the respondents prescribed by FPR 4.7(1)/FPC7 and column (iv) of Appendix 3/column (iii) of Schedule 2 to the respective rules. In all applications under the Children Act 1989 there are categories of persons who (if they exist) must always be joined in the proceedings as respondents. They are:

- every person whom the applicant believes to have parental responsibility for the child
- where the child is the subject of a care order, every person whom the applicant believes to have had parental responsibility immediately prior to the making of the care order
- in the case of an application to extend, vary or discharge an order, the parties to the proceedings leading to that order
- in specified proceedings, the child.

In addition to these respondents, in applications under Schedule 1 to the Children Act 1989 (financial provision) those persons whom the applicant believes to be interested in or affected by the proceedings, must also be joined.

4.13 A person who is not a respondent may request to be joined as a party to the proceedings, by virtue of FPR 4.7(2)/FPC 7(2).

In order to be joined he must file a request to the court in writing. If the person who wishes to become a party has parental responsibility for the child, the court must grant his request without a hearing or any representations, in accordance with FPR 4.7(4)/FPC 7(4). A party to the proceedings may also file a request in writing that another person be joined as a party. Similarly, if a party wishes to cease to be a party, or wishes another party to cease to be a party, he may file a request in writing. (A suggested form of written request is set out at para **4.7**.)

Persons to whom notice must be given (FPR 4.4(3)/FPC 4(3))

4.14 An applicant, besides serving a copy of his application on each respondent as required by FPR 4.4(1)(b)/FPC 4(1)(b), must give written notice of the proceedings to the persons set out in FPR Appendix 3, column (iii)/FPC Schedule 2, column (ii). The purpose of this is to inform those persons who have an interest in the child that legal proceedings are being taken in respect of him, and to give them the opportunity to apply to be joined as parties. As with respondents, there are certain categories of person who must be given notice of any application in respect of a child. They are:

- any local authority providing accommodation for the child
- any person who is currently caring for the child
- if the child is alleged to be staying in a certified refuge (section 51(1) or (2) of the Children Act 1989) the person who is providing the refuge.

Where the application is for a section 8 order, in addition to those listed above, the applicant must also give notice to every person whom he believes:

- to be named in a court order which is still in effect with respect to the child (unless he believes that it is not relevant)
- to be a party to pending proceedings in respect of the child (unless he believes that they are not relevant)
- to be a person with whom the child has lived for three years or more prior to the application.

Where the application is for an order under section 5(1) (appointment of a guardian), if the father of the child does not have parental responsibility he must also be given notice (if he does have parental responsibility he will be a respondent). In

the case of applications under Parts IV and V of the Children
Act 1989 reference should be made to FPR Appendix 3/FPC
Schedule 2.

SERVICE

Service of documents and notices (FPR 4.8/FPC 8)

4.15 When an application or other document has been filed
it will generally be required by the rules to be served on, that
is to say sent or given to, every other party to the proceedings.
The Act and the rules provide a number of ways of effecting
service. There are special provisions in FPR 4.8(4)/FPC 4(4) in
respect of service of documents on a child, but any document
may be served by delivering it personally to the person being
served - ie by handing it to him in person. Where a person
wishes to enforce a residence order under section 14(2) of the
Children Act 1989 it must be served in accordance with section
108(8) either by being served personally, or by being posted to
him by registered post, or recorded delivery, at his last known
address. Service of documents otherwise is dealt with in FPR
4.8/FPC 8, and the method of service will depend upon whether
the person to be served is acting in person, or by solicitor, or
is a child. If the person to be served is not known to be acting
by solicitor the service may either be personal, or by first class
post to, or by delivery at, his residence or last known residence.
If the person is known to be acting by solicitor then documents
may be delivered at, or sent by first class post to, the address
which the solicitor has given for service; where that address
includes a document exchange box number the document to be
served may be left at that document exchange or at a document
exchange which sends documents to that document exchange
on every business day. Service via a solicitor may also be effected
by sending a legible copy of the document to the solicitor's office
by facsimile. Service of a document on a party who is a child
may be the subject of a direction of the court, but where no
such direction has been given the document should be served
on the child's solicitor, or if no solicitor has been instructed
upon the guardian ad litem. If neither solicitor nor guardian
ad litem has been appointed, then the leave of the court must
be sought to serve the document upon the child in accordance
with FPR 4.8(4)(c)/FPC 8(4)(c). If the court refuses leave then
it must give a direction under paragraph (8) of the rule that
the requirement under the rules, or any other rules, that the

document be served shall not apply, or that service shall be effected in some other way. In summary, service is effected by:

Party acting in person –
- by handing it to him, or
- by delivery at his residence or last known residence, or
- by sending by first class post to his residence or last known residence.

Party acting by solicitor –
- by delivery at the solicitor's address for service
- by sending by first class post to the solicitor's address for service, or
- where the solicitor has a document exchange or FAX number, by delivery via the document exchange or by FAX.

Child –
- by delivery to the child's solicitor, or if none
- by delivery to the child's guardian ad litem, or if none
- WITH LEAVE OF THE COURT to the child.

Whether there is a solicitor acting for a party can usually be ascertained by telephoning the court and asking for the name and address for service of the solicitor on the record for that party. The court staff will also usually be able to provide the name and address for service of any guardian ad litem.

Service on behalf of a child

4.16 Service on behalf of a child who is a party to proceedings must be effected by the child's solicitor, or if no solicitor is instructed by the guardian ad litem. If the child has neither then the court must serve documents on behalf of the child.

Time to allow for service

4.17 Paragraph (6) of rule 4.8 creates a rebuttable presumption that a document served by first class post was received on the second business day after posting (ie a weekday, other than Christmas and Boxing Days or a bank holiday). Similarly in the case of a document served on a solicitor via a document exchange. Accordingly, where one of these methods is used, an additional two *working* days must be included in any calculation regarding the service of a document within a particular time limit (eg see entries in column (ii) of FPR Appendix 3/FPC

Schedule 2). An example of such a calculation is given below in the case of a directions hearing of an application under section 5(1) (appointment of a guardian) which is to take place on 3 January 1992, which is a Friday:

Notice required (App 3, col (ii))	14 days
Bank holiday Wednesday 1 January	1 day
Christmas Day (Wed) & Boxing Day (Thurs)	2 days
Saturdays & Sundays (3 weekends)	6 days
Total	23 days

Personal service, or service by delivery at an address or by FAX, must therefore take place 23 days before 3 January on Wednesday 11 December 1991 at the latest; a document to be served by first class post or by document exchange must be posted, or delivered to the document exchange, no later than Monday 9 December. In this example the court official who fixed the date of the hearing, in accordance with FPR 4.4(2)(a)/FPC 4(2)(a), would have to have done so by 9 December at the very latest in order to allow sufficient time for the applicant to comply with the cumulative effects of FPR 4.4(1)(b)/FPC 4(1)(b), column (ii) of FPR Appendix 3/FPC Schedule 2 and FPR 4.8(6)/FPC 8(6).

Statement of service

4.18 The applicant is required to file a statement of service before, or no later then the time of, the first appointment for directions or the hearing. The statement must confirm that a copy of the application has been served on each respondent, and every person to whom notice of the proceedings must be given has been notified (see para **4.14**). The statement must also indicate the date and time of service, where and how it was effected, or where service was by post, the date, time and place of posting. A practice form, CHA72, is available in district registries, county courts and the Principal Registry of the Family Division, and may also be used in magistrates' courts. An example is set out overleaf.

Statement of Service

To The   [High] [County] [Magistrates'] Court

The child is [＿＿＿＿＿] a [boy] [girl] born on [＿＿＿＿]   Case no [＿＿＿＿]

You must
- give details of service of the application on each respondent
- give details of service on persons to whom notice has to be given
- file this form with the court on or before the first directions appointment or hearing of the proceedings

You should
- if the person's solicitor was served, give his/her name and address
- if the guardian ad litem was served on behalf of the child, give his/her name and address
- if service was by first class post, give the date, time and place of posting

Name of person	Address of the person served	Method of service	Date served/ posted (1st class)	Time served/ posted (1st class)	Where served/ posted (1st class)

I am [＿＿＿＿] ☐ the applicant ☐ solicitor for the applicant ☐ guardian ad litem ☐ an officer of the court

Service of the [application] [notice of proceedings]
has been carried out according to the rules of court   Signed [＿＿＿＿＿＿]   Date

ANSWER TO APPLICATION

4.19 An answer to an application, where the application is contested, sets out the case for the respondent and provides for the respondent to make an application himself, if he wishes. The rules provide for three ways in which an answer may be made, two of which are specific and the third of which is general. The two specific cases require an answer to be made on prescribed forms in Appendix 1/Schedule 1; they are:

- on an application for a section 8 order – in form CHA 10A
- on an application under Schedule 1 (financial provision) – in form CHA 13A.

and in each of those cases the answer must be filed and served on each of the other parties to the application within 14 days of service of the application. With regard to applications other than the two specific cases mentioned above, an answer may be filed and served not less than two *working* days before the date which has been fixed for the application to be heard. A suggested form for a written answer in such cases is shown overleaf.

CONFIDENTIALITY AND NOTIFICATION OF CONSENT

Confidentiality of documents (FPR 4.23/FPC 23)

4.20 The rules prohibit any disclosure of a document which is held by the court (eg any document which has been filed) and which relates to proceedings under the Children Act 1989, without the leave of the judge or district judge, or the justices' clerk or the court in the case of magistrates' courts. The general rule does not apply to:

- a party
- the legal representatives of a party
- a guardian ad litem
- a welfare officer
- the Legal Aid Board

all of whom may have disclosed to them any document in the proceedings, nor does it apply to the record of any order.

RESPONDENT'S ANSWER

To the _____ [High][County][Magistrates'] Court

Case No _____

The child's full name is _____

My full name is _____

My full address for service is _____

_____

My solicitor's name and address is _____

_____

Tel no _____ FAX _____ Ref _____

[I do not accept that I should be a respondent to this application

because _____

_____]

Do not include the following ● to ● if you do not accept that you should be a respondent

●[Everything in the application is true to the best of my knowledge]

[I believe the application to be untrue in the following respects:

_____

_____

[The court should know the following about this application:

_____

_____

[I wish to oppose this application because _____

_____

_____]

[I intend to make an application for_____

_____]●

I declare that the information I have given is true and correct to the best of my knowledge

Signed _____ date _____

Notification of consent to FAO, change of name of child in care and to child going or living abroad (FPR 4.24/FPC 25)

4.21 There are three circumstances in which consent of those concerned must either be given orally in court, which will invariably be in the course of proceedings relating to an application, or in writing signed by the person giving his consent. In other words, consent must be explicitly personal and cannot, for example, be signified by a letter from a solicitor instructed by the individual concerned. The circumstances are:

- the making of an FAO where the court must obtain the consent of every person named in the order, except the child (section 16(3))
- changing the surname of a child, or removing him from the United Kigdom for one month or more, if the child is in care, requires the consent of every person who has parental responsibility for the child (section 33(7)
- a local authority arranging, or assisting in arranging, for a child in their care to live outside England and Wales; requires the consent of every person who has parental responsibility for the child (Schedule 2, paragraph 19).

In each of the above circumstances the approval of the court is also required, of course; in the first case by way of an order of the court's own motion, and in the other two cases by way of an application to the court. A suggested form of consent is set out overleaf. Although not required by the rules, this form could be used for consent under section 13(1) in private law cases.

4.21 *Procedure up to directions or other hearing*

FORM OF CONSENT

To the _____ [High][County][Magistrates'] Court
Case No _____

Section [16(3)] [13(1)] [33(7)] [Schedule 2, paragraph 19] of the Children Act 1989.

The child's full name is _____

My full name is _____

My address is _____
_____

[I am a person to be named in the Family Assistance Order which the court proposes to make under section 16 of the Children Act 1989 in respect of the child. I consent to the making of that order.]

[I am a person with parental responsibility for the child and I consent to [the child being known by a new surname] [the child being removed from the United Kingdom for a period of one month or more, from _____ 199 ___ to _____ 199 ___ .]

[the child living outside England and Wales in _____ .]

Signed _____ Date _____ 199__

CHAPTER 5

Procedure at and after hearings

DIRECTIONS FOR THE CONDUCT OF PROCEEDINGS

The directions hearing (FPR 4.14/FPC 14)

5.1 A key stage in most proceedings under the Children Act 1989 is the hearing for directions, which will always be necessary in a matter of any complexity. This is a preliminary hearing, the date of which is usually fixed in accordance with FPR 4.4(2)(a)/FPC 4(2)(a) when an application is filed. The directions hearing enables a district judge/justices' clerk (or a single justice) to take control of the proceedings by giving directions about those steps which must be taken by the parties before the substantive hearing of the application and, most importantly, to define a timetable for the action to be taken by each of the parties. If the need arises during the course of the proceedings, any of the parties may request a directions hearing (see para **5.3**). The directions which may be given are a matter for the court, which has a wide discretion to order any relevant step to be taken, but they include:

- the timetable for the proceedings
- varying the time within, or by, which action must be taken
- the attendance of a child
- the appointment of a guardian ad litem
- service of documents
- submission of evidence, including experts' reports
- welfare reports
- transfer to another court
- consolidation with other proceedings.

It is a requirement of section 11(1) of the Children Act 1989 that when any question of making a section 8 order arises, or any other question arises with respect to a section 8 order, the court must draw up a timetable. Similarly, a court hearing an application under Part IV must also draw up a timetable in accordance with section 32 (but see also chapter 8). It is likely that the court will draw up a timetable in any application of substance because, by virtue of section 1(2) of the Children Act 1989, the court must have regard to the principle that any delay in determining a question in relation to the upbringing of a child is likely to prejudice its welfare. The setting of a timetable will usually be, therefore, a feature of the initial directions hearing. Where any rules of court set a time limit within which an act must be done in Children Act proceedings then, by virtue of FPR 4.15(1)/FPC 15(4), the time limit may only be extended by directions given under FPR 4.14/FPC 14. In order to minimise delay, FPR 4.15/FPC 15 goes on to require the district judge/ justices' clerk, or the court staff, to fix a date for the next hearing either at the adjournment or conclusion of any directions hearing (unless the proceedings have been determined), or as soon as practicable after the directions hearing has taken place. The court will give notice of the date to the parties, and the guardian ad litem or welfare officer if one has been nominated.

5.2 Unless the court directs that a hearing shall take place in court, all directions appointments in proceedings, and the hearing of applications, under the Children Act 1989 take place in the High Court and a county court in chambers (FPR 4.16(7)). If a magistrates' court considers it expedient in the interest of the child it will hear the proceedings in private (FPC 16(7)).

5.3 Directions may be given, or varied, or revoked of the court's own motion. In most proceedings, however, the initiation of a directions hearing will usually be on the written request of a party. FPR 4.14 (3)(b) and (c) /FPC 14 paragraph 5(b)(c) provides for the giving, variation or revocation of directions on the written request of a party, who must specify the direction which is sought, file the request and serve it on the other parties. If the consent or agreement of the other parties is obtained, and the written request is signed by each, or his representative, then the request is simply filed for the court to consider (see para **5.4**). Where there are several parties, unless the other parties, or their representatives, are readily available and there is no difficulty in obtaining the necessary signatures on a single document, it is acceptable for a copy of the request to be sent to each for separate signature, provided of course that all the copies of the request which have been signed are filed together. A request for directions to be made, varied or revoked might take the following form.

APPLICATION FOR DIRECTIONS TO BE
[GIVEN][VARIED][REVOKED]

[Rule 4.14(3)[(b)][(c)] of the Family Proceedings Rules 1991] [Rule 14(5)[(b)][(c)] of the Family Proceedings Courts (Children Act 1989) Rules 1991]

To The _____ [High][County][Magistrates'] Court

Case No _____

The name of the child is _____

I _____[Applicant][Respondent] apply for the following directions [to be [varied][revoked]]:

[The other parties to these proceedings consent to [this][these] direction[s]-

Name _____ [Respondent][Applicant]

I consent _____

[Solicitor on behalf of _____]   ]

The applicant is [a parent] [a person with parental responsibility] [another party to the proceedings _____] [a person seeking leave to make this application] [the child]

My title is   Mr[ ] Mrs[ ] Miss[ ] Ms[ ] Other _____

My full name is   _____

My full address is   _____

_____

_____

My telephone no is _____

My solicitor is   _____

_____

_____

Tel: _____ Fax _____ Ref _____

5.4 When a written request is received by the court which requires a hearing (i e it does not have the consent of all the parties), the court staff will fix a date for hearing the request, usually in consultation with the party making it or their solicitor. The date of the hearing must be at least four working days ahead (ignoring Saturday, Sunday and any bank holiday) so as to allow two days for delivery of notices by first class post, unless the party making the request wishes to arrange for immediate delivery upon the other parties or their solicitors, when two days' notice is required. The court staff will then send a notice of the date of the hearing to the other parties. If the request for directions is by consent the court may simply grant the request and inform the parties of the decision. The court may wish, however, to hear argument about the request in which case a date for hearing the request will be fixed, and the court staff will send a notice to each party giving not less than two working days' notice. A note will be taken by the district judge/justices' clerk, or a court clerk, of the directions which have been given, varied or revoked. Any party who was not present at a directions hearing, or if there was no hearing all the parties, will be sent a copy of the note by the court as soon as practicable.

Urgent applications for directions

5.5 Where a party wishes to request the court to make, vary or revoke directions as a matter of urgency, in other words on less than two days' notice (i e not including Saturday, Sunday or a bank holiday), the request may be made orally and, if necessary, without notice to the other parties. The party wishing to make a request in this way may only do so if he has obtained the leave of the court, but leave may be obtained in a case of real urgency by telephoning the court and, indeed, the request itself could be dealt with by telephone. It is more likely that an oral request will be made during the course of a hearing when the other parties are present.

Section 8 order under section 11(3) or interim care or supervision order under section 38(1) (FPR 4.14(7)/FPC 14(7))

5.6 By virtue of section 11(3) of the Children Act 1989 the court may make a section 8 order, and by virtue of section 38(1)(a) it may make an interim care or supervision order, at any time during the course of an application even though it is not in a position to dispose finally of those proceedings. The rules therefore enable a party to ask the court to make a section 8 order, or an interim care or supervision order, in a request for directions as an interim measure pending the final outcome of the proceedings. For example, upon a substantive application for a residence order the court might be asked, by way of an application for directions, to make a prohibited steps order pending the resolution of the proceedings where the applicant believes that the respondent, with whom the child is living for the time being, may remove the child from the United Kingdom. The procedure for obtaining directions urgently, whether by an oral or written request, with or without notice, which is explained in para **4.25**, will apply to a direction in relation to an interim order as it does to other directions.

Order of court's own motion (FPR 4.14(8)/FPC 14(10)

5.7 The court may give directions for the conduct of proceedings where it decides that it may need to exercise its power to make an order of its own motion, eg a section 8 order under section 10(1)(b) or an interim care order under section 38(1)(b). In such a case the court will give the parties to the proceedings notice of its intention to give directions. It will invite the parties to make written representations, or if they wish to be heard on the matter it will fix a date for the parties to attend the court, giving them not less than two days' notice of the date.

Directions on transfer (FPR 4.14(9)/FPC 14(11)

5.8 If a case is transferred from one court to another, eg from a magistrates' court to a county court, or from a county court to the High Court, any directions which were in force immediately before the transfer took place will continue in force in the court to which the case has been transferred. The directions will remain in force until they are revoked or varied by the 'receiving' court, and they must be read subject to any changes in terminology that may be needed to make them apply appropriately in the 'receiving' court. The proceedings will be brought before the court for review shortly after transfer by virtue of FPR 4.15 (2)(a)/ FPC 15(5)(a) (see para **5.10**).

TRANSFER

Transfer from magistrates' court to county court and from county court to high court (FPR 4.6/FPC 6)

5.9 Transfer of proceedings from one court to another is governed by the Children (Allocation of Proceedings) Order 1991, and the transfer of public law proceedings from a magistrates' court to a county court, and vice versa, is dealt with in articles 7, 9 and 11 (see paras **8.50–8.53**). Other transfers of proceedings are dealt with in articles 6, 8, 10, 12, 13, 15, 16 and 17. A transfer of proceedings between magistrates' courts is dealt with in article 6, and a transfer from county court to county court in article 10. The question of transfer will usually be dealt with at the directions appointment, but any party may apply to the court for a direction for transfer at any stage in the proceedings. Transfers between magistrates' courts apart (where there are five criteria), there are two criteria for transfer from one tier of courts to another, both of which must be satisfied. *The common criterion upon which the decision to transfer must be based in every case is whether the transfer is in the interests of the child, having regard to the principle in section 1(2) of the Children Act 1989 that delay in determining any question relating to the child's upbringing is likely to prejudice the welfare of the child.* The other criterion of appropriateness varies slightly as between magistrate's courts, county courts and the High Court. Articles 8, 10, 12 and 13 confer the power to transfer as follows:

- *Article 8: magistrates' court to a county court*, if the magistrates' court considers the proceedings can be dealt with *more appropriately* in that county court
- *Article 10: county court to county court*, where the *sole* criterion is the interests of the child
- *Article 12: county court to High Court*, if the county court considers the proceedings are *appropriate* for determination in the High Court
- *Article 13: High Court to county court*, if the High Court considers the proceedings are *appropriate* for determination in a county court.

The criteria which govern transfers between magistrates' courts in addition to the delay criterion are:

- *Article 6: magistrates' court to magistrates' court*, if a transfer is considered to be in the interests of the child because it is likely to accelerate significantly the determination of the proceedings, because it would be appropriate to transfer the proceedings to be heard with other family proceedings, or for some other reason; and the 'receiving' justices' clerk consents to the transfer.

Where the destination of the proceedings upon transfer is a county court, articles 15 to 17 of the Children (Allocation of Proceedings) Order 1991 regulate to which category of county court (see para **4.1**) the proceedings may be transferred. In general, proceedings transferred to a county court must go to a *divorce* county court. The exceptions to this general rule are:

- where proceedings, other than an application for a section 8 order, are transferred so that they may be consolidated with other proceedings (they are transferred to the county court in which the other proceedings are pending)
- where an application for a section 8 order is transferred from the High Court, unless it is being transferred for consolidation, it must be transferred to a family hearing centre
- where a county court, which is not a family hearing centre, is notified that an application for a section 8 order, or proceedings under sections 12 or 18 of the Adoption Act 1976, will be opposed the proceedings must be transferred to a family hearing centre for trial.

Action required on transfer or refusal to transfer (FPR 4.6(4) and 4.15(2)(a)/FPC 6)

5.10 Where a justices' clerk receives a written request from a party to transfer proceedings he must issue a certificate in Form CHA64 in FPC Schedule 1 granting, or in Form CHA65 refusing, the request in accordance with the relevant above-mentioned criteria. A certificate granting a request must be sent to the parties, any guardian ad litem and to the receiving magistrates' or county court. Where the request to transfer to a county court is refused the applicant may file an application to the county court in Form CHA58 in FPR Appendix 1, together with a copy of the certificate in Form CHA65, and serve copies of both on all parties to the proceedings *within two days* of receiving Form 65. On the fourth day after the application has been filed (unless the parties agree to earlier consideration) the county court must consider the application and whether to grant it, in which case the court must inform the parties, or to hear the application with not less than one day's notice to the parties. Whenever proceedings are transferred from a magistrates' court to a county court, the county court must consider whether it is in the interests of the child to transfer the proceedings to the High Court, but only if the proceedings are appropriate for determination in the High Court (rule 4.6(4)). The county court must either:

- decide that an order is not needed,
- make an order of its own motion,
- fix a date for the parties to be heard on the question whether the case should be transferred and notify them, or
- invite the parties to make written representations on the question within a specified period.

If the county court orders the case to be transferred to the High Court, the court staff will notify the parties accordingly. In every court when proceedings are transferred, the court, or the listing officer, must fix a date for the proceedings to come before the court to which they are being transferred as soon as possible after the transfer (rule 4.15 (2)(a)(i)). This requires the court staff to establish when the receiving court can list the case for a directions appointment or hearing. The court, or the court staff, will notify the parties and any welfare officer and/or, guardian ad litem who has been appointed of the date so fixed.

AFFIDAVITS AND WRITTEN STATEMENTS

Use of documents and written statements (FPR 4.17/FPC 17)

5.11 In the High Court and county courts in proceedings under the Children Act 1989, which are governed by Part IV of the rules, affidavits may not be used. Instead, FPR 4.17 requires written statements to be filed. This facilitates uniformity of procedure, which is necessary in particular for cases which are transferred from magistrates' courts to county courts or the High Court. Since magistrates' courts have never used affidavits in their procedure it was simpler to require evidence by statement than to introduce the added complication of affidavits into the magistrates' courts system, which has had to accommodate itself to a significant departure from a largely oral, summary tradition by considering written evidence extensively. Each party who intends to adduce oral evidence must file and serve on the other parties, and any welfare officer or guardian ad litem who may have been appointed, written statements of the substance of that evidence (FPR 4.17/FPC 17). This applies to evidence to be given at a directions appointment or any hearing in the proceedings.

The statements must be filed at, or by, the time the court directs. If the court does not set a time, then the statements must be filed and served before the hearing or appointment at which oral evidence is to be given. There are additional restrictions in respect of proceedings for a section 8 order which are dealt with in para **5.12**. Each statement must be dated and signed by the person making it, and it must also contain a declaration by the person making it that the maker believes it to be true and understands that it may be placed before the court. Similarly, copies of any documents, including experts' reports, upon which a party intends to rely must also be filed and served on the other parties etc, before the hearing or at such other time as the court may direct. A party may not adduce evidence, nor seek to rely on any document, where he has failed to comply with these requirements, unless he obtains the leave of the court to do so. An example of how a statement of evidence might be set out follows.

STATEMENT OF EVIDENCE

Section _____ of the Children Act 1989

In The _____ [High] [County] [Magistrates'] Court

Case No. _____

This is the statement of _____

Address: _____

_____

I believe the above statement to be true and I understand that my statement may be placed before the court.

Signature _____ Date _____ 19____

Documents in proceedings for a section 8 order

5.12 There are restrictions upon the filing of documents in proceedings for a section 8 order. By virtue of FPR 4.17(4)/FPC 17(5), a party is prohibited from filing or serving any document other than as may be required by, or authorised in, the rules. Nor may a party vary in any way a form which is prescribed by the rules so as to give information, or make a statement, which is not required or authorised by the form. If for any reason a party wishes to depart from those requirements he must first obtain the leave of the court to do so. Furthermore, in proceedings for a section 8 order a party is not permitted to file a statement or a document, in compliance with FPR 4.17(1)/FPC 17(1) until such time as the court may direct. In other words, the party must wait until the first direction's hearing and await, or seek, a direction of the court about the timing of the filing of statements and other documentary evidence.

Supplementary and amended statements (FPR 4.19/FPC 19)

5.13 A supplementary statement, that is to say a statement which is supplementary to one which has already been served, may be filed and served on the other parties to the proceedings, provided that this is done in compliance with any direction which the court has given about the timing of statements. However, if a party wishes to *amend* a document which has already been filed and served he must obtain the leave of the court, and unless the court otherwise directs (eg during the course of a hearing) the request for leave must be in writing (FPR 4.19 (1)/FPC 19(1)). Although the rules are not explicit on this point, it is obviously necessary for the court to be told the terms of the amendment which the party is seeking to make. The court will either grant the request and inform the person who made it, or it will invite the parties, or particular parties, to make representations to the court within a specified period as to whether the request should be granted. Where the request is granted, the person amending the document must file it in its amended form, and serve it on all upon whom it was served previously. The amendment must be identified in the amended version of the document - eg by highlighting it, underlining it, or printing it in **bold** or *italics*.

Expert evidence (FPR 4.18/FPC 18)

5.14 Experts' reports are treated in the same way as any other documentary evidence. There is, however, a very important restriction on the commissioning of a report from an expert where the expert is required to examine medically or psychiatrically, or otherwise assess, the child in order to prepare a report for use in the proceedings. In every case the leave of the court must be obtained. The application for leave (see para **4.7** for a suggested format) must be served on all the parties, and the guardian ad litem if appointed, unless the court directs otherwise. If leave has not been obtained for the examination or assessment to be carried out no evidence arising out of the examination or assessment may be put before the court, unless it gives the party leave to do so. The court will clearly require compelling reasons for the failure to obtain leave, or for allowing the evidence to be adduced.

TESTS TO DETERMINE PATERNITY

Blood tests

5.15   Section 20 of the Family Law Reform Act 1969 (as amended by the Family Law Reform Act 1987 and section 89 of the Children Act 1989) enables any court in civil proceedings which involve the question of a person's paternity to direct the use of blood tests to establish whether or not there are sufficient genetic similarities between two or more people to prove that they are related. A sample cannot be taken from a person without his consent or, in the case of a mental patient or a child under the age of 16, the consent of the person who has the care of him (section 21 of the 1969 Act). If a person fails to comply with a direction of the court for blood tests, the court may draw such inferences, if any, from that fact as appear proper to the court in the circumstances (section 23). The 1969 Act does not confer an unfettered discretion on the court, and it must in any event be construed with section 1(1) of the Children Act 1989 where the issue impinges upon the upbringing of a child.[1] If the test will be in the interest of the child the High Court or a county court may restrain the mother from leaving the jurisdiction by exercising its power under section 37 of the Supreme Court Act 1981, as applied in a county court by section 38(1) of the County Courts Act 1984.[2] The procedure for ordering blood tests is contained in the Magistrates' Courts (Blood Tests) Rules 1971 (SI 1971 No 1991) in magistrates' courts, in CCR Order 47, rule 5 in county courts, and RSC Order 112 in the High Court. Blood tests must be conducted in accordance with the Blood Tests (Evidence of Paternity) Regulations 1971 (SI 1971 No 1861 – as amended).[3] As with applications made under Part IV of the Family Proceedings Rules 1991 or the Family Proceedings Courts (Children Act 1989) Rules 1991, an application for blood tests must be made by filing the application in the court and sending a notice to every other party in the proceedings not less than two days before the date fixed for it to be heard. The application must specify who is to carry out the tests if the person whose paternity is in issue is under the age of eighteen. If the direction involves taking a sample from a person who is not a party to the proceedings the notice of the application must be served on her personally, and the court may make her a party to the proceedings (CCR, Order 47, rule 5(3); RSC Order 112, rule 4). Where the court decides to give a direction for blood tests it must specify in the direction the person who is to carry out the tests, and that person must be the person specified in the application unless the court considers that it would be inappropriate to specify that person, in which case it must refuse the application. A list of medical practitioners appointed by the Home Secretary for testing blood samples, some of whom are able to carry out DNA profiling, is held in every county court office in 'Court Business' item B2001 or may be obtained on inquiry to a magistrates' court office. The court is unlikely to decline to make a direction on the ground that the person specified is inappropriate if one of these practitioners has agreed to undertake tests. When the court makes a direction for blood tests a copy of the direction will be sent to every party, and any other person from whom the direction involves the taking of samples. Until the court receives a report from the blood tester the proceedings will stand adjourned. When the report is received a copy is sent to every person to whom a copy of the directions were sent.

¹ *S v S* [1972] AC 24, [1970] 3 All ER 107, HL; *Re JS (a minor)* [1981] Fam 22, [1980] 1 All ER 1061, CA.
² *Re I (a minor)* (1978) the Times, 22 May, (1986) 137 NLJ 613.
³ Amending instruments are SIs 1975 No 896, 1978 No 1266, 1979 No 1226, 1982 No 1244, 1986 No 11357, 1987 No 1199, 1989 No 776, 1990 No 359, 1990 No 1025, 1991 No 12 and 1991 No 839.

WELFARE REPORTS AND GUARDIANS AD LITEM IN MATRIMONIAL PROCEEDINGS

Welfare officer (FPR 4.13/FPC 13)

5.16 For the purposes of the rules a 'welfare officer' is any person who has been asked to prepare a welfare report under section 7 of the Children Act 1989. She may be either a probation officer, an officer of a local authority (ie a social worker) or some other person the local authority considers appropriate (eg a fee-paid social worker or a social worker employed by a charitable organisation). In practice, in the county courts and the High

Court the court welfare officers are probation officers who have been nominated by the Chief Probation Officer for the area to undertake this role, and who in some areas form a civil work unit. Where the court considers that it will be assisted by a welfare report, or it accedes to an application by a party for a welfare report, it will usually ask at a directions hearing for a report to be prepared (see para **5.1**). The court may ask for the report to be made orally or in writing, but it will usually ask for a written report unless the issues upon it wishes the welfare officer to report are very minor or there is great urgency. It is generally recognised as good practice for the court to specify the issues with which it is concerned; to fail to do so leaves the welfare officer with little choice but to investigate all the circumstances of the child's family which may entail a great deal of wasted effort if there are only one or two issues with which the court is concerned. It is open to the welfare officer to seek a direction from the court as to the matters upon which it wishes her to report if it does not make this clear in its request. A report in contested proceedings should provide the court with reliable factual observations and information about the child and his relationship with each relevant adult, and his siblings, and their circumstances.[1] Although it may be necessary occasionally for more than one welfare officer to prepare the report, for example where the parties live at considerable distances from one another, a single report by one officer is more satisfactory.[2] The contents of a welfare report are excepted from the rules of evidence by the provisions of section 7(4) of the Children Act 1989. The court may take account of any statement made, and any evidence given in respect of matters referred to, in a report to the extent that the court regards the statement or evidence as relevant to the question which it is considering. A welfare officer may therefore properly include matters of hearsay, that is to say what she has been told by other persons, provided that they are relevant to the issues.

[1] *Scott v Scott* [1986] 2 FLR 320, [1986] Fam Law 301, CA; see also *Practice Direction* [1987] FCR 48, [1986] 2 FLR 171 which appear likely to be applied to equally to cases under the Children Act 1989.
[2] See *Practice Note (Welfare Reports)* (1973) 117 Sol Jo 88.

Timing and disclosure of the report (FPR 4.13/FPC 13)

5.17 When, in the usual way, a welfare officer makes a written report she must file a copy of it with the court by the date by which the court has directed the report shall be filed. If the court does not direct a particular date, then the welfare officer must file her report at least five days before any hearing at which she has been given notice that her report will be given or considered. The welfare officer must attend such a hearing, unless she has been excused by the court from attending. On receipt of the report the court staff will send a copy of the report to each of the parties and, if one has been appointed, to the guardian ad litem. Any party may question the welfare officer about her report at the hearing, and it is therefore a sensible precaution for any party wishing to do so to confirm to the court as soon as possible that they require the attendance of the welfare officer. It is a contempt of court in the High Court or a county court, and contrary to FPR 4.23/FPC 23, for a welfare report, or any material part of its contents, to be disclosed to any person without the leave of the court or the district judge/justices' clerk, except to a party or his or her legal representatives, a guardian ad litem (if appointed), the Legal Aid Board or a welfare officer preparing a further or fresh report.

Guardian ad litem in matrimonial proceedings in the High Court or a county court

5.18 A guardian ad litem may be appointed in matrimonial proceedings where a child needs to be represented on certain applications, under FPR 2.57. The applications are a variation of settlement which may affect the child's interests and any other ancillary application where the court thinks it necessary. There is a more general power to appoint a guardian ad litem in 'private law' proceedings under the Children Act 1989 under FPR 9.5. If in any family proceedings, that is to say any of the business which is of the sort which may be dealt with in the Family Division of the High Court, the court considers that a child ought to be separately represented it may appoint the Official Solicitor, or some other 'proper' person, to be the child's guardian ad litem. Before making the appointment it must be satisfied that the proposed guardian ad litem consents, and the Official Solicitor will usually only consent where the case is in the High Court or otherwise there is some particular reason why he should be appointed. A 'proper' person would be someone who has both the ability and the independence to represent the child impartially. There is no provision for a guardian ad litem to be reimbursed any expenses he may incur, and it is invariably desirable for the court to ask one or more of the parties to be prepared to bear the costs of the guardian ad litem. If the child is made a party to the proceedings he may, of course, become entitled to an order for costs in the usual way, but such an order will not enable the guardian ad litem to recover a fee for acting as such. An order appointing a guardian ad litem may be made by the court of its own motion, or it may direct a party to make an application for a guardian ad litem to be appointed in which case it must stay the proceedings until an application has been made. A party may also apply, without direction, for a guardian ad litem to be appointed, and the proposed guardian ad litem may apply himself. On an application by a party the written consent of the guardian ad litem must be filed, unless the court directs otherwise. The guardian ad litem may wish to withhold his consent until given an undertaking by the applicant that he will be reimbursed his expenses and, if appropriate – eg the proposed guardian ad litem is an independent social worker – a fee. If the proposed guardian ad litem is not to be the Official Solicitor then the applicant must also file with the consent a certificate by a solicitor that the proposed guardian ad litem has no interest in the proceedings adverse to that of the child, and that he is a proper person to be a guardian. Once appointed the guardian ad litem is treated as a party to the proceedings for the purposes of any requirement in the rules for a document to be served on, or a notice to be given to, a party.

HEARINGS

Attendance at directions appointment and hearing (FPR 4.16/ FPC 16)

5.19 Whenever the court gives a party notice of a directions appointment he is required to attend, unless the court/justices' clerk decides that his presence is not required at that hearing – in which case he will be told so when given notice of the hearing. The court may decide that a party, including a child, may be absent from all or any part of proceedings. It may do so if it considers that because of the evidence which is likely to be given, or the matters which will be discussed, it is in the interests of the child that the party be absent. The party must be represented, however, by a guardian ad litem or a solicitor. Before doing this the court must give the guardian ad litem and the solicitor for the child (if they have been respectively appointed or instructed), and the child, an opportunity to make representations about whether it is in the interests of the child that he, or another party, should be excluded from all or part of the proceedings. *If the applicant appears* at a hearing or directions appointment but any respondent does not, the court/ justices' clerk may proceed in the absence of the respondent, or respondents, but must be satisfied that he, or they, received reasonable notice of the hearing, or that the circumstances of the case justify proceeding. *If the applicant does not appear* the court may either refuse the application or, if sufficient evidence has been received previously, it may carry on the hearing without the applicant, provided that one or more of the respondents has appeared. *If no one appears* at the appointed time and place for a directions appointment or a hearing, the court may refuse the application.

The hearing (FPR 4.21/FPC 21)

5.20 At the substantive hearing of an application, or in a directions appointment, the normal order of giving evidence is for the applicant to open his case and to adduce his evidence. Any party with parental responsibility for the child will follow with his witnesses, and then any other respondents who wish to call witnesses. If a guardian ad litem has been appointed she will give evidence last, and if there is no guardian ad litem but the child is a party, the child is the last to give evidence. This sequence may be varied by directions of the court, both as to the order of speeches and as to the order in which witnesses shall be called. At the final hearing in the proceedings the court must deliver its judgment as soon as practicable, and this will be frequently delivered ex tempore though where the judgment is lengthy and complicated it may be reserved for subsequent delivery, either orally or by being handed down in writing to the parties. When it makes an order, or refuses an application, the court must state any findings of fact and its reasons for the decision. In a magistrates' court the justices' clerk must record in writing the name(s) of the justice(s) constituting the court and, in consultation with them, the reasons for the court's decision and any findings of fact. Any order which is made must be recorded in the appropriate form in Appendix 1/Schedule 1 to the rules, or when there is no such form, in writing. Form CHA 56 is a form of general order which will be appropriate in most circumstances where a specific form is not provided. The order form is completed by the court or a member of the court's staff, and a copy is served on each party and on any person with whom the child is living. If an order under any of the following sections is made ex parte, it becomes the duty of the applicant to serve, within 48 hours of the order being made, a copy of the order in the form indicated:

- a prohibited steps or specific issue order under section 8 – Form CHA8 Form CHA9
- section 44 (EPO) – Form CHA35
- section 48(4) (search order for another child) – Form CHA42
- section 48(9) (warrant of assistance) – Form CHA44
- section 50 (RO) – Form CHA46
- section 75(1) (cancelling registration of a child-minder) – Form CHA60: magistrates' courts only
- section 102(1) (search warrant for certain premises): Form CHA60: magistrates' courts only

The appropriate form must be served on each party and on any person who has the actual care of the child and who had such care immediately prior to the making of the order. Where a hearing or directions appointment takes place in the High Court or a county court outside the normal opening hours of the court office,[1] the judge or the proper officer must take a note of the substance of the proceedings.

[1] Usually 10.00 am to 4.30 pm, Monday to Friday except Bank Holidays; during certain holiday periods court office may only be open for part of the day.

Evidence (FPR 4.17 and 4.20/FPC 17 and 20)

5.21 At a hearing or directions appointment a party may only adduce evidence where its substance is contained in a written statement, or statements, which has been served on the other parties, and any welfare officer or guardian ad litem who may have been appointed, in accordance with FPR 4.17(1)/FPC 17(1), unless the court gives leave to the contrary (see para **5.11**). Nor may a party seek to rely on any document, including an expert's report, unless a copy of that document has been served on each party etc, or the court gives him leave to do so. The report of a welfare officer which has been served on the parties, and read by the court, may be the subject of questions by any party at a hearing during which the report is given or considered (see para **5.17**). Section 7(4) of the Children Act 1989 makes any statement in a report, and any evidence given in respect of matters referred to in a report, admissible regardless of any enactment or rule of law which would otherwise make it inadmissible, provided that in the opinion of the court it is relevant to the question which the court is considering. Hearsay evidence when given in connection with the upbringing, maintenance or welfare of a child is admissible in any civil proceedings, including of course family proceedings, before the High Court or a county court, by virtue of the Children (Admissibility of Hearsay Evidence) Order 1991 (SI 1991 No 1115). Similarly, in family proceedings[1] in a magistrates' court hearsay evidence is admissible by virtue of that order. The evidence of any child may be heard by the court if, in the opinion of the court, the child understands that it is his duty to speak the truth and he has sufficient understanding to justify his evidence being heard (section 96(2) of the Children Act 1989). The court/justices' clerk, or a member of the court staff, must keep a note of the substance of the oral evidence given at a hearing or a directions appointment (FPR 4.20/FPC 20).

[1] Family proceedings are defined in section 8(3) and (4) as including any proceedings under Parts I, II and IV (but *not* V) of the Children Act 1989, the Adoption Act 1976 and the Domestic Proceedings in Magistrates' Courts Act 1978.

APPEALS

Appeal from a decision of a district judge (FPR 4.22)

5.22 In proceedings in a county court appeal lies from any decision of a district judge to the judge of the court in which the decision was made (ie to a circuit judge in practice). FPR 4.22 governs appeals under the Children Act 1989. The appellant is required to take the following action in order to bring an appeal:

- draft a notice of appeal setting out the grounds on which he relies
- obtain a certified copy of the application and of the order appealed against, and any order staying its execution
- obtain a copy of any notes of evidence from the court
- obtain a copy of any reasons given from the court.

The appellant must make copies of each of the above documents for each of the other parties and any guardian ad litem who may have been appointed, and then file the notice of appeal and the other documents and serve copies on each party, and on any guardian ad litem. The *notice of appeal* must be filed and served within 14 days after the decision against which the appeal is brought, or with the leave of the judge within such other period as he may direct. The other appeal documents must be filed and served as soon as practicable afterwards, subject to any direction which the judge may give on the matter.

Appeal from a magistrates' court to the High Court

5.23 An appeal lies to the High Court against the making of, or refusal to make, any order (other than an interim maintenance order) under the Children Act 1989 by a magistrates' court. The appellant must follow the same steps in respect of such an appeal as those set out in para **5.22**, and the procedure is also the same. Unless the President of the Family Division directs otherwise such appeals will be heard by a single judge, and there appears to be no reason why such an appeal should not be heard in a provincial first tier centre. A district judge may hear an application to:

- withdraw the appeal
- dismiss the appeal with the consent of all the parties
- amend the grounds of the appeal.

On an appeal from a magistrates' court to the High Court, the latter may make such orders as may be necessary to give effect to its determination of the appeal, and any such order may be accompanied by such incidental or consequential orders as appear to the court to be just. Any order made by the High Court on appeal (other than an order directing the rehearing by a magistrates' court of an application) may be treated for the purpose of enforcement and any power to revive, vary or dischage orders, as if it were an order of the magistrates' court.

Variation or affirmation of decision on appeal and cross-appeals

5.24 It is open to a respondent on appeal, both in the High Court and in a county court, to contend:

- that the decision of the district judge or the magistrates' court, as the case may be, should be varied in any event or if the appeal is allowed in whole or in part
- that the decision should be affirmed on grounds other than those relied on by the district judge or the magistrates' court, as the case may be

- by way of cross-appeal, that the decision of the district judge or the magistrates' court, as the case may be, was wrong in whole or in part.

If he wishes to do so he must file a notice in writing setting out the grounds on which he relies, and serve it on all the other parties to the appeal *within 14 days* of receiving the notice of appeal. A suggested notice of appeal is set out opposite.

NOTICE OF APPEAL

To The [High] _____ [County] Court   5

                                   Case No _____

Appeal against the [decision][order] of [District Judge _____]

[the family proceedings court of _____ PSD]

made on the _____ day of _____ 199____

Appellant _____

                                    and

1st Respondent _____

2nd Respondent _____

3rd Respondent _____

Name[s] of child[ren] in respect of whom the appeal is made:

_____

_____

_____

The grounds of my appeal are:

_____

_____

_____

My title is Mr[ ] Mrs[ ] Miss[ ] Ms[ ] Other _____

My full name is   _____

My full address is   _____

                     _____

My telephone no is _____

My solicitor is   _____

                     _____

                     _____

          Tel: _____ Fax _____ Ref _____

I declare that the information I have given is correct and complete
to the best of my knowledge. Signed _____

          Date _____

COSTS

5.25 In magistrates' courts, at any time in any application made, or in any proceedings brought, under the Children Act 1989 or any statutory instrument made under it, or under any amendment made by the Act in any other enactment, a court may make an order that one party shall pay the whole, or any part of, the costs of another party. The court must give the party against whom it is considering whether to make an order for costs an opportunity to make representations as to why the order should not be made (FPC 22). In the High Court costs are dealt with in the usual way under RSC O.62, and in a county court under CCR O.38.

SECTION 37 INVESTIGATION

Section 37 direction — investigation by local authority (FPR 4.26/FPC 27)

5.26 Where, in the course of any family proceedings (see note to para **5.21** in which a question arises with respect to the welfare of a child, it appears to the court that it might be appropriate to make a care or supervision order, the court may direct a local authority to investigate the child's circumstances. The local authority may only be one within whose area the child is ordinarily resident, or otherwise the local authority within whose area any of the circumstances arose in consequence of which the direction is given. On giving a direction the court must adjourn the proceedings and the proper officer/justices' clerk or the court must record the direction in writing. As soon as practicable after the direction has been given, the proper officer/justices' clerk must serve on the parties to the proceedings and on the local authority (if it is not a party) a copy of the direction. The court may direct the proper officer/justices' clerk to serve on the local authority copies of documentary evidence which has been, or is to be, adduced in the proceedings. The local authority must then carry out an investigation and consider whether it should:

- apply for a care or supervision order
- provide services or assistance for the child or his family
- take any other action with respect to the child.

If the local authority decides not to apply for a care or supervision order with respect to the child it must inform the court in writing, within *eight* weeks of the date of the court's direction, of:

● the reasons for its decision
● any service or assistance which they have provided, or intend to provide
● any other action which it has taken or proposes to take.

Where the local authority decide not to apply for a care or supervision order thay must consider whether it would be appropriate to review the case at some future date, and if so they must decide the date upon which the review is to begin. Such a decision would clearly fall into the third category of matters to be reported to the court. The court's power under section 37(1) replaces the power which the court had under several enactments (eg section 43 of the Matrimonial Causes Act 1973) to make a care order of its own motion or on the application of a local authority. The question of whether intervention by the state is necessary has become, therefore, a matter entirely for the appropriate local authority after it has investigated the child's circumstances. A court may only direct the local authority's attention to the matter; it has no further discretion to exercise once it has done so. The question of the making of a care or supervision order will only come before it if the local authority decides to make an application. Where a county court which is not a care centre (see para **4.1**) has ordered an investigation, it must order any application for a care or supervision order by the local authority to be made in a nominated care centre.

CHAPTER 6

Financial provision for children

Powers of the High Court and the county courts

6.1 Schedule 1 of the Children Act 1989 governs the making of orders for financial provision for children and, as mentioned in section 15(1) of the Act (as amended by schedule 16 to the Courts and Legal Services Act 1990), consists primarily of the re-enactment of provisions of section 6 of the Family Law Reform Act 1969, the Guardianship of Minors Acts 1971 and 1973, the Children Act 1975 and sections 15 and 16 of the Family Law Reform Act 1987, with consequential amendments and minor modifications. The substance of the law in relation to the provision of financial relief for children is therefore left unchanged by the Children Act 1989. Paragraphs 1 and 2 of Schedule 1 to the Children Act 1989 deal respectively with the court's power to make orders against parents and in respect of persons over the age of 18. The orders which the High Court and county courts may make against either or both parents of a child are:

● maintenance orders ('periodical payments')
● secured maintenance orders
● lump sum orders
● transfers of property
● settlements.

All orders except the latter (settlements) may be made to the applicant for the benefit of the child, or to the child himself. A settlement of property to which a parent is entitled, either in possession or in reversion, must be made to the benefit of the child, to the satisfaction of the court. These powers may be exercised at any time until the child attains the age of 18. Maintenance orders may be varied or discharged by a subsequent order made on the application of the parent paying maintenance or the person receiving it, and on varying or discharging a maintenance order the court may make an order for the payment of a lump sum in accordance with paragraph 5(3). Only one order for a settlement or for a transfer of property may be made against a parent for the same child, but there is no limit to the number of maintenance or lump sum orders which may be made in respect of a child before he attains the age of 18. The court may exercise these powers of its own motion when it makes, varies or discharges a *residence* order, or where the child is a ward of court. The court has power also to make maintenance and lump sum orders against either or both of the parents of a person who has reached the age of 18 if *either* of the following criteria are met:

- the applicant is, or would be or, if an order were made, receiving instruction at an educational establishment or undergoing training for a trade, profession or vocation whether or not in paid employment
- there are special circumstances which justify the making of an order

and the following circumstances prevail:

- there was no maintenance order[1] in force in respect of the child immediately before his 16th birthday
- the parents of the child are not living with each other in the same household.

These powers may also be exercised at any time and the court may make further orders while a pre-existing order is in force. A lump sum order may be made to defray expenses or liabilities incurred in connection with the birth of the child, or in maintaining the child, which were reasonably incurred before the order was made (paragraph 5(1)). The court may provide for a lump sum order to be paid by instalments (paragraph 5(5)), and such a provision may be varied on the application of the payer or recipient in the terms of the number of instalments, the amount of each instalment and the date on which any instalment becomes payable (paragraph 5(6)).

---

[1] Maintenance order in this context means a periodical, or secured periodical, payments order under Schedule 1 to the Children Act 1989, or under section 6(3) of the Family Law Reform Act 1969, sections 23 or 27 of the Matrimonial Causes Act 1973 or Part I of the Domestic Proceedings and Magistrates' Courts Act 1978.

6.2 *Financial provision for children*

Powers of magistrates' courts

6.2 Magistrates' courts may exercise the same powers as the High Court and county courts in respect of maintenance orders and lump sums, but they are limited by paragraph 5(2) to an amount not exceeding £1,000 when making a lump sum order (but this does not prevent magistrates from making a further order up to that amount when varying or discharging a maintenance order – paragraph 5(3) and (4)). They do not have the power to make an order for secured periodical payments, or for a settlement or for a transfer of property. None of those powers was conferred under the preceding legislation, chiefly because the exercise of such powers calls for a command of the law of property which is outside the normal range of expertise of justices and their clerks, and the magistrates' courts have traditionally been courts of summary justice. Although the traditional argument is waning few clerks, and proportionately even fewer justices, would claim to be experts in the law of property. By virtue of section 92(4) of the Children Act 1989, a magistrates' court is not competent to deal with an application, or make an order, involving the administration or application of any property belonging to, or held in trust for, a child or any income from it. It is therefore the case that if an application is to be made for a secured order, a settlement or a transfer of property in proceedings in respect of a child it should be commenced in a county court or in the High Court.

Criteria for making orders

6.3 The basic criterion for making any order for financial relief is that the court must consider the financial situation of each of the relevant persons and, of course, of the child and come to a decision which will do justice to them, having regard to all the circumstances of the case. To assist it in doing this the court is provided with details of the financial and housing situation of each party in a Statement of Means which the applicant and respondent are required to complete (in form CHA14). The court is directed in particular, by paragraph 4 of Schedule 1, to take into account:

- the income, earning capacity, property and other financial resources which each person concerned (see below) has or is likely to have in the foreseeable future
- the financial needs, obligations and responsibilities which each

108

person concerned has or is likely to have in the foreseeable future
- the financial needs of the child
- the income, earning capacity (if any), property and other financial resources of the child
- any physical or mental disability of the child
- the manner in which the child was being, or was expected to be, educated or trained.

The persons concerned in relation to a child under the age of 18 are:
- any parent of the child (see next para)
- the applicant for the order
- any other person in whose favour the court proposes to make the order,

and in relation to a person aged 18 or over instead of 'any parent', the father and mother of the child are the persons concerned. Where the court is considering an order against a spouse, or former spouse, who is not the natural parent of the child, ie in favour of a 'child of the family', it must have regard to whether that person has assumed responsibility for the maintenance of the child, and if so:
- the extent to which he met that responsibility
- the basis on which he met that responsibility
- the length of the period during which he met that responsibility
- whether he met that responsibility knowing the child was not his child.

The court must also have regard to the liability of any other person to maintain the child. It should be noted that no order under Schedule 1 may be made against a guardian.

Applications for financial relief

6.4 The making of applications is governed by the Family Proceedings Rules 1991(FPR), rr 4.4 and 4.7 and the Family Proceedings Courts (Children Act 1989) Rules 1991(FPC), rr 4 and 7 (see para **4.7**). The persons who may apply for an order for financial relief *against a parent* are a parent, a guardian or a person in whose favour a residence order in respect of a child has been made. 'Parent' in this context means not only the child's mother or father but also a husband or wife, or former husband or former wife, in relation to whom the child is a 'child of the family'; that is to say a child who has been treated by both parties to a marriage as a child of their marriage (other than as a foster child placed by a local authority or voluntary organisation). The respondents will be those persons described in column (iv) of Appendix 3 to the Family Proceedings Rules 1991 and column (iv) of Schedule 2 to the Family Proceedings Court (Children Act 1989) Rules 1991, namely:

- every person whom the applicant believes to have parental responsibility for the child
- those persons whom the applicant believes to be interested in or affected by the proceedings.

In addition the applicant must give notice of the proceedings to certain other persons mentioned in column (iii) of FPR Appendix 3/column (iv) of FPC Schedule 2; these are:

- a local authority providing accommodation for the child
- any person caring for the child at the time when the proceedings are commenced
- if the child is staying in a refuge certificated under section 51(1) or (2) of the Children Act 1989, the person providing the refuge.

The applicant must take the following steps:

- complete an application in Form CHA13
- complete a statement of means in Form CHA14
- file both in the court with a copy for each respondent
- obtain a date and time for the directions appointment from the court (which will be inserted on the Notice of Hearing)
- serve a copy of the Application, the Notice of Hearing and the Statement of Means on each respondent *not less than 14 days* prior to the date fixed for hearing
- send a copy of the Notice of Hearing, suitably adapted, to each person to whom notice of the proceedings must be given.

It follows from the requirement to give 14 days' notice of a hearing (weekends and bank holidays not counting) that the hearing must be fixed at least three weeks from the date of application. Once made an application may only be withdrawn with the leave of the court (see para **4.9**).

Answer to application for financial relief

6.5 An answer to an application for financial relief must be made in form CHA13A, a copy of which must be filed with a copy for each of the other parties to the application within 14 days of service of the application (see also para **4.19**).

Interim orders

6.6 Where an application is made to a court for financial relief against a parent, or for a person over 18, the court has the power under paragraph 9 of Schedule 1 to make an interim maintenance order pending the final outcome of the application. Such an order may require either, or both, parents to make periodical payments; the frequency of payment and the length of time for which they will continue are at the discretion of the court but they must cease when the application is disposed of. The court may also give directions in relation to an interim order. Payments may not be back-dated to a date before the date of the application, but they may be ordered to commence on some future date. Where an interim order is to end on a given date it may be varied by the court substituting a later date. The principle of minimising delay applies to applications for financial relief since they are proceedings in which a question with respect to the upbringing of a child arises, and although the timetabling provision in section 11 does not apply, no doubt the court will usually have it in mind to give directions to ensure that the matter is disposed of as quickly as practicable.

Financial statements and affidavits

6.7 On an application under Schedule 1 the rules in Part IV of the Family Proceedings Rules apply, by virtue of rule 4.1(2)(d), except where financial relief is also sought by, or on behalf of, an adult. An application for financial relief for an adult must be made under some other enactment (e g the Matrimonial Causes Act 1973) and the procedure relevant to that class of application will apply. In the High Court and county courts such an application may be required to be made by affidavit. Where the application is in respect of a child alone, and on an application under paragraph 2 of Schedule 1 of the Children Act 1989, 'child' includes a person who has reached the age of 18, and in a magistrates' court the financial statements by applicant and respondents must be in Form CHA 14. Any other statement which is to be adduced orally at any hearing must be in the form required by FPR 4.17(1)(a)/FPC 17(1)(a) (see para **5.11**), and served on the other parties before the hearing. Evidence may not be adduced orally, nor may any document (e g bank statement) be relied upon, at a hearing unless a copy of a statement of the substance of the evidence, or the document, has been served on the other parties in accordance with FPR 4.17(1)/FPC 17(1), without the leave of the court. A document which has been filed or served may not be amended without the leave of the court,which is normally requested in writing (see para **5.13**).

Duration of orders

6.8 An order for periodical, or secured periodical, payments may begin with the date of the application, or any later date, but may not in the first instance extend beyond the child's 17th birthday unless the court thinks it right to specify a later date. A shorter period may be specified by the court. In any event, such an order may not extend beyond the child's 18th birthday unless it appears to the court that *either* of the following conditions is met, namely that:

- the child is, or will be or, if an order were made, would be receiving instruction at an educational establishment or undergoing training for a trade, profession or vocation whether or not in paid employment
- there are special circumstances which justify the making of an order.

All orders for periodical payments made against a parent while the child is under the age of 18 cease to have effect if the parent making payments and a parent receiving the payments live together for more than six months. Any periodical payments order which is not secured ceases to have effect on the death of the payer.

Variation and revocation of periodical payments orders

6.9 The court may vary a maintenance order made under the Children Act 1989 or, when the court makes a residence order, an order under some other enactment requiring a person to contribute to a child's maintenance. In the latter case variation could include an alteration in the amount payable, or the substitution of the person in whose favour the residence order is made for the person to whom the maintenance is otherwise payable. When the court is considering a question of variation or discharge of an order for financial provision it must also have regard to all the circumstances of the case, and in these the Act includes any change in the matters mentioned in para **6.3**. The court may suspend the operation of an order, or any part of it, for a period and revive it, or any suspended provision, as the case may be. It may also postpone a variation of the order to come into effect at some future date, or bring the variation into effect retrospectively but no earlier than the date of the application for the variation. When the child in question has attained the age of 16 he may apply for a variation of an order which is still in force himself. If an order ceased to have effect on the child's 16th birthday, or on some other date before the child's 18th birthday, he may apply for the order to be revived, and the court may make an order reviving the order which has ceased to have effect if *either* of the following criteria are met:

• the applicant is, or will be or, if an order were made, would be receiving instruction at an educational establishment or undergoing training for a trade, profession or vocation whether or not in paid employment
• there are special circumstances which justify the making of an order.

The revival order may commence on any date on or after the date of the application, at the discretion of the court. A revived order may be varied under paragraph 6(5) of Schedule 1 on the application of the child or the payer. A guardian may apply for an order against a parent to be varied or discharged, after the death of either parent.

Variation of maintenance agreements

6.10 The court has power under paragraphs 10 and 11 of Schedule 1 to the Children Act 1989 to alter a maintenance agreement relating to a child. The agreement must be one which is, or was, made in writing between the father and mother of the child which contains any provision with respect to:

• the making of payments
• the securing of payments
• the disposition of property

- the use of property

for the maintenance or education of the child. These provisions are referred to in paragraphs 10 and 11 as 'financial arrangements', and the powers of the court under those paragraphs only extend to such 'financial arrangements'. Where a party seeks to alter a maintenance agreement with respect to a spouse, then he or she must do so under section 35 or section 36 of the Matrimonial Causes Act 1973 in accordance with rules 3.2–3.4 of the Family Proceedings Rules 1991, even if an alteration is also sought in the agreement with respect to a child. An application to alter 'financial arrangements', however, may be made to a magistrates' court, a county court or the High Court under Schedule 1 if the parties to the agreement are domiciled or resident in England and Wales, and in the case of a magistrates' court at least one of the parties must be resident in the relevant commission area. The power to alter a maintenance agreement may be exercised if the court is satisfied of *either* of the following matters:

- by reason of a change in the circumstances in the light of which any 'financial arrangements' were made (including a change foreseen by the parties), the agreement should be altered so as to make different 'financial arrangements'
- the agreement does not contain proper 'financial arrangements' with respect to the child.

If it is satisfied, the court may vary or revoke any 'financial arrangements' contained in the agreement as it appears to it to be just in all the circumstances. A magistrates' court may only increase, reduce or terminate periodical payments where the agreement contains provision for such payments; it may also only insert a provision for maintenance payments to be made in respect of a child where the agreement contains no provision for the making of any periodical payments. These powers apply to agreements made before 14 October 1991. The duration of the term for which the payments changed or added by the order may run is limited to the child's 17th birthday in the first instance, unless the criteria in paragraph 3 of Schedule 1 are met (see para **6.8**).

6.11 The High Court and a county court have power under paragraph 11 of Schedule 1 to alter a maintenance agreement which provides for maintenance for a child to continue after the death of a party to the agreement. This power may be exercised after the death of that party, if he dies domiciled in England

and Wales, on the application of his personal representatives or of the surviving party. The application must be made within six months of the date on which probate or letters of administration are obtained in respect of the dead party's estate, or the leave of the court must be obtained to make the application after that date. By virtue of paragraph 11(4) of Schedule 1, a grant of representation relating only to settled land, trust property and real estate or personal estate may be disregarded in certain circumstances. An application to a county court may only be made if it would have jurisdiction to make an order under the Inheritance (Provision for Family and Dependants) Act 1975 in relation to the dead party's estate.

Financial provision for children abroad

6.12 Paragraph 14 of Schedule 1 to the Children Act 1989 enables a court to make a maintenance order for a child who is living outside England and Wales against a parent living in England and Wales, if the child is living with any of the following:

- another parent of his
- a guardian of his
- a person in whose favour a residence order is in force with respect to the child.

The applicant for the order must be one of those persons mentioned above. It follows that a child may not make an application himself, but he may apply for a variation of an order made by virtue of paragraph 14(1) when he has attained the age of 16. An order for the maintenance of a person over the age of 18, it would appear, cannot be made if that person lives outside England and Wales since paragraph 14 does not mention paragraph 2 of the Schedule (orders for financial relief of persons over 18).

Local authority contribution to a child's maintenance

6.13 Local authorities have a discretion, conferred by paragraph 15 of Schedule 1 to the Children Act 1989, to assist with the cost of accommodation and maintenance of a child. This only applies where the child lives, or is to live, with a person as a result of a residence order, and the person with the residence order in his favour is not the parent, or the husband or wife of a parent, of the child. But see para **10.3** (Local authority support for children).

Appeals

6.14 An appeal against:

- the making, variation or revocation of an order
- the terms of an order
- a refusal to make, vary or revoke an order

other than an interim maintenance order, lies from a magistrates' court to the High Court, and from a district judge to a circuit judge. An appeal from a circuit judge, or from a district judge of the Principal Registry of the Family Division, lies to the Court of Appeal. Where an appeal from a magistrates' court to the High Court relates to an order for periodical payments, the High Court may order its decision to take effect from such date as it sees fit. If on such an appeal the High Court reduces the amount of payment or discharges the order it may:

- order the payee to pay to the payer such sum in respect of payments already made it sees fit
- remit the whole or any part of arrears which have accrued under the order being appealed.

For matters relating to appeals generally see paras **5.22–5.24.**

CHAPTER 7

Emergency protection of children

Introduction

7.1 Part V of the Act introduces new provisions for the protection of children into an area which in the past has been fraught with difficulties and controversy. Enquiries into the deaths of children where complaints of lack of action have been made can be contrasted with events where precipitate action has been condemned as infringing on the personal rights and liberty of children and parents. The new framework attempts to encompass the protection of children at risk, while acknowledging and strengthening the position of parents; endeavouring to recognise what will often be competing or conflicting interests.

Child assessment orders

7.2 Section 43 of the Act creates the CAO, which has no parallel in the previous legislation. The order will enable an assessment of a child's health and welfare to be made where concern exists, but where evidence or information, justifying a child's compulsory removal from home, is lacking.

Grounds for a CAO

7.3 A CAO may only be applied for by a local authority or 'authorised person' (defined by section 31(9) and currently restricted to the NSPCC). Here there is an immediate contrast to the Emergency Protection Order where, under section 44(1)(a) theoretically anyone can apply (see para **7.9** post). On application for a CAO the court may make an order if satisfied that each of the following three conditions is met:

- the applicant has reasonable cause to suspect that the child is suffering, or is likely to suffer, significant harm

- an assessment of the state of the child's health or development, or of the way in which he has been treated, is required to enable the applicant to determine whether or not the child is suffering, or is likely to suffer, significant harm, and
- it is unlikely that such an assessment will be made, or be satisfactory, in the absence of an order under this section (section 43(1)).

The section requires all three elements to be made out; and the court, on considering such an application, must apply the welfare principle and the presumption of no order (section 1(1) and (5)). In contrast to an EPO the court must be satisfied of the applicant's belief regarding risk of harm, and then consider and evaluate the factual circumstances of the case. As a CAO is not classified as family proceedings under the Act, the court is not required to consider the welfare checklist in section 1(3) and must either make or refuse to make the order applied for although, reflecting the flexibility of remedies available under the Act, the court can treat an application for a CAO as if it were an application for an EPO in certain circumstances (see para **7.6** post). Unlike an EPO, the court, for the purpose of this application, means a full court, emphasising the non-emergency nature of the CAO and would be a full inter-partes hearing.

Duration and effect of CAO

7.4   The order will specify the nature of the assessment to be carried out and the date by which it is to begin. The order will commence on this date, and will have effect for such period as the court decides. While a shorter period may be specified, the order cannot, in any event, exceed seven days in total. Unlike the EPO there is no power for this maximum period to be extended (section 43(5)). The order imposes a duty on any person who is in a position to produce the child, to produce him to the person named in the order and to comply with any directions relating to assessment that the order may specify. The Act does not restrict the type of assessment which can be ordered; this could range from medical or psychiatric examination to any necessary examination of a child's intellectual, social or behavioural needs. However, any person carrying out all or part of the assessment must do so in accordance with the terms of the order, so the court must be quite specific when framing the CAO (section 43(7)). However, a child of sufficient understanding to make an informed decision may refuse to submit to any examination or other form of assessment (section 43(8)). Whether such enfranchisement of mature adolescents, which principle runs through the Act, will frustrate this, or other orders available under the Act, in practice remains to be seen.

7.5 The child may be kept away from home under a CAO only in accordance with the court's directions, where this is necessary for the period or periods specified in the order (section 43(9)). The CAO does not authorise a child's removal from home under any other circumstances. If, following assessment, removal is necessary to safeguard a child, an application would have to be made for an EPO. Where the order authorises removal, it must also contain such directions as the court thinks fit with regard to contact the child is to have with other persons while away from home (section 43(10)). This restriction of removal from home reflects the difference between the CAO and EPO. Removal should be restricted to the extent that it is necessary for the assessment to be carried out, and contact restricted only when this would lead to the execution of the order being frustrated.

7.6 The choice of CAO or EPO, which will largely depend on degree of urgency and level of concern, initially rests with the authorised person applying. However, reflecting the flexibility allowed the court under the Act, the court is the final arbiter of choice. Thus section 43(3) allows a court, where the situation is more serious than originally thought, to treat the application for a CAO as an application for an EPO. More particularly, the court is precluded from making a CAO where it is satisfied grounds exist for making an EPO and that it ought to make such an order (section 43(4)). Any person making an application for a child assessment order must take such steps as are reasonably practicable to ensure that notice of the application is given to:

- the child's parents
- any person who has parental responsibility for the child
- any person caring for the child
- any person with a contact order in force in respect of the child
- any person allowed contact by virtue of an order under section 34 and
- the child,

before the hearing of the application (section 43(11)). Any of the above persons or such other persons as the court grants leave to may apply to the court for the CAO to be varied or discharged (section 43(12)). As the application must be heard by a full court, opposition to the order by parties can be vented at the full inter-partes hearing. An appeal against the making or refusing to make a CAO will lie to the High Court (section 94) (see para **5.23**). Under section 91(14), on disposing of an application for a CAO, the court may order that no further such application may be made in respect of the child concerned by any person named (including the local authority), without leave of the court. In any event no further application for a CAO may be made with respect to the child concerned within six months, without the court's leave (section 91(15)).

Emergency protection orders

7.7 Unlike the CAO, a non-urgent remedy available to address narrow or specific issues, the EPO is an order, albeit transitory, which enables a child to be retained in, or removed to, a place in order to safeguard his welfare. Section 44(1) of the Act allows an EPO to be granted in any of three sets of circumstances. Akin to the CAO, this order is not within the definition of family proceedings; therefore the court must make or refuse to make an order, and while regard must be had to the principles of section 1(1) and (5) of the Act, the checklist in section 1(3) will not apply.

Grounds

7.8 The main ground for obtaining an EPO is that the court is satisfied that there is reasonable cause to believe the child is likely to suffer significant harm if he is not removed to accommodation provided by or on behalf of the applicant, or if he does not remain in the place in which he is then being accommodated (section 44(1)(a)).

- 'Harm' in this context is defined in section 31(9) and means ill-treatment or the impairment of health or development (section 105(1))
- 'Development' means physical, intellectual, emotional, social and behavioural development
- 'Health' means physical and mental health

- 'Ill-treatment' includes sexual abuse and forms of ill-treatment which are not physical
- 'Significant' means, from its dictionary definition, considerable, noteworthy or important. This could exist in the seriousness of the harm or the implication of it and will be a matter for the court to consider in each case.

Where the question of whether harm suffered by a child is significant turns on the child's health or development, his health or development shall be compared with that which could reasonably be expected of a similar child.

7.9 The class of applicant here is in theory wholly unrestricted. However, while a concerned relative or neighbour may be able to act independently of the authorities to protect a child in the first instance, a local authority may take over the order along with its concomitant powers and responsibilities, if this is considered by them to be in the child's best interests. (Emergency Protection Orders (Transfer of Responsibilities) Regulations 1991, SI No 1414). Unlike the CAO and the remaining grounds under section 44, this ground requires the court, not the applicant, to be satisfied that there is reasonable cause to believe the child is likely to suffer significant harm. This ground contains therefore a prospective element and would encompass a situation where no actual harm has been suffered but there is reason to believe this is likely unless an order is made.

7.10 The second ground applies only to local authorities and allows them to apply for an EPO where they are unable to gain access to a child at risk during the course of an investigation. In this case the court must be satisfied that enquiries are being made with respect to the child under section 47(1)(b), and those enquiries are being frustrated by access to the child being unreasonably refused to a person authorised to seek access, and that the applicant has reasonable cause to believe that access to the child is required as a matter of urgency (section 44(1)(b)). Under section 47(1)(b) a local authority has a duty to make enquiries whenever they have reasonable cause to suspect that a child in their area is suffering, or likely to suffer, significant harm (see para **7.19**). The third ground, although similar, is extended to cover application by authorised persons (currently only local authorities and the NSPCC). Such a person may apply for an EPO where access is refused, and the court may only make the order if satisfied that the following conditions are fulfilled:

- the applicant has reasonable cause to suspect that a child is suffering, or is likely to suffer, significant harm
- the applicant is making enquiries with respect to the child's welfare, and
- these enquiries are being frustrated by access to the child being unreasonably refused to a person authorised to seek access and the applicant has reasonable cause to believe that access to the child is required as a matter of urgency (section 44(1)(c)).

The second and third grounds require a reasonably held suspicion by the applicant that the child is suffering, or likely to suffer, significant harm, together with unreasonable refusal of access, which the applicant has cause to believe is required as a matter of urgency. This latter element will be a matter for the court to consider. The court will need to be satisfied on applications for an EPO that the situation demands urgent action. Where immediate danger is lacking but there is need for further investigation of the child's health and development, the CAO should be the option chosen.

Effect of an EPO

7.11 An EPO has three legal effects while in force, which are:
- to direct any person who is in a position to produce the child to the applicant to do so
- to authorise the removal of the child at any time to accommodation provided by, or on behalf of, the applicant and his detention there, or the prevention of a child's removal from a hospital or other place in which he was being accommodated immediately before the order was made, and
- to give the applicant parental responsibility for the child (section 44(4)).

The order must name the child or, if this is not reasonably practicable, it must describe him as clearly as possible (section 44(14)). The order does not authorise the applicant to enter premises and search for the child unless a specific power is included (see para **7.13** post). It will transfer, in effect, both the physical care of a child and the concomitant parental responsibility to the applicant (section 44(4)). However, section 44(5) governs the exercise of those powers under the EPO. It provides that the applicant shall:

- only exercise parental responsibility in order to safeguard the welfare of the child and
- take, and shall only take, such action in meeting this responsibility as is reasonably required to safeguard or promote the welfare of the child (having regard in particular to the duration of the order); and comply with the requirements of any regulations made by the Secretary of State regarding this matter.

Parental responsibility under an EPO is therefore restricted, obviously because of the transitory nature of the order, although a positive duty is imposed on the applicant to take action when necessary to safeguard and promote the child's welfare. Therefore, removal from home of the child is not necessarily automatic once an EPO has been made if this course is not necessary to safeguard the child's welfare. All options providing effective protection for the child will have to be considered by the local authority. Power exists, for example, for a local authority to give assistance to an alleged abuser so he or she may move to alternative accommodation (Schedule 2 Paragraph 5).

ADDITIONAL POWERS TO TRACE CHILDREN AT RISK

Orders to disclose whereabouts

7.12 Where it appears to a court making an EPO that adequate information as to a child's location is not available to the applicant, but is available to another person, it may include in the order a provision requiring that person to disclose any information he has regarding the child's whereabouts (section 48(1)). Disclosure will not be excused on the ground that it might incriminate the informant or his spouse, although any statement or admission will not be admissible in evidence against either of them for any offence except perjury (section 48(2)).

Authority to search premises and search warrants

7.13 There is a distinction in the Act between entry and search of premises by the applicant for an order, and entry and search by the police with or without the applicant in attendance. An EPO may contain a provision authorising the applicant to enter specified premises and search for the child who is the subject of the order (section 48(3)). If, however, there is reasonable cause to believe that there may be another child on those premises with respect to whom an EPO ought to be made, the court may also authorise the applicant to search for that child on the same premises (section 48(4)). If the child concerned is found and the applicant is satisfied that the grounds for making an EPO exist with respect to this child, the authorisation will act as if it were an EPO (section 48(5)). An obligation is imposed on the applicant to notify the court of the outcome of the search for the second child (section 48(6)). Any person intentionally obstructing a person exercising the power of entry and search authorised under section 48(3) or (4) commits an offence punishable on summary conviction by a fine not exceeding level 3 on the standard scale. The above orders should not be confused with the power to issue a search warrant under section 48(9). Anyone, not only the applicant for an EPO, may apply to the court for a warrant which authorises a constable to assist in the exercise of powers under an EPO using reasonable force if necessary. The court may issue the warrant where it appears that a person attempting to exercise powers of entry and search under an EPO has been, or is likely to be, prevented from doing so by being refused access to the child concerned or entry to the premises in question (section 48(9)). The warrant must be addressed to, and executed by, a constable who must allow the applicant to accompany him if he desires and the court does not direct otherwise (section 48(10)). The court may also direct that the constable be accompanied by a registered medical practitioner, registered nurse or registered health visitor, if he chooses (section 48(11)). Wherever reasonably practicable, an order under section 48(4), an application for a warrant and any such warrant granted under section 48(9), must name the child or describe him as clearly as possible. The above orders are not automatic, but complementary, and it may be necessary on occasion to obtain both the EPO and order under section 48 to achieve enforcement of the emergency protection procedures.

Duration

7.14 The duration of an EPO is governed by section 45 of the Act. The maximum length of the order, initially, is limited to eight days, although the court can specify a shorter period. Where the court wishes to make an eight-day order but the last day would fall on a public holiday (Christmas Day, Good Friday, a bank holiday or a Sunday) the court may specify a period which ends at noon on the first later day which is not such a holiday section 45(2). It is clearly intended that this period will allow a local authority sufficient time in which to obtain adequate evidence to pursue an application for an interim care order if this is deemed necessary. However, the Act recognises that on occasion this period will be insufficient and allows the court a discretion to extend the EPO for a period not exceeding seven days. The court may only extend the order if satisfied, on the application only of local authorities or authorised persons (the NSPCC) that there is reasonable cause to believe that the child concerned is likely to suffer significant harm if there is no extension (section 45(5)). Whatever difficulties face a local authority there can only be one extension (section 45(6)).

Parental contact

7.15 In accord with the presumption of reasonable contact which applies to children in care and the subject of a CAO, section 44(6) and (13) creates a similar presumption with regard to EPOs. The local authority must allow the child reasonable contact, subject to such directions as the court considers appropriate, with:

- his parents
- any other person with parental responsibility for him
- any person with whom he was living immediately before the making of the order
- any person in whose favour a contact order is in force
- any person allowed to have contact with the child by virtue of an order under section 34 and
- any person acting on behalf of any of those persons (section 44(13)).

The court may give directions regarding contact between the child and any named person (section 44(6)(a)) and may do so either on making the EPO or at any time while it is in force (section 44(9)(a)). In both cases the court can impose conditions; for instance contact should only take place in the presence of a named third party. As with much else in the Act, the court is given the flexibility to control or even prohibit contact in the child's best interests.

Medical and other assessments

7.16 On making an EPO or at any time while the order is in force, the court has power to direct medical, psychiatric or other assessments of the child (section 44(6)(b) and (9)(a)). Alternatively, the court may either order that there is to be no such examination or assessment, or prohibit them unless it directs otherwise (section 44(8)). However, recognising the personal integrity of mature adolescents, a child of sufficient understanding to make an informed decision may refuse to submit to any examination or assessment (section 44(7)). Directions regarding contact or medical examination or other assessment may be varied at any time on the application of any person included in FPC 2(4)/FPR 4.2(4), namely, parties to the application for the order in respect of which it is sought to vary the directions, the guardian ad litem, the local authority in whose area the child resides and any person named in the directions (section 44(9)(b)). The respondents to an application to vary directions are the parties to the proceedings leading to the order, any person who was caring for the child prior to the making of the order, and any person whose contact with the child is affected by the directions (FPC Schedule 2, column (iii)/FPR Appendix 3, column (iv)).

Duty to return child

7.17 An EPO allows an applicant to remove or detain a child. However, the exercise of this power is subject to the principle underlying section 44(10); basically a child should not be removed from parental care longer than is strictly necessary. The applicant must either return the child, or allow him to be removed where it appears safe to do so, this duty arises even though the EPO is still in force (section 44(10)). The applicant must return the child to the care of the person from whose care he was removed. However, if this is not reasonably practicable, the child must be returned to:

- his parent;
- any person who has parental responsibility for the child; or
- such other person as the applicant (with the agreement of the court) considers appropriate (section 44(11)).

The EPO will remain in force until its expiry date even if the child is returned home under the above provisions. However, section 44(12) safeguards the position of the child, in that in the event of a further change of circumstances, while the EPO remains in force, the applicant may again exercise his powers to remove the child if this action appears necessary.

7.18 Although an EPO application, in theory, can be heard inter partes, the necessity for immediate action probably means that, pragmatically, most applications for an EPO will be heard ex parte (see para **7.33**). Indeed, on occasion, to put parties on notice of an application may exacerbate a child's situation. However, an EPO may be challenged on its merits, if made ex parte, by an application to discharge it. The child, his parents, anyone having parental responsibility or any person with whom the child was living prior to the application may make such an application (section 45(8)). No application for discharge of an EPO can be heard by the court before the expiration of 72 hours from the time of the making of the order (section 45(9)). However, no person can apply to discharge the order if they were given notice of the original hearing and were present (so would have had the opportunity to challenge at this stage), nor can there be any application to discharge an extended EPO (section 45(11)). Although the decision itself to extend can only be made at an inter partes hearing so there would have to be an opportunity for representations, that no extension should be granted. These provisions minimise disruption to the local authority over what is a short period in which to investigate the particular circumstances of the case. Unlike the CAO, no appeal lies against the making of, or refusal to make an EPO or against any direction given by the court in connection with such an order. Finally, a court hearing an application for, or relating to, an EPO may take account of any statement contained in any report in the course of, or in connection with, the hearing or any evidence given during the hearing which is, in the court's opinion, relevant to the application (section 45(7)). The main differences between the orders are:

Section 43 CAO	**Section 44 EPO**
Non-urgent	Urgent
Inter partes	Ex parte
Full court	Court or single justice
Can convert to EPO	Cannot convert to CAO
Applicant - local authority/ NSPCC	Applicant - any person
Duration seven days: no extension	Duration eight days: one extension of seven days
Appeal to High Court	No appeal

Investigative duties of local authorities

7.19 The Act imposes an active duty on local authorities to investigate any case where it is suspected that a child is suffering, or is likely to suffer, significant harm. This obligation is embodied in section 47(1). Where a local authority:

- is informed that a child who lives, or is found, in its area:
  - (i) is the subject of an emergency protection order; or
  - (ii) is in police protection or
- has reasonable cause to suspect that a child who lives, or is found, in its area, is suffering, or is likely to suffer, significant harm,

the authority must make, or cause to be made, such enquiries as they consider necessary to enable them to decide whether they should take any action to safeguard or promote the child's welfare. The duty therefore is focused on whether a child is at risk of harm, and not merely whether there exist grounds for court proceedings.

7.20 The Act is very specific about the nature and purpose of any enquiries, and this duty applies equally to an authority which has obtained an EPO in relation to a child (section 47(2)). The enquiries must be directed, in particular, towards establishing:

- whether the authority should make any application to the court, or exercise any of their other powers under the Act, with respect to the child;
- whether, in the case of a child:
  - (i) with respect to whom an emergency protection order has been made; and
  - (ii) who is not in accommodation provided by or on behalf of the authority,
  it would be in the child's best interests (while an emergency protection order remains in force) for him to be in such accommodation and
- whether, in the case of a child who has been taken into police protection, it would be in the child's best interests for the authority to ask for an application to be made under section 46(7) (ie for an EPO, see para **7.26**).

The first consideration above will involve the local authority considering whether to apply to a court for an EPO, care or supervision order, or whether to exercise their powers under Part III of the Act (see chapter 10). The local authority must take such steps as are reasonably practicable to obtain access to the child, or arrange for someone else to obtain access on their behalf, unless satisfied that it already has sufficient information about him to decide what action, if any, to take (section 47(4)). If access is refused or information about the child's whereabouts withheld, the local authority must apply for an emergency protection order, or care or supervision order, unless satisfied that the child's welfare can be satisfactorily safeguarded without this (section 47(6)). The Act requires the local authority to consult with the local education authority where matters connected with the child's education require investigation (section 47(5)). If, as a result of enquiries, the local authority concludes it should take action to safeguard or promote a child's welfare, it must do so, so far as this is within its power and reasonably practicable (section 47(8)). Other local authorities, health authorities and local education and housing authorities will have a statutory duty to assist an investigating authority if requested unless it would be unreasonable to expect them to do so in all the circumstances of the case. The Secretary of State will have power to extend this duty to other persons or agencies (eg NSPCC). So the Act now makes provision for co-operation between statutory and voluntary agencies in the investigation of suspected harm and the protection of children at risk. Where, on concluding its enquiries, a local authority decides not to seek a statutory order, it must consider whether it would be appropriate to review the case at a later date; if so it must fix a date on which the review is to begin (section 47(7)).

Abduction and recovery of children

7.21 Sections 49 to 51 of the Act deal with the abduction and recovery of children who are in care or subject to emergency orders. In addition the work of organisations in providing safe houses for runaway children is recognised by exempting them from criminal liability for abduction.

Offence of abduction

7.22 Section 49(1) makes it an offence to abduct a child in care, or who is subject to an emergency protection order or in police protection. The offence is committed by any person who, knowingly and without reasonable excuse:

● takes a child to whom this section applies away from the responsible person
● keeps such a child away from the responsible person or

- induces, assists or incites such a child to run away from the responsible person.

The responsible person, in each case, is the person who for the time being has care of the child by virtue of the above-mentioned orders (section 49(2)). This class of responsible person could include for instance foster parents. The section is silent regarding the wishes of the child concerning where he desires to live, therefore whether a person charged with such an offence will be able to advance the child's wishes as a reason for committing the offence and therefore providing the defence of reasonable excuse is open to question.

Recovery orders

7.23 Section 50 provides the court with power to make a recovery order where there is reason to believe that a child to whom this section applies is unlawfully taken away or is being unlawfully kept away from the responsible person; or has run away or is staying away from the responsible person; or is missing (section 50(1)). The responsible person means any person who for the time being has care of the child by virtue of a care order, EPO or an order pursuant to section 46 of the Act. Recovery orders can only be made in relation to children covered by section 49 (section 50(2)). Where an order is made under this section it:

- operates as a direction to any person who is in a position to do so to produce the child on request to any authorised person;
- authorises the removal of the child by the authorised person;
- requires any person with information as to the child's whereabouts to disclose it if requested to do so to a constable;
- authorises a constable to enter specified premises and to search for the child, using reasonable force if necessary (section 50(3)).

'Authorised person' for the above purposes means any person specified by the court, any constable and any person authorised to exercise any power under the recovery order by a person with parental responsibility under a care order or EPO (section 50(7)). Applications for recovery orders may be made by any person with parental responsibility for the child under the care order or EPO or by a designated officer where the child is in police protection (section 50(4)). The order must name the child and applicant (section 50(5)). The court may only specify premises that are to be entered and searched by a constable under section

50(3) where there are reasonable grounds for believing the child to be on them (section 50(6)). Where a person is authorised he must, if asked to do so, produce some duly authenticated document showing he is authorised. Obstructing a person exercising his power to remove a child is an offence (section 50(8) and (9)). Where an authorised person requires someone to disclose information concerning the child's whereabouts, that person cannot be excused from non-compliance on the grounds that it might incriminate himself or his spouse (section 50(11)). Finally, a recovery order made in England or Wales also has effect in Scotland as if made there (section 50(13)).

Refuges for children at risk

7.24 Organisations which provide safe houses or refuges for runaway children at risk of harm will be exempted from criminal liability for abduction under section 47. This protection will encompass voluntary homes or registered childrens' homes formally certified as a refuge by the Secretary of State in accordance with the Refuges (Children's Homes and Foster Placement) Regulations 1991 (SI 1991 No 1507), made under section 51(4). The regulations specify how certificates are issued, when they may be withdrawn and conditions which must be complied with while such certificates are in force (section 51(1)). The certificate may also be granted in relation to a foster parent who has been requested to provide a refuge by a local authority or voluntary organisation. Foster parent in this case means a local authority foster parent or a foster parent with whom a child is placed by a voluntary organisation (section 51(2) and (3)). Such a person will also be exempt from criminal prosecution in providing the refuge (section 51(6)). However, the Act does not prevent application for a recovery order, in respect of children in certified refuges, to discover their whereabouts and secure their return.

Police power for removal and accommodation of chidren

7.25 Section 46 modifies emergency powers of the police to remove and accommodate children on a short term basis in urgent situations. Provision is made for the child to be transferred to local authority accommodation as soon as practicable and reflecting the nature of these powers the police are not given parental responsibility in such cases.

7.26 Where a constable has reasonable cause to believe that a child would otherwise be likely to suffer significant harm, he may remove the child to suitable accommodation and keep him there; or take such steps as are reasonable to ensure that the child's removal from any hospital, or other place, in which he is then being accommodated is prevented (section 46(1)). This power of removal does not carry a right of entry. Therefore, in cases where entry is likely to be refused an application for an EPO together with a warrant order section 48 would be necessary. A constable for the purpose of section 46(1) would be a police officer of any rank, however, the case must be inquired into by an officer specifically designated for this purpose as soon as reasonably practicable (section 46(3)(e)). On completing inquiries this designated officer must release the child unless he considers that there is still reasonable cause for believing that the child would be likely to suffer significant harm if released (section 46(5)). In any event the child may be kept in police protection under these powers for up to seventy-two hours only; if the child's continued detention is necessary, this must be authorised by an EPO; such an application may be made by the designated officer on behalf of the local authority whether or not the authority know of it or agree to its being made (section 46(6) and (7) and (8)). Where such an order is granted, the maximum duration of eight days for an initial EPO runs from the date of the child's removal into police protection.

7.27 The Act imposes specific requirements on any officer when he initially takes a child into police protection; apart from ensuring inquiries are made by the designated officer. As soon as reasonably practicable he must inform the local authority in whose area the child was found of the steps which have been, and are proposed to be, taken and the reasons for taking them. Details must be given of the child's present accommodation to the authority where he ordinarily resides, if different from where the child is found. He must, if the child is capable of understanding, inform the child of the steps which have been taken, the reasons for this and steps which may be taken. If reasonably practicable he must also discover the wishes and feelings of the child. The child must be moved to accommodation provided by or on behalf of a local authority or designated as a refuge (see para **7.24**), if he was not so accommodated on removal. Finally, the officer must, as far as is reasonably practicable, notify the child's parents, those with parental responsibility or any person with whom the child was living prior to removal, of the steps taken, the reasons for this, and of any further steps which may be taken.

Parental responsibility and parental contact – child in police protection

7.28 In relation to a child in police protection neither the constable concerned nor the designated officer acquire parental responsibility for him. However, the designated officer must do whatever is reasonable in all the circumstances of the case to safeguard or promote the child's welfare, having regard, in particular, to the length of time he may remain in police protection (section 46(9)). It is the responsibility of the designated officer to allow specified individuals such contact with the child as, in the opinion of the designated officer, is both reasonable and in the child's best interests. This class of individuals comprises the child's parents, persons with parental responsibility, anyone with whom the child was living prior to coming into police protection, anyone who has the benefit of a contact order or a section 34 contact order or anyone acting on behalf of any of these persons (section 46(10)). Once the child is moved into accommodation provided by or on behalf of the local authority, this duty will be transferred to the authority (section 46(11)). The withholding of parental responsibility from the police is obviously in line with the fleeting nature of police protection; and consistent with this, there is no presumption of contact, unlike the CAO or EPO, which is left to the discretion of the designated officer.

PROCEDURAL AND RELATED MATTERS

7.29 The procedure to be followed under Part V of the Children Act 1989 is that laid down in the Family Proceedings Courts (Children Act 1989) Rules 1991 and the Family Proceedings Rules 1991, for which see chapters 4 and 5.

General: attendance of the child

7.30 In any proceedings under Part V the court is empowered to order the attendance of the child, although this power is at the court's discretion and can be exercised at whatever stage of the proceedings as the court may specify. If the order is not complied with, or the court feels it will not be complied with, a constable or other specified person may be authorised to bring the child to court and enter and search premises where he has reasonable cause to believe the child to be. The court may also order anyone in a position to do so to bring the child to court and order anyone who is thought to have information about the child's whereabouts to disclose this (section 95). This attendance of the child in certain cases may assist the court. However it should also be noted that the child would be entitled to attend by virtue of his party status in any event; the mature adolescent may avail himself of this.

Evidence

7.31 It will be possible under section 96(1) and (2) for a court to admit the unsworn evidence of a child where the court considers that while the child does not understand the nature of the oath, he does understand the duty to tell the truth. It is important to remember that while hearsay evidence is admissible in family proceedings by virtue of the Children (Admissibility of Hearsay Evidence) Order 1991, Part V applications fall outside the ambit of this order, and on such applications, therefore, the restrictive rules of hearsay will apply. The general rule against self-incrimination is removed in Part V applications (section 98) and admission of evidence in applications for an EPO is governed by section 45(7) (see para **7.18**). For a detailed discussion on evidence in Part IV and V proceedings see chapter 5.

Appointment of guardian ad litem (section 41: FPC 10/FPR 4.10)

7.32 A guardian must be appointed in proceedings under Part V (including applications to discharge) as soon as practicable after commencement of proceedings unless the justices' clerk/ district judge or the court considers such an appointment is not necessary to safeguard the interests of the child. The guardian shall, unless this has already been done, appoint a solicitor for the child (FPC 11/FPR 4.11). For a detailed discussion of the guardian ad litem's powers and duties see paras **8.55-8.57**).

Urgent applications (FPC 4(4)/FPR 4.4(4))

7.33 Certain applications may be made ex parte in cases of urgency. In addition to some section 8 orders (see para 4.8), an application for an EPO (section 44), a warrant authorising a constable to enter and search for a child (section 48) or an RO (section 50) may be made ex parte, with the leave of the justices' clerk/district judge. If leave is granted the applicant must file an application in Form CHA34 (EPO), Form CHA43 (section 48 warrant) or Form CHA45 (RO), as the case may be, in respect of each child. Where the application is made by telephone the form must be filed within 24 hours, or as the justices' clerk directs. In the case of an EPO the applicant must serve a copy of the application on each respondent (see respondents listed in para 7.16) within 48 hours after the making of the order. If the court refuses to make an order ex parte it may direct that the application be made inter partes. In a magistrates' court these applications may be granted by a single justice who is a member of the Family Panel.

Time for service of applications

7.34 The time which must be allowed for the service of an application on the respondents to proceedings under Part V varies according to the nature of the application. The minimum number of days which must be allowed between service and a subsequent directions, or other, hearing is governed by FPC 4(1)(b) and Schedule 2, column (ii)/FPR 4.4(1)(b) and Appendix 3, column (ii). Unless an application is served upon the respondent, or his solicitor, in person or delivered at his address, two working days must be allowed in addition to the time for service where the application is sent by first class post, or in the case of a solicitor via a document exchange service. The times required for service are as follows:

- 1 day   section 44(1) – EPO
                section 44(9) – variation of direction in EPO
                section 45(4) – extension of period of EPO
                section 45(8) – discharge of an EPO
                section 46(7) – application for EPO by designated officer
                section 48(9) – warrant of assistance
                section 50(1) – RO
- 2 days   section 43(12) – CAO: variation or discharge
- 7 days   section 43(1) – CAO

CHAPTER 8

Care and supervision

Introduction

8.1 Part IV of the Act introduces a statutory framework, allowing a child, his parents, or others connected with him to participate fully, which governs compulsory public intervention in the family life. The conditions for admission into care under the previous legislation not only differed but were contained in a number of separate statutory procedures. The Act removes those inconsistencies and creates one new statutory ground which has to be established in any proceedings in which a care or supervision order is sought. In line with this principle of only one route existing into care, section 100(2) of the Act removes from a local authority the option of commencing wardship proceedings where they seek to obtain a care or supervision order or other control of a child on an extra-statutory basis.

8.2 Section 31 allows a court to place a child in the care, or under the supervision, of any local authority on the application of a local authority or authorised person (section 31(1)). Currently the only other body authorised by the Secretary of State is the NSPCC. However, where the NSPCC (or any other body which may be authorised in future) wish to commence proceedings, before making application if it is reasonably practicable to do so, it must consult with the local authority in whose area the child ordinarily resides (section 31(6)). Indeed, if a child is the subject of either existing care proceedings or an existing care or supervision order, the court is precluded from entertaining an application by the NSPCC (section 31(7)). The court may not make a care or supervision order in relation to a child who has reached the age of seventeen, or sixteen where the child is married (section 31(3)). A care order is defined as an order which places the child with respect to whom the application is made, in the care of a designated local authority. A supervision order is defined as an order putting the child under the supervision of a designated local authority or of a probation officer. This authority must be either the authority within whose area the child is ordinarily resident, or the authority within whose area any circumstances arose in consequence of which the order is made (section 31(1)(a) and (b) and (8)). An application under section 31 can be made on its own or in any other family proceeding (section 31(4)). However, in whatever proceedings these orders are sought, they can only be made if the grounds in section 31(2) are satisfied.

Grounds

8.3 Section 31(2) provides that a court may only make a care or supervision order if it is satisfied:

- that the child concerned is suffering, or is likely to suffer, significant harm and
- that the harm, or likelihood of harm, is attributable to the care given to the child, or likely to be given to him if the order were not made, not being what it would be reasonable to expect a parent to give him; or the child being beyond parental control.

  — 'Harm' is defined as meaning ill-treatment or the impairment of health or development.
  — 'Development' means physical, intellectual, emotional, social or behavioural development.
  — 'Health' means physical and mental health.
  — 'Ill-treatment' includes sexual abuse and forms of ill-treatment which are not physical.
  — Where the question of whether any harm suffered by a child is significant turns on the child's health or development, his health or development shall be compared with that which could reasonably be expected of a similar child (section 31(9) and (10)).
  — 'Significant' means, from its dictionary definition, considerable, noteworthy or important. This could exist in the seriousness of the harm or the implication of it, and will be a matter for the court to consider in each case.

First and foremost, the principles embodied in section 1 of the Act apply to applications under section 31. Therefore the court must have regard to the welfare principle in section 1(1) and section 1(5) precludes the court from making an order unless it considers it better for the child than not doing so. Local authorities are under a duty to promote the welfare of children in need and as far as is consistent with this duty, to promote the upbringing of children by their families (section 17(1)). Local authorities should, therefore, fully explore voluntary arrangements, through provision of services, to the child and his family before commencing an application under the Act. Section 1(5) would in effect prevent children being placed in care where albeit home circumstances may not be adequate, there is no evidence an order would improve the situation. The welfare checklist in section 1(3) also applies to applications under Part IV (reproduced in full in Chapter 3), unlike applications involving the emergency protection of children. However, the provisions in section 1 will only become relevant to the court's considerations once the grounds in section 31 are satisfied. The statutory threshold in section 31(2) must be crossed initially, then all the circumstances of the case looked at in light of the section 1 principles.

Harm

8.4 The grounds in section 31(2) contain a prospective element, therefore a local authority may possibly seek an order on the basis of apprehended harm. However, it will still not be possible for orders to be sought in relation to an unborn child; a local authority will have to wait until a child has an existence independent of that of the mother. The definition of harm is comprehensive enough to cater for all forms of neglect or abuse; the level required for the threshold criteria to be satisfied being significant.

Where harm relates to a child's health or development, his health or development shall be compared with that which could reasonably be expected of a similar child. Similar in this context may need to take account of the environmental, social and cultural characteristics of the child. The need to personalise the standard required to the child in question takes account of the fact that special care or attention may be needed for some children and not others. Account must be taken of the attributes and consequent needs of the child before the court. The standard of health and development against which to measure the child is that which it is reasonable to expect and not the best that could possibly be achieved. Otherwise a child could be removed from home because other arrangements cater for his needs better than his parents' care, which offends against one of the underlying principles of the Act, that of non-intervention unless necessary. Finally, the issue of whether harm is likely will be a matter for the court to assess; and the court will need to balance the chance of harm occurring against the magnitude of harm if it occurs.

8.5 Section 31(2) contains a causative element in that harm or its likelihood must be linked to either a deficiency in, or unacceptable standard of, care for the child or to the fact that the child is beyond parental control: no order can be made unless both limbs of the test in section 31(2) are made out.

Parental care

8.6 Any harm, or likelihood of harm, to the child must result from shortcomings in parental care — whether this results from inadequacy or incapability of providing reasonable care, or because parents, despite their best efforts, are not able to meet a child's needs or are unwilling to utilise any relevant services. The standard of parental care is objective, but not in a way which demands the same minimum standard for all children; it must be judged on whether the care provided is reasonable for the child in question. The focus of the court's attention is child-centred. The test in section 31(2)(b)(i) therefore, requires the court to consider whether the care given to the child, bearing in mind the child's particular needs or attributes, is what it would be reasonable to expect a parent to give him. The court must then decide whether the care given by the parents in question matches up with this standard.

Parental control

8.7 The alternative condition applies where the harm or likelihood of harm is attributable to the child being beyond parental control. It will be immaterial whether this is due to the parents or the child, but lack of control without attendant evidence of harm will not of itself allow a child to be taken into care. Providing the threshold conditions are satisfied, and the standard of proof required will be on the balance of probabilities, the court must apply the provisions of section 1: whether an order will promote a child's welfare or whether no order at all is appropriate. At this stage it will be incumbent on an applicant, more so than under the previous legislation, to provide the court with details of their plans for the child, to enable the court to decide what order, if any, is appropriate for the child.

Timetable and delay and venue

8.8 A court hearing any application under Part IV of the Act must have regard to the general principle in section 1(2) that any delay in the determining of the application is likely to prejudice the welfare of the child concerned. To this end the court must draw up a timetable, and more specifically give appropriate directions to ensure this timetable is adhered to, in order to ensure the application is disposed of expeditiously (section 32). As a general rule all Part IV applications will be commenced in a magistrates' court. However, the Children (Allocation of Proceedings) Order 1991, SI 1991 No 1677, makes provision for transfer of such applications between magistrates' courts, from magistrates' to county courts, appeals against refusal to transfer and the criteria for such transfers. For a detailed discussion of allocation procedure and the specific rules regarding timetabling, see paras **1.44** and **5.1**. The order and the relevant rules (FPR 4.14 and 4.15/FPC 14 and 15) are also reproduced in the Appendices.

EFFECT AND DURATION OF PART IV ORDERS

Care orders

8.9 A care order, other than an interim care order, continues in force until the child reaches the age of eighteen, unless brought to an end earlier (which circumstances are discussed in this chapter post). A local authority named in a care order has a duty to receive the child into its care and keep him in its care while the order remains in force (section 33(1)). If a care order application was made by an authorised person (ie NSPCC) and the local authority was not informed in accordance with section 31(6) (para **8.2** ante) the child may be kept in that person's care until received into local authority care (section 33(2)). Section 33(3) provides that while a care order is in force the designated local authority shall:

● have parental responsibility for the child and
● have the power (subject to the following provisions of this

section) to determine the extent to which a parent or guardian of the child may meet his parental responsibility for him.

Parental responsibility is defined in section 3(1) as 'all the rights, duties, powers, responsibilities and authority which by law a parent of a child has in relation to the child and his property'. The duties of a designated local authority in respect of a child in its care will encompass provision of accommodation and maintaining him, safeguarding and promoting his welfare, and ensuring effect is given to its other welfare responsibilities under Part III of the Act. Especially important in this context is a general duty of consultation imposed on local authorities when a child is in their care by virtue of a care order. Section 22 provides that before making any decision with regard to such a child, as far as is practicable, the local authority shall ascertain the wishes and feelings of:

- the child
- his parents
- any person with parental responsibility for the child
- any other person whose wishes and feelings the authority consider relevant.

The authority must give due consideration to the wishes and feelings of the above class of persons before making such decision. In respect of the child concerned, his age and understanding will be a factor, as will his religion, racial origin, cultural and linguistic background.

8.10 However, an innovation in care proceedings is introduced by section 2(5) and (6) of the Act. A parent or other person with parental responsibility for a child does not lose this even when a care order is made. Parental responsibility is shared, but despite the parent or guardian retaining parental responsibility and the local authority acquiring it by virtue of a care order, the Act does contain restrictions on how the respective parties will be able to exercise such responsibility. With regard to parents or guardians, the fact they retain parental responsibility will not entitle them to act in any way which would be incompatible with any order made with respect to the child under the Act (section 2(8)). In addition to this the local authority, by virtue of section 33(3)(b), will have the power to determine the extent to which a parent or guardian of a child may meet his parental responsibility. But this power may not be exercised unless the local authority is satisfied that it is necessary to do so to safeguard or promote the child's welfare (section 33(4)). A local authority may therefore prevent a parent, when this is justified in the child's interests, from undermining its decisions; and in the case of a child allowed home, this power may be utilised where a clear conflict arises between a parent and the local authority. However, while this overriding power of veto exists, when a child is returned home by a local authority during the currency of a care order, nothing will prevent a parent or guardian from doing what is reasonable in all the circumstances of the case, for the purpose of safeguarding or promoting the welfare of the child, while in their care. In effect, the sum of these provisions is that while parental responsibility is shared, and the status of parents or guardians appears to be enhanced, the local authority has the power to control the exercise of parental responsibility of parents or guardians, and so in reality the ascendancy lies with the local authority, as it must if the order is to have any efficacy.

8.11 However, the parental responsibility acquired by the local authority is hedged with a number of restrictions. It may not cause the child to be brought up in any religious persuasion other than the one he would have been brought up in if the order had not been made. It may not appoint a guardian for the child or consent to either an order freeing the child for adoption or to an adoption order. Power to consent to adoption or a child's marriage will remain with a parent or guardian (section 33(9)). Finally, while a care order is in force no person may cause the child to be known by a new surname or remove him from the UK without either the written consent of every person who has parental responsibility or the leave of the court (section 33(7)). However, there is no restriction on taking the child out of the UK for a period of less than one month or where the local authority has made arrangement for the child to live outside England and Wales under paragraph 19 of Schedule 2 of the Act (section 33(8)(a) and (6)).

Parental contact

8.12 A local authority is under a general duty by virtue of Schedule 2, paragraph 15, to promote contact between children it is looking after and their families; however section 34(1) of the Act creates a statutory presumption of reasonable contact between children subject to care orders and a specified class of persons. This comprises his parents, any guardian or person in whose favour a residence order was in force immediately before the care order was made, or in the same circumstances, a person who had care of the child by virtue of an order made in the exercise of the High Court's inherent jurisdiction. Parent in this context would include an unmarried father. However, there is no presumption of contact in favour of other blood relatives or members of an extended family. In the case of such persons, if they desire contact, either reliance could be placed on the local authority's duty under Schedule 2, paragraph 15 or application would have to be made to the court for an order allowing contact with the child. Before making a care order, the court must consider the arrangements the local authority has made, or proposes, for affording any person contact with the child in question; and invite the parties to the proceedings to comment on such arrangements (section 34(11)). If parties and the local authority reach agreement over contact the court may not need to make an order under section 34 and areas of potential disagreement in the future may be defused. Attendant on this requirement, the court also has power, if it considers such an order should be made, to make an order for contact, notwithstanding that there has been no application for contact in respect of the child (section 34(5)). An order for contact may be made at the same time as the care order itself, or during the currency of the care order, and may impose such conditions regarding contact as the court considers appropriate; for instance that contact is supervised or prescribing its frequency and duration (section 34(7) and (10)).

8.13 While the court is under a duty to consider contact arrangements and can make orders for contact of its own motion, section 34 makes specific provision regarding applications for an order. Any of the persons entitled to the presumption of contact under section 34(1) may apply without restriction, or any other person, with leave of the court. On the hearing of such applications, the court may order such contact as it considers appropriate between the child and applicant (section 34(3)). Such applications can be made at the initial hearing for a care order or at any time while the care order subsists. Applications under this provision could be made by relatives or others connected with the child, or where parties are dissatisfied with the arrangements made or proposals for contact.

8.14 Application can also be made regarding contact by the child or the local authority, and the court is empowered to make such order as it considers appropriate with respect to contact

143

between the child and a named person (section 34(2)). Allowing a local authority recourse to the court would allow it to resolve disputes over contact with a parent or other person; and thereby have the precise extent of their responsibilities with regard to contact defined. Provision for the child to apply may be useful if he wishes to maintain contact with a relative or friend not otherwise entitled to contact. A local authority may refuse to allow contact, in an emergency, which it otherwise must allow either as a result of the presumption under section 34(1) or any order under section 34, if it is satisfied it is necessary to do so in order to safeguard or promote the child's welfare. The refusal must:

- be decided upon as a matter of urgency; and
- not last for more than seven days (section 34(6)).

After seven days, or in any other case which does not fall within the above criteria, the local authority will have to apply to the court for an order authorising it to refuse to allow contact between the child and any person entitled to the presumption of contact (whether or not an order is in force with respect to them) or any person named in an order under section 34 (section 34(4)). A child may also apply for an order refusing contact between himself and any person. A court has power to vary or discharge an order for contact on the application of the local authority, child or person named in the order (section 34(9)). There is provision for the Secretary of State to make regulations applying to, the steps to be taken by an authority refusing contact in an emergency, on which basis parties may depart by agreement from the terms of an order allowing or authorising refusal of contact and notification by the local authority of any variation or suspension of voluntary contact arrangements (ie not under a section 34 order) (section 34(8)).

8.15 Section 91(17) provides that where an application for contact is refused by the court, the applicant may not make a further application for such an order in respect of the same child until the expiration of six months from the refusal, unless he obtains leave of the court to do so. The court should also consider its general power, particularly in the case of a vexatious litigant, to order that no application for an order under the Act of any specified kind, may be made with respect to a child by any person named in such order without the court's leave. This power arises whenever the court disposes of any application for an order under the Act (section 91(14)).

Supervision orders

8.16 A court can make a supervision order as an alternative to a care order. The child is placed under the supervision of a designated local authority, or in certain circumstances, a probation officer. The order is governed by section 35 of the Act and Parts I and II of Schedule 3. The statutory basis for making a supervision order is identical to that for a care order embodied in section 31(2) of the Act (see para **8.3**). The court cannot designate a local authority as supervisor unless either the authority agree; or the child lives, or will live within its area (Schedule 3, Part II, paragraph 9(1)). A court cannot designate a probation officer as supervisor unless the relevant local authority request this and there is a probation officer working with another member of the household to which the child belongs (Schedule 3, Part II, paragraph 9(2)). The making of a supervision order automatically terminates any earlier care or supervision order in respect of the child which would otherwise continue in force (Schedule 3, Part II, paragraph 10).

Duration

8.17 A supervision order will cease to have effect one year after the date on which it was made. While every order in the first instance can only last for twelve months, the supervisor may apply to the court to extend, or further extend the order; the court may extend the order in this case for such period as it may specify. However, a supervision order may not be extended, or further extended, so that it would last in total for more than three years beginning with the date on which it was initially made (Schedule 3, Part II, Paragraph 6). In any event a supervision order would cease to have effect on the child reaching eighteen years of age (section 91(13)). These provisions ensure the order is kept under the scrutiny of the court. A supervision order will also cease to have effect if steps are taken or orders made under the Child Abduction and Custody Act, 1985 (which provides for recognition and enforcement of foreign custody orders).

Duties of supervisor

8.18 While a supervision order is in force it is a supervisor's duty:

- to advise, assist and befriend the supervised child
- to take such steps as are reasonably necessary to give effect to the order
- where the order is not wholly complied with, or
- the supervisor considers that the order may no longer be necessary: he must to consider whether or not to apply to the court for its variation or discharge (section 35(1)).

In addition the Secretary of State is given power to make regulations concerning the exercise of local authority functions and expenditure in respect of supervision orders (Schedule 3, Part II, Paragraph 11). The Act therefore places a duty on the supervisor to monitor the effectiveness of the order, and where it proves ineffective or its purpose has been achieved, to take positive action. All other matters relating to supervision orders are embodied in Schedule 3, Parts I and II.

Specific requirements

8.19 A supervision order may require the child to comply with any directions given by the supervisor to do all or any of the following:

- to live at a specified place or places for certain periods of time
- to present himself to a specified person or persons at times and places as stated
- to participate in specified activities at certain times.

It is for the supervisor, not the court, to decide whether, and to what extent, directions are given to the child and the form of directions in any individual case is also a matter for the supervisor's discretion (Schedule 3, Paragraph 2(2)). However, this power must be read in conjunction with paragraph 7, which places an overall limit of 90 days on any particular activity under the above provisions (or such shorter period as the court may specify in the order). In calculating the number of days, any day on which the child fails to comply with the supervisor's directions may be disregarded.

8.20 In the case of very young children the imposition of the requirements contained in paragraph 2 of Schedule 3 may often be unrealistic. However, the Act now allows a court to impose requirements under a supervision order on any 'responsible person'. In relation to the supervised child, this is either a person who has parental responsibility for him or any other person with whom he is living (Schedule 3, Paragraph (1)). Paragraph 3 details requirements which the order may impose on the responsible person, with the caveat that such requirements may only be imposed with the consent of the responsible person concerned. The order may require the responsible person:

- to take all reasonable steps to ensure that the supervised child complies with any direction given by the supervisor
- to take all reasonable steps to ensure that the child complies with any requirement in the order concerning psychiatric or medical examination or treatment and
- to comply with any directions given by the supervisor requiring him to attend a specified place or to take part in specified activities (paragraph 3).

This last direction could, for instance, require a parent to attend instruction classes in child care. The direction given by the supervisor in this case may specify also whether or not the child is to attend with the supervised person. However, the proviso in paragraph 7 that the total number of days must not exceed ninety or such lesser number as specified in the order during which the responsible person may be required to comply with any or all of the above requirements, also applies in the case of the responsible person. Paragraph 3 also may require any responsible person to keep the supervisor informed of his address where this differs from the child's.

8.21 Complementing the above requirements, paragraph 8 provides that a supervision order may require the child to keep his supervisor informed of any change in his address and to allow the supervisor to visit him at the place where he is living. Similar duties are imposed on the responsible person who must inform the supervisor of the child's address, if this is known to him, when requested to do so; and must allow the supervisor reasonable contact with the child where he is living with him. A supervisor who is denied access under these provisions may apply to the court for a warrant under section 102 of the Act. If it appears to the court on the application of the supervisor that he has been refused access to premises or access to the child concerned, or he is likely to be prevented from exercising such powers, it may issue a warrant authorising any constable to assist the supervisor in exercising these powers, using reasonable force if necessary. The warrant must be addressed to, and executed by, a constable. The applicant may accompany the constable if he desires and the court does not direct otherwise. Where it is reasonably practicable the warrant must name the child, where it does not it must describe him as clearly as possible. A court may direct that the constable executing the warrant may be accompanied by a registered medical practitioner, registered nurse or registered health visitor, if he chooses (section 102).

Psychiatric and medical examinations – paragraph 4

8.22 A supervision order may require the child to submit to a medical or psychiatric examination. The order may provide for the child to be examined on one occasion, or for examination to take place from time to time as directed by the supervisor. The examination must be carried out by, or under the direction of, a registered medical practitioner specified in the order. The order must also specify where any examination shall take place, at which the child is to attend as a non-resident patient. A child cannot be required to attend a hospital or a mental nursing home as an in-patient for the purpose of examination unless the court is satisfied, on the evidence of a registered medical practitioner that:

- the child may be suffering from a physical or mental condition that requires, and may be susceptible, to treatment; and
- a period as a resident patient is necessary if the examination is to be carried out properly.

Where a child has sufficient understanding to make an informed decision, the court cannot include the requirement for examination in an order unless it is satisfied that the child consents. In this case the child's wishes are conclusive. The other constraint in respect of including an examination requirement in a supervision order is that the court must also be satisfied that satisfactory arrangements have been, or can be, made for the examination. When including an examination requirement, the court may, with consent of the responsible person, require him to take all reasonable steps to ensure the child is examined in accordance with the order (paragraph 3(1)(b)).

Psychiatric and medical treatment – paragraph 5

8.23 A court, when making or varying a supervision order may include a medical treatment requirement if satisfied on the evidence of a registered medical practitioner that the child's physical condition requires, and may be susceptible to, treatment and that, where the child has sufficient understanding to make an informed decision, he consents to its inclusion – so again the child's wishes are conclusive. Also the court must be satisfied arrangements have been, or can be, made for the treatment. No requirement for treatment can be included unless all three requirements are met. The period of treatment must be specified in the order, as must whether the child is to be a resident or non-resident patient. The treatment must be by, or under the direction of such registered medical practitioner as the order may specify. If the child is to be a non-resident patient the order may specify the place where treatment is to take place; if the child is to be a resident patient the treatment must take place at a health service hospital. Where the court proposes to include a mental treatment requirement the same conditions and restrictions, in particular consent of the child when relevant, apply with three exceptions. First the evidence regarding the mental condition of the child must be supplied by a doctor approved under section 12 of the Mental Health Act 1983 and secondly, the court must be satisfied that the child's mental condition does not warrant detention under that Act. Finally, where the child is to be a resident patient this must be in a hospital or mental nursing home; so the requirement the hospital must be a health service hospital is not mandatory in the case of psychiatric treatment. The doctor by whom, or under whose direction, the child is undergoing treatment must make a written report to the child's supervisor if he is unwilling to continue with the treatment or he is of the opinion that:

- the treatment should continue beyond the period specified in the order
- the child needs different treatment
- he is not susceptible to treatment
- he does not require further treatment.

The supervisor must refer such a report to the court which may make an order cancelling or varying the treatment requirement. As with medical or psychiatric examination, the court may include a requirement, with consent of the responsible person, that he take all reasonable steps to ensure the child receives treatment in accordance with the order (paragraph 3(1)(b)).

Section 8 orders

8.24 It must be remembered that all applications under Part IV come within the definition of 'family proceedings' in section 8(3) of the Act. The welfare checklist in section 1 requires the court to consider, amongst other matters, the range of powers available to the court in the proceedings before it. It is always incumbent upon the court in any Part IV application to consider whether another order than the one sought would be more appropriate, and the court has power to make any of the orders under section 8 (for detailed discussion see paras **1.7** and **4.10**) either on an application or, where there is no specific application, but the court of its own volition feels such an order is more appropriate than a care or supervision order (section 10(1)). Any person entitled to apply for a section 8 order or granted leave to do so may make application for such an order in care proceedings (section 10(2)). For example, the court, on a Part IV application, may nevertheless feel that the child's interests would be better served by the making of a residence order in favour of a relative. A residence order, if appropriate, may be made in care proceedings whether or not the statutory ground in section 31(2) is satisfied. The wide options available to the court in family proceedings would also mean that a residence order could be coupled with a supervision order; however in this case the section 31(2) ground must be met. The one restriction in this range of possible orders, is that no court may make a care order and a section 8 order. The only section 8 order which may be made in respect of a child in care is a residence order, the effect of which discharges the care order. In addition no local authority may apply for, or court make, a residence or contact order in its favour (section 9(1) and section 91(1)).

Interim orders

8.25 Where, in any proceedings for a care or supervision order, the proceedings are adjourned, or the court gives a direction under section 37(1) (ie local authorities' duty to investigate: see para **8.43**), the court may make an interim care or supervision order (section 38(1)). The court will normally be a full court; however where there is a written request for an interim order which contains the consent of, and is signed by the parties or representatives and any guardian ad litem; or a previous interim order has been made in the same proceedings; or the terms of the order sought are the same as the last such interim order, then the order can be made by a single justice or justices' clerk. (FPC 28).

8.26 The court cannot make an interim order unless satisfied that there are reasonable grounds for believing that the circumstances with respect to the child are as mentioned in section 31(2) (section 38(2)). There must, therefore, be sufficient evidence to justify a reasonable belief that grounds for a full order may exist. Also it must be remembered that the grounds in section 1 apply, so the court should not make an interim order unless it considers that doing so would be better for the child than making no order (section 1(5)).

8.27 It should be borne in mind that the court may make a residence order under section 8 as an interim measure when adjourning a Part IV application or giving a direction under section 37(1) (section 11(3)). A residence order, for instance, which names the person with whom the child is to live, could be made in favour of a relative or other person connected with the child. However, where the court chooses this option it must also make an interim supervision order unless it is satisfied that the child's welfare will be satisfactorily safeguarded without this (section 38(3)). Provisions regarding duration of interim orders would not apply to a residence order, but would operate if an interim supervision order was also made (see following para). This power would allow the child to be placed with a suitable person during the course of proceedings, with the additional safeguard of statutory supervision.

8.28 Section 38(4) governs the duration of interim orders. It provides that an interim order (care or supervision) shall have effect for such period as may be specified in the order, but will cease on whichever of the following events occurs first:

• the expiry of the period of eight weeks beginning with the date on which the order is made;
• if the order is the second or subsequent such order, the expiry of the relevant period (ie four weeks beginning with the date on which the order is made or eight weeks from the original order whichever is the later) (section 38(5)).

Apart from these situations an interim order terminates on the disposal of the application for a care or supervision order, or where a direction is given under section 37(1) (see para **8.43**), at the end of the eight week period or such other period as the court directed for the authority to report on its investigation. In short, a first interim order may be made for up to a maximum of eight weeks beginning with the date on which it was made. A second or subsequent order may last for up to four weeks beginning with the date on which it is made, or where the first order was for less than eight weeks, for up to eight weeks from when the first order was made. Thereafter the four-week limit will apply on each subsequent interim order. The court will still need to be satisfied that the criteria in section 31(2) and section 1(5) are met, whenever there is an application for an interim order. In determining the period of an interim order the court must consider whether any party who was, or might have been opposed to its making was in a position to argue his case against the order in full (section 38(10)). Therefore, a shorter order may on occasion be necessary to allow a party to contest a further interim order application.

Medical and psychiatric examination

8.29 When a court makes an interim care or supervision order it may give such directions as it considers appropriate with respect to the medical or psychiatric examination or other assessment of the child; however if the child is of sufficient understanding to make an informed decision he may refuse to submit to such examination or assessment (section 38(6)). As well as authorising examination or assessment, the court may expressly prohibit it, or prohibit it unless there is a direction otherwise (section 38(7)). Paragraphs 4 and 5 of Schedule 3 to the Act (see para **8.22**) do not apply in relation to interim supervision orders (section 38(9)). The provisions of section 38(6) and (7) above, may be used by parties to care applications where they either need to have a child assessed, or where they wish to prevent another party from doing this. Courts may find this power useful to order, when necessary, joint assessments, to minimise the number of assessments a child has to undergo, which can be intrusive at a time when the child needs more support than under normal circumstances. Directions for medical examination or other kinds of assessment may be given when the interim order is made or during its currency. These may be varied at any time on the application of the class of persons detailed in FPC 2(1)/FPR 4.2(1), namely parties to the proceedings in which such directions are given, and any person named in such directions (section 38(6) and (8)).

Effect of interim orders

8.30 Interim care and supervision orders are similar in nature to the full orders; however the length of order is finite and determined by the court and the court may give directions. Otherwise by virtue of section 31(11), on an interim care order, the local authority will acquire parental responsibility while the order subsists. Additionally, the provisions of section 34 regarding contact with children in care will apply during the period of an interim care order. So the court must consider proposals for contact and invite parties to comment; and may make an order for contact on application by parties or of its own motion. The local authority during the currency of an interim care order is also required to comply with responsibilities regarding children in its care under Part III of the Act. An interim supervision order does not confer parental responsibility on the local authority. Contact between the child and other parties in this case would be through the use of section 8 orders (section 11(3)).

DISCHARGE AND VARIATION OF CARE AND SUPERVISION ORDERS

8.31 A care order (including an interim care order) may be discharged by the court on the application of the child, any person who has parental responsibility for him or the local authority designated by the order (section 39(1)). This class of applicants would include a parent (including an unmarried father who had parental responsibility by virtue of a court order or by agreement) or a guardian. However, a non-parent, who had the benefit of a residence order prior to the care order being made will not be able to apply, as by virtue of section 91(2) the care order discharges any order under section 8. However, such a person may seek a residence order under section 8 (with leave of the court) in respect of the child. A residence order made in respect of a child in the care of a local authority automatically discharges any care order in force (section 91(1)). When considering whether to grant leave to a person to make application for a section 8 order the court must have regard to such factors as the applicant's connection to the child, local authority plans for the child's future, wishes and feelings of the parents and any risk of disrupting the child's life to the extent he would be harmed (section 10(9)). The court may substitute a supervision order for the care order on an application to discharge, even if the grounds in section 31(2) no longer subsist at the time (section 39(4)).

Alternatively on discharging a care order the court may make a residence order if it feels this is the most appropriate order to benefit the child.

Supervision orders

8.32 A supervision order (including an interim supervision order) may be discharged, or varied, by the court on the application of the child, any person with parental responsibility, or the supervisor (section 39(2)). A person who is not entitled to seek a discharge of the order, but with whom the child is living, may apply for any requirement under the order to be varied in so far as such requirement affects him (section 39(3)). However, it must be noted that on discharging a supervision order, the court cannot make a care order unless the section 31(2) criteria are satisfied. If a local authority wish to replace a supervision order with a care order they would have to commence proceedings anew under section 31; and if a care order was made in these proceedings, this would discharge the supervision order automatically (section 91(3)). On the discharge of a supervision order, it is open to the court to make a section 8 residence order in an appropriate case.

Grounds

8.33 The Act contains no specific grounds for discharge or variation of orders. However, the principles in section 1 of the Act; will apply, including the welfare of the child being paramount (section 1(1)) and that no variation or discharge should be ordered unless that would be better than leaving the order in operation (section 1(5)) in conjunction with the welfare checklist in section 1(3). The principles will accordingly govern the exercise of the court's discretion when hearing such applications.

8.34 A positive duty is placed on a local authority to consider at least at every statutory review of a case of a child in its care, whether to apply for the discharge of the care order (section 26(2)(e)) and a similar duty, requiring a supervisor to consider whether or not to apply for variation or discharge of a supervision order is imposed when the order is not being complied with or he considers it is no longer necessary (section 35(1)(c)).

8.35 No further application can be made for the discharge of a care or supervision order, or the substitution of a supervision for a care order within six months of a previous application, unless the court grants leave to do so (section 91(15)). This prohibition does not apply to interim orders (section 91(16)). A court is also given a general power when disposing of any application under the Act, to order that there may be no application for an order of any specified kind with respect to the child concerned by any person named in the order, without the court's leave. This provision is aimed, presumably, at the vexatious litigant (section 91(14)).

Appeals

8.36 An appeal lies to the High Court against any order made by a magistrates' court under the Act, or refusal to make an order. Any party to the original proceedings may appeal and this will include the local authority or NSPCC (section 94(1)). A court, if at the time it dismisses an application for a care order, and the child concerned was subject to an interim care order, may make a care order in respect of him pending the appeal. If an application for a care or supervision order is dismissed and at the time the child concerned was the subject of an interim supervision order, the court may make a supervision order in respect of the child pending the appeal. Both the above orders pending appeal may be subject to whatever directions, if any, the court sees fit to include in the order (section 40(1) and (2)). Where a court grants an application to discharge a care or supervision order it may order that, pending appeal, its decision is not to have effect or that the care or supervision order is to continue but subject to such directions as the court sees fit to impose (section 40(3)). In effect in all of the above situations, the immediate status quo is preserved pending determination of the appeal which will ensure that the child is protected and the continuity of his life is not interrupted until the appeal is heard. However, there is no power for the court to preserve the status quo in favour of a parent pending an appeal; the court has no power to defer a care or supervision order from taking effect. Any order under section 40 only has effect for such period as may be specified in the order, but in any event, cannot exceed the appeal period. This will terminate either with the determination of the appeal, or the end of the period within which an appeal may be brought (section 40(4) and (6)). Regarding Part IV or V applications no appeal will lie:

- against the making or refusal to make an EPO or against any direction given in connection with such an order (section 45);
- against a decision by a magistrates' court to decline jurisdiction, where it has this power, because it considers a case can be more conveniently dealt with by another court (section 94(2));
- outside any circumstances the Lord Chancellor may provide for in connection with transfer, or proposed transfer of proceedings under Schedule 11 (section 94(10) and (11)).

Upon an appeal, the High Court may make such orders as may be necessary to give effect to its determination of the appeal and such incidental and consequential orders as appear just (section 94(4) and (5)). Any order made on appeal (other than that directing the application to be reheard by the magistrates) for the purpose of any power to vary, revive, discharge or enforcement must be treated as if it were an order of the original magistrates' court from which the appeal was brought (section 94(9)) (see also paras **5.23** and **5.24**).

Education supervision orders

8.37   In the case of a child not attending school, a specific procedure is introduced by the Act. A court may make an education supervision order if it is satisfied that the child concerned is of compulsory school age and is not being properly educated (section 36(3)). A child is defined as being properly educated if he is receiving efficient full-time education suitable to his age, ability and aptitude and any special educational needs he may have (section 36(4)). It shall be assumed that a child is not being properly educated, unless there is proof to the contrary if:

- he is a registered pupil at a school which he is not attending regularly within the meaning of section 39 of the Education Act 1944 or
- the child is the subject of a school attendance order which is in force under section 37 of the Education Act 1944 which has not been complied with (section 36(5)).

No education supervision order may be made with respect to a child who is in the care of a local authority (section 36(6)). Any local education authority may apply for an order putting the child concerned under the supervision of a designated local education authority. The local education authority designated must be either:

- the authority within whose area the child concerned is or will be living; or
- where the child is a registered pupil at a school and the authority within whose area he lives and the authority within whose area the school is situated agree, it shall be the latter authority (section 36(7)).

Prior to making an application the education authority must consult the social services committee within whose area the child is, or will be, living or where the child is being accommodated by, or on behalf of, a local authority, that authority.

Duration and effect of orders

8.38 An order will initially last for one year beginning with the date on which it is made. Application can be made by the education authority for the order to be extended and this may not be made earlier than three months before the expiry date. The order may be extended more than once, but no one extension may be for a period of more than three years. An order will automatically cease to have effect on the making of a care order or on the child reaching school leaving age (Schedule 3, paragraph 15). Once an order had been made in respect of a child, a school attendance order under section 37 of the Education Act 1944 and any education requirement in a supervision order made in criminal proceedings will cease to have effect. Also while the order is in force sections 37 and 76 of the Education Act 1944 (school attendance orders and pupils to be educated in accordance with parents' wishes) and sections 6 and 7 of the Education Act 1980 (parental preference and appeals against admission decisions) will not apply to the child (Schedule 3, paragraph 13).

Powers and duties of supervisor

8.39 It is a supervisor's duty to advise, assist and befriend and give directions to the supervised child, and his parents, in such a way as will, in the opinion of the supervisor, secure that he is properly educated (Schedule 3, paragraph 12). 'Parent' is defined in accordance with the Education Act 1944 to include a non-parent with parental responsibility or any person who has care of the child. The supervisor has wide powers to decide how a child shall receive his education, and may give directions at any time while the order is in force. However, as far as is reasonably practicable, a supervisor shall ascertain the wishes and feelings of the child and parents, in particular as to where the child should be educated, before giving any directions (Schedule 3, paragraph 12). When setting the terms of any direction, he must give due consideration to such wishes and feelings as he has been able to ascertain with regard to the parents, and child, having regard to the child's age and understanding (paragraph 12(3)). The order may require the child to keep the supervisor informed of any change of address and to allow the supervisor to visit him wherever he is living. A parent must, if requested, inform the supervisor of the child's address, if this is known to him. If the child concerned is living with the parent, he must allow the supervisor reasonable contact with the child (paragraph 16).

Non-compliance with an order

8.40 If the supervisor's directions are not complied with, the supervisor must consider what further steps he must take in exercising his powers under the Act (paragraph 12(1)(6)). Where a child persistently fails to comply with any direction of his supervisor, the education authority must notify the appropriate local authority (ie the authority area where the child lives, or where he is provided with accommodation by a local authority, that authority). When such a notification is given the local authority must investigate the circumstances of the child. The Act is not specific concerning the action the local authority shall take, other than investigate the child's circumstances and decide, in all probability, whether it should take any action under the Act (paragraph 19). Failure to attend school on its own would not meet the statutory criteria in section 31(2) justifying a care order. However, persistent absence from school where this is causing, or likely to cause, significant harm and is attributable to the standard of parenting might fulfil the statutory criteria necessary for state intervention. A parent who persistently fails to comply with a direction given under the order commits an offence. However, it is a defence for the parent to prove that he took all reasonable steps to ensure the direction was complied with or that the direction was unacceptable or that he complied with requirements under an existing supervision order in respect of the child and it was not reasonably practicable to comply with both (paragraph 18) (where a supervision order is in force, made in care or criminal proceedings, the directions of that supervisor will take precedence over those under the education supervision order: (paragraph 14). Once an education supervision order is in force, a parent's duty to comply with sections 36 and 39 of the Education Act 1944 (duty to secure education of children and secure regular attendance of registered pupils) is superseded by the duty to comply with the supervisor's directions (paragraph 13). Paragraph 14 empowers the Secretary of State to make regulations modifying or displacing any other statutory provisions relating to education in so far as they may affect the operation of an education supervision order, if necessary or expedient.

Discharge of orders

8.41 An order may be discharged on the application of the child, a parent or the education authority concerned. No specific grounds are required, but a court must consider the principles in section 1 of the Act: that the child's welfare is paramount, the welfare checklist in section 1(3) and the, 'no order' principle in section 1(5). If a court discharges an order it may direct the local authority within whose area the child is, or will be, living to investigate his circumstances (paragraph 17). Again, the purpose of the investigation is not specified; although the local authority would have to consider whether it is appropriate for it to provide assistance on an extra-statutory basis or commence proceedings under the Act for a care or supervision order.

8.42 Where, following a parent's conviction for an offence under section 37 of the Education Act 1944, or where a person is charged with an offence under section 39 of that Act, the court may direct the local education authority to institute proceedings for an education supervision order with respect to the child. Any direction must be in writing and where a local education authority decides not to apply for such an order, its decision must also be given to the court in writing (FPC 31).

Directions to local authority to investigate

8.43 Section 37 of the Act empowers a court in any family proceedings to direct a local authority to investigate the circumstances of a child. The court may make such a direction in any family proceedings in which a question arises as to the welfare of a child and it appears to the court that it may be appropriate for a care or supervision order to be made (section 37(1)). Whether or not the court makes a direction is within its discretion; section 37 does not impose a positive duty on the court. The local authority is, however, obliged to comply with such a direction and while undertaking an investigation it must consider specifically whether it should:

- apply for a care or supervision order
- provide services or assistance for the child or his family
- take any other action with respect to the child (section 37(2)).

8.44 Following its investigation, if the local authority decides not to apply for a care or supervision order with respect to the child, it must inform the court of:

- the reasons for its decision;
- any service or assistance which it has provided or intends to provide for the child and his family;
- any other action which it has taken or proposes to take in relation to the child (section 37(3)).

8.45 On giving a direction the court must adjourn the proceedings and the justices' clerk/proper officer or the court must record the direction in writing. A copy of the direction, as soon as practicable after it is given, must be served by the justices' clerk/proper officer on the parties to the proceedings and on the local authority, where it is not a party. In addition, the justices' clerk/proper officer must serve copies of such documentary evidence which has been, or is to be, adduced in the proceedings as the court may direct. Any report back to the court by the local authority on any of the matters in section 37(3) must be in writing (FPC 27/FPR 4.26). The information must be given to the court within eight weeks, beginning with the date of the direction unless the court directs otherwise (section 37(4)). An authority directed to investigate must be either the authority in whose area the child ordinarily resides, or the authority in whose area the circumstances arose in consequence of which the direction is given. Where an authority declines to apply for an order under Part IV, it must consider whether it is appropriate to review the child's case at a later date; if so, it must determine the date on which the review is to begin.

8.46 An authority complying with a court's direction will have to balance compulsory intervention against voluntary assistance and co-operation and decide which course will best protect the welfare of the child. However, while the authority must undertake the investigation when directed, the final decision regarding what is the most appropriate form of action rests with it. If the court feels a statutory order is called for, and the authority do not, the court has no redress; there is no power for the court to make an order of its own motion or direct an authority to commence proceedings.

MAGISTRATES' COURT ALLOCATION AND REPRESENTATION OF THE CHILD

8.47 The allocation of cases is governed by the Children (Allocation of Proceedings) Order 1991, SI 1991 No 1801 (see also paras **1.44–1.46**), which allocates cases to the magistrates' courts or various categories of county courts according to the criteria set out in the Order (reproduced in Appendix 3 to this book). Procedure concerning applications under Part IV and Part V (for special procedure relating to ex parte emergency applications see paras **4.48** and **7.33**) is identical and is governed by FPC 4/FPR 4.4.

Allocation

8.48 Article 3 of the Allocation of Proceedings Order provides that all applications under Part IV and V of the Act shall be commenced in a magistrates' court. However, there are a number of exceptions. Where the following proceedings arise out of an investigation directed under section 37(1) by the High Court or a county court, article 3(2) and (3) provides that they must be commenced in the court which made the direction, or in such care centre[1] as the court directing investigation orders:

- care or supervision applications (section 31)
- education supervision orders (section 36)
- child assessment orders (section 43)
- emergency protection orders (section 44)
- applications for EPOs by a police officer (section 46(2))
- powers to assist discovery of children (section 48).

In addition where other proceedings under Part IV or V are pending in respect of the same child in the High Court or county court, application should be to these courts as appropriate. Article 4 of the order provides that any applications to vary, extend, or discharge orders or applications whose effect is to vary or discharge, shall be to the court which made the order. Nevertheless, a court still has power to transfer such applications to any other court where transfer criteria are met. The procedure on transfer, or refusal to transfer, is dealt with in paras **5.9** and **5.10**.

¹ Care centre means a court listed in column (ii) of Schedule 2 to the Allocation Order (see para 4).

TRANSFER OF CASES

Transfer between magistrates' courts (article 6)

8.49 A magistrates' court may transfer proceedings within its own tier to another magistrates' court, where it feels this is in the child's interests because:

- the transfer is likely significantly to accelerate disposal of the proceedings or
- it would be appropriate for the proceedings to be heard with other pending family proceedings in the other court or
- for some other reason, and the court which would receive the proceedings consents to such transfer.

Transfer from magistrates' court to county court (article 7)

8.50 Subject to certain exceptions, a magistrates' court may, either on the application of a party or of its own motion, transfer Part IV or V applications to a county court where this is considered to be in the child's interests. However, in deciding whether this is in the interests of the child, there are a number of criteria which must be considered; first:

- the principle in section 1(2) of the Act, namely any delay in determining questions relating to a child's upbringing is likely to prejudice the child's welfare;

and the court must also consider:

- whether proceedings are exceptionally grave, complex, or important, in particular because of:
  - (i) complicated or conflicting evidence about risks involved to the child's physical or moral well-being or other matters relating to the child's welfare;

   (ii)   number of parties;
  (iii) conflict of law with another jurisdiction;
  (iv) novel or difficult points of law;
   (v) a question of general public interest; or
- whether it is appropriate for the proceedings to be heard with family proceedings pending in another court; or
- whether transfer is likely significantly to accelerate the determination of proceedings where no other method of doing so is appropriate (including lateral transfer to another magistrates' court) and delay will seriously prejudice the interests of the child concerned.

The order does, however, prohibit or restrict the transfer of certain kinds of proceedings. Emergency protection applications, namely:

- section 44 emergency protection orders
- duration of EPOs (section 45)
- application for EPO by police officer (section 46(7))
- powers to assist discovery of children (section 48)

shall not be transferred from a magistrates' court. Obviously the delay of a transfer would be prejudicial to a child in such applications. Other Part IV or V proceedings may only be transferred vertically to another tier, where they will be heard together with other family proceedings which are pending in the other court and which proceedings arise out of the same circumstances.

8.51 If a magistrates' court refuses to transfer proceedings under Article 7 of the order, any party to the proceedings may apply to the relevant care centre listed in column (ii) of Schedule 2 to the order which has jurisdiction for the case to be transferred. On hearing this application the district judge may transfer proceedings to the care centre, if, after considering the principles in section 1(2) of the Act and the criteria in Article 7, he considers this to be in the child's interests. The district judge may also, after considering the principle of delay, transfer the proceedings to the High Court if the proceedings are more appropriate for that forum and this would be in the child's interests.

Transfer from county court to magistrates' court (article 11)

8.52 Before hearing the proceedings which have been transferred to it by a magistrates' court, the county court may transfer proceedings back to the particular magistrates' court, when on considering the no delay principle in section 1(2) and the interests of the child, it feels that the criteria cited by the magistrates' court as the reason for the transfer are either not applicable, or no longer applicable, in relation to:

- the exceptionally grave, important or complex nature of the proceedings criteria or
- joining with other family proceedings (because the county court has determined these) or
- the acceleration of determining proceedings (the above criteria are set out in full in para **8.50**).

Before an order is made, the views of the justice's clerk of the relevant court on whether the order should be made must be obtained (FPR 4.6(b)). The Children (Allocation of Proceedings) (Appeals) Order 1991 (SI 1991 No 1801) provides for an appeal against the decision of a district judge to order the transfer of proceedings to a magistrates' court. The appeal may be made to a family division judge in the High Court or to a circuit judge (but all appeals from the principle registry of the family division go to the High Court).

It is important to note Article 21, which provides that if proceedings are commenced or transferred in contravention of the order's provisions, this will not invalidate the proceedings; and no appeal will lie against the determination of proceedings based purely on such contravention.

REPRESENTATION OF THE CHILD

Guardian ad litem (section 41 and FPC 10/FPR 4.10)

8.53 The court is under a positive duty to appoint a guardian ad litem in specified proceedings, unless it is satisfied that it is not necessary to do so in order to safeguard the child's interests (section 41(1)). The proceedings specified are:

- section 31 (care and supervision applications)
- section 37(1) (local authority duty to investigate)
- section 39 (discharge and variation of care and supervision orders)
- section 39(4) (substitute supervision for care order)
- where the court is considering making a residence order in respect of a child subject to a care order
- section 34 (contact orders for children in care)
- Part V applications

- appeals against the making or refusal to make any of the above orders (NB except the making or refusal to make an EPO: section 45(10)),

and other proceedings which may be specified by rules of court but no rules have been made at this time (section 41(6)). The positive duty now makes it probable that guardians ad litem will be appointed in most cases. Perhaps the only type of case where an appointment may not be necessary is that of an older child able to instruct his own solicitor.

Appointment (FPC 10/FPR 4.10)

8.54 As soon as practicable after the commencement of specified proceedings, or the transfer of specified proceedings (defined in section 45(10)) the justices' clerk/district judge or court (which can be a single justice) shall appoint a guardian ad litem unless:

- an appointment has been made by the court which made the transfer and is subsisting, or
- the justices' clerk/district judge or court considers such an appointment is not necessary to safeguard the child's interests.

At any stage in specified proceedings a party may apply, without notifying the other parties (unless the clerk/district judge or court directs otherwise) for the appointment of a guardian ad litem. The justices' clerk/district judge or court must grant this application unless satisfied the appointment is not necessary to safeguard the child's interests; in this case reasons for declining to appoint must be given and a note of them taken by the justices' clerk/proper officer (FPC 10(2) and (3)/FPR 4.10(3)). At any stage in specified proceedings the justices' clerk/district judge or court may appoint a guardian ad litem, whether or not there has been an application for an appointment (FPR 4.10(4)/FPC 10(4)). As soon as practicable after the appointment, or refusal to appoint, a guardian ad litem, the justices' clerk/proper officer must notify the parties; and if appointed, the clerk/proper officer must, as soon as practicable, notify the guardian ad litem and serve on him copies of the application and documents filed with the application (FPC 10(5) and (6)/FPR 4.10(5) and (6)). On appointing a guardian ad litem the clerk or court must consider the appointment of anyone who previously acted as guardian ad litem of the same child (FPC 10(8)/FPR 4.10(8)). The appointment of a guardian ad litem continues for the time specified or until terminated by the court, and on terminating such an appointment, the reasons for this must be given in writing

(FPC 10(9) and (10)/FPR 4.10(9) and (10)). By virture of a direction given by the Lord Chancellor under section 90(3) of the Supreme Court Act 1981 on 7 October 1991, the Official Solicitor may be appointed guardian ad litem in the High Court in 'specified proceedings' under section 41 (see para **8.53**), in the circumstances set out in paragraph 3 of the direction. If the court considers those circumstances exist, then it may appoint the Official Solicitor. They are:

- the child concerned does not have a guardian ad litem *and*
- there are exceptional circumstances which make it desirable in the interests of the welfare of the child that the Official Solicitor rather than a panel member be appointed, having regard to:

  1 any foreign element in the case which would make it likely to require the guardian ad litem to make enquiries, or take other action, outside the jurisdiction of the court
  2 the likely burden on the guardian ad litem where he is to represent several children in the same proceedings
  3 the existence of proceedings relating to the child in any other division of the High Court in which the Official Solicitor is representing the child
  4 any other circumstances which the court considers to be relevant.

The desirability of appointing the Official Solicitor as guardian ad litem might be a matter which should be taken into account by a district judge in deciding, in accordance with article 12 of the Children (Allocation of Proceedings) Order, whether the proceedings are appropriate for determination in the High Court, and that such determination would be in the child's interest (see para **8.51**).

Powers and duties of guardian ad litem (FPC 11/FPR 4.11)

8.55 The guardian ad litem, in carrying out his duty, must have regard to the principles in section 1(2) (delay is likely to prejudice the child's welfare) and section 1(3) (welfare checklist) of the Act. The guardian ad litem must:

- appoint a solicitor for the child, unless this has already been done
- give advice to the child, having regard to his understanding
- instruct the solicitor representing the child on all matters relevant to the child arising in the course of the proceedings (FPC 11(2)/FPR 4.11(2)).

A court may appoint a solicitor for the child where no guardian ad litem is appointed, the child is of sufficient understanding to give instructions to a solicitor and wishes to do so, and the court feels it is in the child's best interests for him to be represented by a solicitor (section 41(3) and (4)). Where it appears to the guardian ad litem that the child is capable of conducting proceedings himself, intends to do so and is instructing his solicitor direct, he must inform the court. From that point he must perform all of his duties other than that of appointing a solicitor, and participate in the proceedings as the justices' clerk/district judge or court directs. He may, with the clerk/ district judge or court's leave, have legal representation in his conduct of these duties (FPC 11(3)/FPR 4.11(3)). The guardian ad litem, unless excused, must attend all directions appointments and hearings of the proceedings and must advise the justices' clerk/district judge or court on:

- whether the child is of sufficient understanding for any purpose, including the child's refusal to submit to examination or other assessment the court has power to direct or order
- the wishes of the child in any relevant matter, including his attendance at court
- the appropriate forum for the proceedings
- the timing of proceedings
- the options available, the suitability of each option and what order should be made in respect of the child
- any other matter on which the justices' clerk or court seeks the guardian ad litem's advice
- any matter concerning which the guardian ad litem feels the justices' clerk/district judge or court should be informed of (FPC 11(4)/FPR 4.11(4)(f)).

Any advice given by the guardian ad litem, subject to the court's order may be given orally or in writing; if oral, the justices' clerk/proper justice or court must make a note of it.

Other duties of the guardian ad litem

8.56 The guardian ad litem must, where practicable, notify any person, if in his opinion that person's joinder as a party to the proceedings would be likely to safeguard the child's interests, of that person's right to apply to be made a party and must inform the justices' clerk or court:

- of any such notification

- of any attempted, but unsuccessful notification and
- of any other person he believes may wish to be made party to the proceedings.

Unless the court otherwise directs, a guardian ad litem must file his written report advising on the interests of the child not less than seven days prior to the final hearing. As soon as practicable, the court must serve this on the other parties. Where there is no solicitor acting for the child, the guardian ad litem must serve and accept service of documents on the child's behalf. Where the child is capable of understanding, he must also explain to the child the meaning and significance of each document's contents. A guardian ad litem is also empowered to make whatever investigations are necessary to enable him to carry out his duties and must specifically:

- contact or seek to interview such persons as he thinks appropriate, or the court directs;
- if he inspects records specified under section 42 (see post), bring to the attention of the court, and others as the court directs, all such records which will assist, in his opinion, the proper determination of the proceedings;
- obtain whatever professional assistance which is available to him and which he thinks is appropriate, or as the justices' clerk or court directs.

Finally the guardian ad litem must provide such other assistance as the justices' clerk or court may require (FPC 11(6)-(10)/FPR 4).

Inspection of local authority records

8.57 The guardian ad litem has the right at all reasonable times to examine and take copies of any records in the possession of a local authority which were compiled in connection with:

- the making, or proposed making, by any person of any application under the Act with respect to the child concerned;
- any functions which stand referred to its social services committee under the Local Authority Social Services Act 1970, so far as those records relate to the child concerned.

Where a guardian ad litem takes a copy of any record he is entitled to examine, the copy or any part of it is admissible as evidence of any matter referred to in any:

- report which the guardian ad litem makes to the court in the proceedings in question; or
- evidence which the guardian ad litem gives in the proceedings.

This is regardless of any enactment or rule of law which would otherwise prevent the record in question being admissible in evidence (section 42). A local authority has no discretion to withhold information, and the provision would appear to be wide enough to encompass case conference minutes and files compiled with a view to adoption. The provision also is limited to a local authority, so it is open to question, when the NSPCC have instituted proceedings, whether they are under a similar duty to disclose. The Act and rules do increase the influence and position of the guardian ad litem; and the beneficiaries of the wide range of information given to the court, through the guardian ad litem, will be children involved in proceedings.

Solicitor for the child

8.58   Whether a solicitor is appointed to represent the child by the court or guardian ad litem, his duties are prescribed by FPC 12/FPR 4.12. He must represent the child in accordance with instructions received from the guardian ad litem unless he considers, taking into account the guardian ad litem's views and any direction given by the court under FPC 11(3)/FPR 4.11(3), that:

- the child wishes to give conflicting instructions to those of the guardian ad litem
- that the child is able, having regard to his understanding, to give such instructions on his own behalf.

(In this case the solicitor must conduct proceedings in accordance with the child's instructions.) Where no guardian ad litem is appointed, and the child is able to instruct a solicitor and wishes to do so, he must act in accordance with the child's instructions; in default of instructions from a guardian ad litem or a child he must act in furtherance of the child's best interests. Where no guardian ad litem is appointed the solicitor shall serve and accept service of documents on the child's behalf and where the child has sufficient understanding, explain to the child the meaning and significance of such documents (FPC 12(2)/FPR 4.12(2)). The court may terminate a solicitor's appointment on the application of the child, after allowing representations from the guardian ad litem and solicitor (FPC 12(3)/FPR 4.12(3)). Similarly, the guardian ad litem may apply to the court for a solicitor's appointment to be terminated (see suggested form below); the court may terminate the appointment after giving the solicitor and child, if competent, the opportunity to make representations (FPC 12(4)/FPR 4.12(4)). The reasons for terminating the appointment must be recorded in writing by the court. A suggested form of application for the termination of the appointment of a solicitor is shown overleaf.

8.58 *Care and supervision*

APPLICATION FOR TERMINATION OF APPOINTMENT OF
SOLICITOR

Application to the _____ [High][County][Magistrates']
Court for the termination of a solicitor's appointment. Case No ____

Section 41 of the Children Act 1989

The name of the child is _____; [s]he

is a [boy] [girl] born on _____ 19 ___, now aged ___

The child lives at _____

_____

_____

I am the guardian ad litem for the child.

My title is Mr[ ] Mrs[ ] Miss[ ] Ms[ ] Other _____

My full name is _____

My full address is _____

_____

_____

My telephone no is _____

I apply for the appointment of _____ solicitor

of _____

_____

_____

appointed by the court to represent the child on _____
199___ to be terminated.

The grounds of my application are:

_____

_____

_____

_____

I declare that the information I have given is correct and complete
to the best of my knowledge _____ date _____ 199___

Time for service of applications

8.59 The time which must be allowed for the service of an application on the respondents to proceedings under Part IV varies according to the nature of the application. The minimum number of days which must be allowed between service and a subsequent directions, or other, hearing is governed by FPC 4(1)(b) and Schedule 2, column (ii)/FPR 4.4(1)(b) and Appendix 3, column (ii). Unless an application is served upon the respondent, or his solicitor, in person or delivered at his address, two working days must be allowed in addition to the time for service where the application is sent by first class post, or in the case of a solicitor via a document exchange service. The times required for service are as follows:

- 1 day   section 102(1)   – warrant to assist in entry/ contact in respect of a child subject to a supervision order
- 3 days   section 31   – care or supervision order
     section 34   – contact to be allowed with named person
     section 38(8)(b) – variation of direction under interim care or supervision order
- 7 days   section 36   – education supervision order
     section 39(8)(b) – discharge and variation of care and supervision orders
     Schedule 3   – extension or discharge of supervision order.

CHAPTER 9

Remedies, enforcement and organisation

Provisions conferring power to make orders under Parts I and II

9.1 There are numerous powers of the court which may be invoked upon application and those contained in Parts I and II of the Children Act 1989 are set out below for ease of reference. They are grouped under relevant headings and provide a means of looking up what remedies may be sought of the court in various circumstances. The enactment conferring the power, and the form of application which should be used to invoke it, is also given as follows:

Section	*Powers and Forms of Application*
	Parental responsibility
4(1)(a)	Conferring parental responsibility on unmarried father – Form CHA1
4(3)	Termination of parental responsibility order or agreement (see para **4.7** for form)
4(3)(b)	Leave for child to make application terminating parental responsibility (see para **4.10** for form)
	Guardianship
5(1)	Appointment of a guardian for a child – Form CHA3
5(11)	Appointment of a guardian of a child's estate – inherent jurisdiction of the High Court (no provision in rules)(see RSC Ord 5, r 4, and Ord 43, r 9; *Nugent v Vetzara* (1886) LR 2 Eq 704)
6(7)	Termination of appointment of a guardian – Form CHA5
6(7)(b)	Leave for child to make application terminating appointment of a guardian (see para **4.10** for form)
	Section 8 orders
10(1)(a)	Section 8 order in family proceedings – Form CHA10

Section	Powers and Forms of Application
10(1)(a)(ii)	Leave to apply for a section 8 order in family proceedings (see para **4.10** for form)
10(2)(a)	Section 8 order in Children Act 1989 proceedings – Form CHA10
10(2)(b)	Leave to apply for a section 8 order in Children Act 1989 proceedings (see para **4.10** for form)

Change of name/removal from UK

13(1)(a)	Grant of leave to change surname of a child subject of a residence order – Form CHA11
13(1)(b)	Grant of leave to remove a child subject of a residence order from the United Kingdom for one month or more – Form CHA11A

Family assistance

16(1)	Family Assistance Order (court's own motion only)
16(6)	Variation or discharge of a section 8 order where the child is also the subject of a Family Assistance Order (reference by probation/local authority officer)

Financial provision

Paragraph of Schedule 1

1(1)(a)	Maintenance (secured/unsecured), lump sum, settlement and transfer of property by or from parent in the High Court or a county court – Form CHA13
1(1)(b)	Maintenance (unsecured) and lump sum in a magistrates' court – Form CHA13
1(4)	Variation or discharge of a maintenance order – Form CHA15
2(1)	Maintenance and lump sum for person over eighteen – Form CHA13
2(5)	Variation or discharge of a paragraph 2(1) order – Form CHA15
5(6)	Variation in respect of instalments payable under an order for the payment of a lump sum (see para **4.7** for form)
6(5)	Revival of lapsed order for child between sixteen and eighteen – Form CHA13
6(7)	Variation or discharge of an order revived under paragraph 6(5) – Form CHA15

Section	Powers and Forms of Application

Paragraph of Schedule 1

6(8)	Variation or discharge of an order under paragraph 1 after the death of a parent on the application of a guardian – Form CHA15
8(2)	Revocation or variation of financial relief order made under another enactment on the making of a residence order – Form CHA15 (adapted)
9(1)(a)	Interim maintenance by a parent on an application under paragraph 1 or 2 – Form CHA13
9(1)(b)	Interim order giving direction on an application under paragraph 1 or 2 – Form CHA13
9(4)	Variation of a date in interim order under paragraph 9 (see para **4.7** for form)
10(3)	Variation or revocation of financial arrangements in a maintenance agreement (limited in a magistrates' court to periodical payments: subparagraph (6)) – Form CHA15 (adapted)
11(1)	Variation or revocation of financial arrangements in a maintenance agreement continuing after the death of a party in the High Court or a county court – Form CHA15 (adapted)
14(1)	Maintenance (secured/unsecured in the High Court or a county court, unsecured in a magistrates' court) by a parent living in England and Wales for a child resident in a country outside England and Wales – Form CHA15

Provisions conferring power to make orders under Parts III, IV and V

9.2 The powers of the court under Parts III to V which can be invoked on application are set out below, together with the enactment conferring the remedy and the appropriate form of application, as follows.

Section	Type of order and form of application

Secure Accommodation

25(2)(b)	Authorisation to keep a child in secure accommodation for a further period – Form CHA17

Section	Type of order and form of application
25(5)	Interim authorisation to keep a child in secure accommodation for a further period – Form CHA17

Care and Supervision

31(1)(a)	Placing a child in the care of a designated local authority – Form CHA19
31(1)(b)	Placing a child under the supervision of a designated local authority or of a probation officer – Form CHA19
38(1)(a)	Interim care or supervision order on adjournment of application for care or supervision order – Form CHA19
38(1)(b)	Interim care or supervision order on giving a direction under section 37(1) for a local authority investigation (oral application)
38(8)(b)	Variation of direction for psychiatric, medical or other assessment of a child – Form CHA55
39(1)	Discharge of care order – Form CHA28
39(2)	Discharge or variation of supervision order – Form CHA28
39(3)	Variation of a requirement in a supervision order – Form CHA28
39(4)	Substitution of supervision order for care order – Form CHA28

Paragraph of Schedule 3

6(3)	Extension of term of supervision order – Form CHA49

Child in Care – Contact/Change of Name/Removal from UK

33(7)(a)	Change of surname of child in care – Form CHA11
33(7)(b)	Leave to take a child in care out of United Kingdom – Form CHA11A
34(2)	Contact between child in care and named person – Form CHA21
34(3)	Contact between child in care and person seeking contact – Form CHA21
34(3)(b)	Leave to apply for order for contact with child in care (see para **4.10** for form)
34(4)	Authority for local authority to refuse contact between child and named person – Form CHA23
34(9)	Variation or discharge of section 34 order – Form CHA55

Section   *Type of order and form of application*

Paragraph of Schedule 2

19(1)   Approving local authority to arrange, or assist in arranging, for a child in their care to live outside England and Wales (see para **4.7** for form)

23(1)   Contribution order for the maintenance of a child looked after by a local authority (see para **4.7** for form)

23(8)   Variation or revocation of a contribution order (see para **4.7** for form)

Education Supervision

36(1)   Education supervision order (ESO) – Form CHA25

Paragraph of Schedule 3

15(2)   Extension of term of ESO – Form CHA51

17(1)   Discharge of ESO – Form CHA53

Care/Supervision Orders Pending Appeal

40(1)   Care order for child subject to an interim care order pending appeal from dismissal of application for care order (oral application)

40(2)   Supervision order for child subject to an interim supervision order pending appeal from dismissal of application for care or supervision order (oral application)

40(5)   Extension of period of an order made under section 40 on appeal against section 40 decision (see para **4.7** for form)

Emergency Protection

43(1)   Child assessment order (CAO) – Form CHA32

43(12)   Variation or discharge of child assessment order – Form CHA55

44(1)   Emergency protection order (EPO) – Form CHA34

44(9)(b)   Giving or variation of direction in an EPO as to contact, medical or psychiatric examination or other assessment – Form CHA36

45(4)   Extension of EPO – Form CHA38

45(8)   Discharge of EPO – Form CHA40

46(7)   EPO for child in police protection – Form CHA34

Section	Type of order and form of application
48(3)	Authorisation to enter and search premises on making EPO – Form CHA34
48(4)	Authorisation to enter and search premises for another child on giving authority under section 48(3) – Form CHA34
48(9)	Warrant of assistance by constable – Form CHA43
50(1)	Recovery order (RO) – Form CHA45
75(1)(a)(i)	Cancellation of registration of child-minder – Form CHA60
75(1)(a)(ii)	Variation of requirement imposed on a child-minder – Form CHA60
75(1)(a)(iii)	Removing, or imposing an additional, requirement on a child-minder – Form CHA60
102(1)	Warrant of assistance by constable to person refused entry to certain premises or access to a child – Form CHA62

Relationship between powers of the court in Parts I,II,IV and V, duties of the local authority in Part III, Parts VI–VIII (childrens' homes and foster care) and adoption

9.3 As was mentioned in para **2.1**, the policy underlying the Children Act 1989 is that it is best for a child if he can be brought up within his family, with both parents playing a full part in his care and upbringing. The powers conferred on the courts by the Act support that policy by facilitating the court in avoiding intervention, unless satisfied that this is the best way to safeguard and promote the welfare of the child. For example, a court may make a residence order under section 10(1)(b) (perhaps in favour of a grandparent) instead of making a care order, make a contact order to encourage contact between the child and a parent, and at the same time make the child the subject of a supervision order or, with the consent of those concerned, make an FAO. To minimise, amongst other things, the incidence and degree of intervention by the state, local authorities are required to discharge various duties in relation to children in need by providing services in accordance with Part III (see para **10.3**). In particular specific duties are set out in Part I of Schedule 2. These include taking reasonable steps designed to reduce the need to bring care or other family proceedings which might lead a child to being placed in local authority care (Schedule 2, paragraph 7), and to prevent children within the local authority's area from suffering ill-treatment or neglect. They may also provide assistance to a person who is likely to cause harm to a child to move from the child's home (Schedule 2, paragraph 5); this is particularly directed at the suspected child abuser who, if he remains in the child's home, may leave the local authority with little alternative but to apply for an EPO to remove the child from the home. By virtue of paragraph 9 of Schedule 2, each local authority is required to provide family centres, which a child or his parents or others looking after him may attend, either on a day basis or residentially, in order to take part in activities and receive advice and counselling. This may be a means of avoiding the need to take a child into care, by providing the family with support while they learn to cope emotionally and socially with the stresses of family life, and improve inadequate parenting skills. Section 20 of the Children Act 1989 requires a local authority to provide accommodation for a child in certain circumstances and enables them to provide accommodation if they consider that this would safeguard or promote the child's welfare. They will usually do so by placing him with a foster parent, in a community home, a voluntary home or a registered children's home. Part VI, in dealing with community homes, imposes a duty upon each local authority to make available community homes for children accommodated by them and for purposes connected with the welfare of children. Voluntary organisations may accommodate children under Part VII in community homes, voluntary homes (ie carried on by voluntary organisations) or children's homes registered under Part VIII. Any child being looked after by a local authority, ie who is either being provided with accommodation or is in their care by virtue of a care order, may be placed with a foster parent or in one of these homes. It is the local authority's duty, however, to promote and maintain contact between a child they are looking after and the child's family, any person who has parental responsibility for him and any friend or other person connected with him. Indeed, so far as is reasonably practicable and consistent with his welfare, the local authority looking after a child must arrange for him to live with a person, or persons, in those categories (section 23(6)). Inevitably there will be cases where it is not conducive to the child's welfare for him to continue to have contact with his family, and the local authority must plan for his long-term future by way of adoption. The local authority will either seek an order freeing the child for adoption under section 18 of the Adoption Act 1976 (so that it may the more readily place a child with foster parents as prospective adopters), or where the child has been placed with foster parents who wish to adopt him, it will make a report to the court on their suitability in accordance with section 23 of the 1976 Act.

Enforcement of orders generally

9.4 The enforcement of orders is differentiated as between magistrates' courts and the High Court and county courts, as well as between financial and other orders. Unlike the other aspects of jurisdiction, enforcement has not been aligned on a common basis for the three tiers of court, save with regard to residence orders (see para **9.5**). The methods of enforcement which are generally available in each tier of court are supplemented by specific provisions in the Children Act 1989, namely section 14 in respect of residence orders and paragraph 12 of Schedule 1 in respect of an order for the payment of money made by a magistrates' court. The enforcement of residence orders in magistrates' courts is also dealt with in FPC 24, and the enforcement of orders in family proceedings in the High Court and county courts is dealt with in FPR Part VII.

Enforcement in magistrates' courts

9.5 An order for the payment of money made by a magistrates' court under the Children Act 1989 is enforceable as a maintenance order within the meaning of section 150 of the Magistrates' Courts Act 1980. The payer, under a magistrates' court order for payments, must give notice of any change of address to any person specified in the order, and for failure to comply with this requirement he may be fined (Schedule 1, paragraph 12). A residence order may be enforced under section 14 of the Children Act 1989 as soon as a copy has been served on the person who is in breach of the order. It is enforced under section 63(3) of the Magistrates' Courts Act 1980, as if it were an order requiring the person who is in breach of it to produce the child to the person in whose favour the order is in force. In contrast with paragraph 12 of Schedule 1, there is no restriction limiting the scope of section 14 to an order made in a magistrates' court. It appears to be open, therefore, to a person in whose favour a residence order has been made in the High Court or a county court to enforce it in a magistrates' court. The person wishing to enforce the order is required by FPC 24 to file a written statement describing the alleged breach of the arrangements settled in the order. The justices' clerk then fixes a date and time for the hearing, and gives notice of that date and time to the parties concerned as soon as practicable. There are no enforcement provisions in the Children Act 1989 or the Family Proceedings Courts (Children Act 1989) Rules 1991 in respect of other categories of order, and enforcement of other orders, eg a contact order, must be pursued by way of a complaint to the court under section 63(3) of the Magistrates' Courts Act 1980.

Enforcement in the High Court and county courts

9.6 Apart from the provision in section 14 of the Children Act 1989 for the enforcement of a residence order mentioned in para **9.5** (which is not restricted to an order made in a magistrates' court), an order made under the Children Act 1989 in the High Court or a county court must be enforced in the appropriate way in accordance with the procedure in those courts. FPR 7.1 deals with the enforcement of an order for the payment of money, and requires an affidavit to be filed before any process for enforcement is issued (eg a warrant of execution) in which the amount due is verified and in which it is shown how that amount is arrived at. Orders issued out of the Principal Registry of the Family Division in proceedings treated as if pending in a county court, are treated as county court orders. FPR 7.2 to 7.6 make various modifications to the RSC and CCR for the purpose of enforcement of orders made in family proceedings, and reference must be made to the rules in question. Several procedural provisions in relation to committal in family proceedings are contained in FPR 7.2. Subject to RSC Ord 52, r 6 (certain applications for committal to be heard in open court), in the High Court applications for committal are made by summons. A district judge may deal with urgent applications for the discharge of a person committed or the discharge by consent of an injunction granted by a judge (which would presumably include an order such as a prohibited steps order which is in the nature of an injunction). Apart from the specific matters dealt with in these rules, and the modifications made to the judgment summons procedure by FPR 7.4–7.6, enforcement by committal in family proceedings in the High Court or a county court is governed by RSC Ord 45, rr 5, 6 and 7 and CCR Ord 29, respectively.

Fees in Children Act proceedings

9.7 Fees in the High Court and county courts are regulated by the Family Proceedings Fees Order 1991 (SI 1991 No 2114). The order requires a fee to be paid on the making of certain applications. There are exemptions from paying fees for a person who:

- is in receipt of legal advice or assistance under the Legal Aid Act 1988
- is in receipt of income support or family credit under Part II of the Social Security Act 1986
- is a minor, or is a person over 18 who is in receipt of, or is applying for, maintenance from a parent under paragraph 2 of Schedule 1, and is *not* the beneficiary of a trust fund in court of more than £50,000.

Where it appears that the payment of any prescribed fee would involve undue hardship owing to the exceptional circumstances of the particular case, the fee may be remitted. The fees are set at four levels – £50, £30, £20 and £15. The highest level is payable, for example, on an application for a care or supervision order, ESO or CAO; the next level on application for other substantive orders (eg section 8 orders); the third level is paid on application for leave to make an application, or termination, variation or discharge of an order under the Children Act 1989. The fourth level, at £15, is payable on commencing an appeal under section 94 (magistrates' court to High Court), or under paragraph 23(11) of Schedule 2 (local authority contributions), and for other interlocutory applications including an application to a county court to transfer up proceedings from a magistrates court. No fee is payable on an application for an EPO or an RO.

Guardian ad litem panels

9.8 By virtue of the Guardian ad Litem and Reporting Officer (Panels) Regulations 1991 (SI 1991 No 2051), every guardian ad litem who is appointed under FPR 4.10/FPC 10 will be a member of a panel constituted under the regulations. Local authorities are required by regulation 2 to establish such panels, and provision is made in the regulations for a panel manager to be appointed to manage the work of the guardians ad litem on each panel, to ensure that they undergo appropriate professional training and to oversee the standards of reporting and the work of the guardians ad litem generally. The expenses, fees and allowances of panel members are dealt with in regulation 9.

Family proceedings panels

9.9   Panels of justices have been elected to form the family proceedings courts panels which, in effect, replace the domestic court panels which have been dissolved with effect from 14 October 1991. The Family Proceedings Courts (Constitution) Rules 1991 (SI 1991 No 1405) made provision for the election and constitution of the panels, and also for the eligibility of justices for election, and the removal of a justice from the panel by the Lord Chancellor on the ground of unsuitability. A justice appointed to the panel must be 'suitable to serve as a member of the panel', and apart from temperament and aptitude she must be prepared to undertake training to equip her to sit as an expert tribunal in children matters. Every stipendiary magistrate is a member of the panel for his petty sessions area ex officio, but he is expected to sit in a family proceedings court only if he has undertaken the relevant training. In the inner London area and the City of London the constitution of family proceedings courts is governed by the Family Proceedings Courts (Constitution) (Metropolitan Area) Rules 1991 (SI 1991 No 1426). Under those rules the members of the family proceedings court panel for the metropolitan area are not elected; they are nominated by the Lord Chancellor.

Care centres and family hearing centres

9.10   The county courts are categorised for the purpose of family proceedings by the Children (Allocation of Proceedings) Order 1991. Family hearing centres are those courts set out in Schedule 1 to the rules, and care centres are those courts set out in column (ii) of Schedule 2 to the order. Their locations are shown in the maps in Appendix 4. The purpose in creating these centres is to improve the handling of family business. By concentrating family work in the centres a relatively small number of specialist judges, specified under section 9 of the Courts and Legal Services Act 1990, can be effectively deployed to ensure that family cases are heard with a minimum of delay and that continuous hearings can be assured (ie running from day to day when necessary, without lengthy adjournments). Although all the care centres are also family hearing centres where any family proceedings may be heard, public law proceedings may not be transferred to a family hearing centre which is not a care centre. A limited number of circuit and district judges, who have undertaken training, have been specified by the Lord Chancellor to exercise this jurisdiction under section 9 of the Courts and Legal Services Act 1990 in the Family Proceedings (Allocation to Judiciary) Directions 1991, and their sittings are geared to ensure that urgent cases can be heard at the care centres with a minimum of notice.

Family court business committees

9.11 At each of the 51 care centres there is a 'designated family judge', who has been designated by the Lord Chancellor, and who has the primary responsibility for hearing child care cases transferred from the magistrates' courts (or exceptionally begun in the care centre). The designated judge is also the chairman of a local implementation committee for that care centre and its catchment area of magistrates' courts, known as the family court business committee (FCBC). The terms of reference of each FCBC are to:

- make sure that arrangements are working properly at a local level, in particular allocation and transfer arrangements, meeting agreed targets where appropriate
- seek to achieve administrative consistency between the two tiers of courts
- ensure that the guardian ad litem and probation services are aware of the needs of the courts, but avoid making unreasonable demands on those two services and
- liaise with the local court user committees.

The members of the FCBC, in addition to the designated judge as chairman, are the local courts administrator as vice-chairman, a district judge and representatives from the justices' clerks of courts operating family panels, the local authority social services and legal departments, the local guardian ad litem panel and the area legal aid board. The secretariat are provided by the courts administrator's staff, and any matters which it is wished should be put before the FCBC should be addressed to the courts administrator (listed in the telephone directory under Lord Chancellor's department).

Family court services committees

9.12 The family court services committees (FCSC) are part of the committee structure which has been established to ensure the Children Act 1989 works as intended. Each of the 51 care centres also has a FCSC chaired by the designated care judge (see para. 9.11), and serviced by the Courts Administrator. The terms of reference of the FCSCs are:

● to promote discussion and encourage co-operation between the professions, agencies and organisations involved in family proceedings
● to consider and make recommendations for the resolution of problematical issues which arise in the conduct of family proceedings, with particular reference to the practice of:
  (a) the courts
  (b) the legal profession
  (c) the medical profession
  (d) the health authorities
  (e) the social services
  (f) the education authorities
  (g) the police
● to identify any necessary improvements to the service provided to the parties to family proceedings by the courts or other agencies and professions and
● to liaise with the family court business committees.

The core membership of the FCSCs, in addition to the judge chairman, is suggested as including a solicitor in private practice, a solicitor from a local authority legal department, a barrister, a probation officer, a representative of the area health authority, a police officer, a magistrate, a justices' clerk, a district judge, a medical practitioner (possibly a paediatrician or child psychiatrist), a guardian ad litem and a social worker. The courts administrator provides the secretariat. An FCSC might also include a health visitor, a GP, an education welfare officer, an NSPCC representative, a representative of local voluntary groups, a CAB representative and a family law academic. Unlike the FCBCs which are court business-oriented, the FCSCs are oriented towards the issues arising from the conduct of family proceedings. These issues might include, for example, assessment techniques and the handling of refusal to consent to treatment or assessment, local services that divert children from court proceedings, availability of expert witnesses and the operation of the criteria,

FAOs and CAOs. A formal link with the associated FCBC is provided by the common chairmanship and secretariat.

Children Act Advisory Committee

9.13 The overall operation of the Children Act 1989 is monitored by the Children Act Advisory Committee (CAAC) whose members are appointed by the Lord Chancellor, in consultation with the Home Secretary, the Secretary of State for Health and the President of the Family Division. The first chairman is the Honourable Mrs Justice Booth, and the members include another family division judge (the Honourable Mrs Justice Bracewell), a circuit judge, a district judge, a magistrate, a justices' clerk, a director of social services, a guardian ad litem panel manager, the Official Solicitor and representatives of the three government departments. Its terms of reference are:

'To advise the Lord Chancellor, the Home Secretary, the Secretary of State for Health and the President of the Family Division on whether the guiding principles of the Children Act 1989 are being achieved and whether court procedures and the guardian ad litem system are operating satisfactorily.'

Although there are no formal links between the CAAC and the FCSCs and FCBCs, minutes of the FCSCs are copied to the CAAC secretariat, and each circuit administrator for the 6 circuits which administer the court service in England and Wales (but not the magistrates' courts), is required to produce an annual report on the work of the FCSCs on their circuits, highlighting problems and points of interest. These reports are submitted to the CAAC. FCSCs, of course, may draw urgent matters to the attention of the CAAC at any time.

CHAPTER 10

Local authority support for children and families

Local authority duty to safeguard and promote welfare of children

10.1 Upon every local authority in England and Wales, section 17 of the Children Act 1989 lays a duty to safeguard and promote the welfare of children within their area who are 'in need' (see para **10.2**). So far as it is consistent with that general duty, the local authority must promote the upbringing of a child 'in need' by his or her family. In relation to such a child, 'family' includes any person who has parental responsibility for the child, or any other person with whom the child has been living. The local authority must do so by providing a range and level of services appropriate to the needs of those children, and it is empowered to provide any such service to the family, or a member of the child's family, with a view to safeguarding or promoting the child's welfare. It is axiomatic that before seeking to invoke the powers of the court to intervene in the family life of a child under Parts IV or V, the local authority must discharge its duty to support the child in the family. Whenever a court is considering whether to make a care or other order under Part IV it must have regard to the welfare checklist in section 1(3), which includes a requirement to consider how capable each of his parents, or any other relevant person, is of meeting the child's needs. It is relevant for the court to consider whether the parent might meet those needs with assistance from the local authority (the services provided to a family by the local authority may include giving assistance in kind or, in exceptional circumstances, in cash). For example, on an application by a local authority for a care order a court may make a residence order, and whether it makes such an order or not, if it considers the circumstances exceptional, it may make a FAO under section 16, requiring the local authority to make an officer available to advise, assist and befriend any

person named in the order. More usually the court will want
to be satisfied that the local authority has adequately discharged
its duties under Part III of the Act, and under Part I of Schedule
2, and that there is nothing more that the local authority could,
and should, do so that the court can be sure that to make an
order is better than to make no order at all.

Identification of children in need

10.2 Children 'in need' is defined by section 17(10) for the
purposes of Part III and Schedule 2. There are two basic categories:
the disabled child and the child who, unless the local authority
provides services for him or her:

- is unlikely to achieve or maintain a reasonable standard of
  health or development
- is unlikely to have the opportunity of maintaining a reasonable
  standard of health or development
- is likely to suffer significant impairment, or further impairment, to health or development.

'Health' means physical or mental health, and 'development'
means physical, intellectual, emotional, social or behavioural
development. A disabled child is one who is:

- blind, deaf or dumb
- suffers from mental disorder of any kind
- is substantially and permanently handicapped by illness,
  congenital deformity or other prescribed disability.

Every local authority is required, by paragraph 1 of Schedule
2, to take reasonable steps to identify the extent to which there
are children in need and, by paragraph 2, to maintain a register
of disabled children in their area. In respect of a child appear-
ing to be in need the local authority may assess the child's
needs for the purposes of the Children Act 1989 at the same
time as it assesses his or her needs under any other enactment,
including:

- the Chronically Sick and Disabled Persons Act 1970
- the Education Act 1981
- the Disabled Persons (Services, Consultation and Representation) Act 1986

so that a comprehensive assessment may be made.

10.3 *Local authority support for children and families*

Provision of services

10.3 The range and level of services which a local authority is required to provide, mentioned in para **10.1**, is at the discretion of each local authority, since even where the Act makes the provision mandatory it is generally to be provided as they consider appropriate, and the level and scope of the service is a matter of judgment for the local authority. Nevertheless, section 17 (2) confers specific powers and duties as set out in Schedule 2. Section 17 also goes on to require local authorities to facilitate the provision of services by others, in particular voluntary organisations, and they may make arrangements for any person to act on their behalf. The services provided may include assistance in kind, or exceptionally in cash (see para **10.6**). The services to be provided must include:

- day care for pre-school under-five year olds in need (and may include other children) – section 18 (see para **10.4**)
- care or supervised activities for school children in need out of school hours and in the school holidays – section 18
- accommodation for a child in need who requires accommodation because no one has parental responsibility for him, or he is lost or abandoned or the person who has been caring for him cannot do so for the time being or permanently – section 20
- accommodation for any child over sixteen in need whose welfare appears likely to be seriously prejudiced by lack of accommodation – section 20 (see para **10.5**)
- accommodation and maintenance for a child the local authority is looking after – section 23
- advising, assisting and befriending a child looked after by the local authority, or who has been looked after or accommodated institutionally or fostered – section 24
- services for disabled children – Schedule 2, paragraph 6
- services for children living with their families such as advice, activities, home help and travel – paragraph 8
- family centres – paragraph 9.

Every local authority must also publish information about the services which they provide under sections 17, 18, 20 and 24, and where appropriate about the services provided by others, in particular such services provided by voluntary organisations. They must also take reasonable steps to ensure that those likely to need the services learn of them. The local authorities are also required by Schedule 2, paragraph 4(1) to provide services so as to prevent children in need within their area suffering ill-treatment or neglect, and by paragraph 7 to reduce the need to bring care and supervision, or other family proceedings which might lead to care, wardship or criminal proceedings. The family centres which local authorities must provide are centres where a child, his parents, any other person with parental responsibility for him or who is looking after him, may attend for occupational, social, cultural or recreational activities, or for advice, guidance or counselling residentially or non-residentially.

Day care

10.4 Day care, in the context of section 18, is any form of care or supervised activity made available to children during the day. It may take, therefore, many forms such as playgroups, child-minding, day fostering, nursery schools, holiday play schemes or supervised playgrounds. The provision of day care for pre-school children in need (as defined in section 17(10): see para **10.2**) must be undertaken by every local authority, as appropriate, by virtue of section 18 of the Children Act 1989. Local authorities are also required to provide school children in need with such care and supervised activities (that is, activities supervised by a responsible person) as is appropriate, out of school hours and in holiday periods. In addition they have a discretion to provide day care for pre-school children who are not in need, and they may extend care and supervised activities to school children who are not in need. They also have a discretion to provide facilities for people who are caring for children in day care, or who accompany a child at any time while the child is in day care. Those facilities may include training, advice, guidance and counselling. The steps which local authorities are required to take by paragraph 7 of Schedule 2 to reduce the need to bring care, criminal and other proceedings with respect to children in their area, and to encourage children not to commit criminal offences, might well include the provision of day care and supervised activities. Such provision would also fall within the categories of services which the local authority must make available to comply with paragraph 8 of Schedule 2, with respect to children in need while living with their families. It would clearly help them to discharge their duties under paragraph 4 of the Schedule, to prevent children within their area from suffering ill-treatment or neglect, and under paragraph 6, to minimise the effect of the disabilities of disabled children and to give disabled children the opportunity to lead lives which are as normal as possible.

Provision of accommodation

10.5 A most important element in the range of local authority duties in respect of children in need is the provision of accommodation, which is required in a variety of circumstances and may be discharged in a number of ways. A child who is provided with accommodation by a local authority is by virtue of section 22(1)(b) 'looked after' by the local authority (see para **10.6**). Accommodation must be provided for a child in two general sets of circumstances. The first relates to the child whose well-being is at risk because of lack of accommodation or care for him. The second relates to the child who has been removed, or is being kept away, from home. Each local authority, by virtue of section 20(1) and (3), must accommodate a child in need who appears to require accommodation because:

- there is no one with parental responsibility for him
- he has been lost or abandoned
- the person caring for him is prevented for some reason from providing him with suitable accommodation or care
- even though he is over the age of 16, they consider that his welfare is likely to be seriously prejudiced if they do not.

In accordance with section 21(1) and (2) they must also provide:

- accommodation for any child removed or kept away from home under Part V
- accommodation for any child in police protection (section 46(3)(f) when requested by the police to accommodate the child (and for other children detained by the police, or on remand or subject to a supervision order in criminal proceedings with a condition of residence).

A local authority may provide accommodation for a child who is not 'in need' if they consider that this would safeguard or promote his welfare, regardless of whether a person who has parental responsibility for the child can accommodate him. These provisions enable a local authority to look after not only the child who has no one to care for him, but also the child who needs temporary care, for example while a single parent is in hospital, or a respite for a parent who has a disabled child requiring 24-hour care. The local authority must take account of the child's wishes, so far as they can ascertain them, which may be problematical of course with a very small or severely handicapped child, and give those wishes due consideration before providing accommodation under section 20, so far as is reasonably practicable and consistent with the child's welfare. They may not, however, provide accommodation for a child under section 20 if any person who has parental responsibility for him objects, if that person is willing and able to provide, or to make arrangements to provide, accommodation for him. Furthermore, any person with parental responsibility for a child may remove him at any time from accommodation provided by the local authority. However, the right of a person with parental responsibility for a child to object, or to remove the child, is overridden if a person in whose favour a residence order for the child has been made, or who has care of the child in wardship, has agreed to the child being looked after by the local authority. If more than one person is named in a residence or wardship order, they must all agree if the rights of a person with parental responsibility for the child are to be overridden. A child aged 16 or over may give his agreement to the provision of accommodation by the local authority, in which case the rights of a person with parental responsibility for him to object or to remove him are of no effect. A local authority may provide accommodation in a community home which takes children over the age of 16 for any person aged between 16 and 21, if they consider that this would safeguard or promote his welfare. This enables a local authority to ease the transition of a child from care to independent living, and for example to maintain the child in a safe environment while he becomes established in regular, full-time work and can begin to fend for himself. By virtue of paragraph 5 of Schedule 2, a person whose presence in the household which a child is living in, is not conducive to the child's well-being, because the child is suffering, or is likely to suffer, ill-treatment at his hands, and who can be persuaded to leave, may be given assistance by the local authority to obtain alternative accommodation, and the assistance may be given in cash. This may help the local authority to avoid seeking an EPO or a care order to remove the child from his home by in effect removing the possible cause of harm. The form which local authority provided accommodation may take for children being looked after by the local authority is:

- a foster parent
- a community home
- a voluntary home

- a registered children's home
- a special home provided by the Secretary of State (there are currently two of these homes known as youth treatment centres)
- other arrangements which the local authority consider appropriate and which are in accordance with regulations made by the Secretary of State (eg semi-independent living hostels or arrangements with suitable landlords for rented accommodation for older children).

A local authority foster parent may be a family, a relative of the child or any other suitable person, on terms agreed with the authority. The accommodation provided must be near the child's home, and if more than one child from a family is being accommodated they must be kept together, so far as is reasonably practicable and consistent with the welfare of each child (but subject to the other provisions of Part III). Accommodation for a disabled child must not be unsuitable for his particular needs – so far as this is practicable.

Children looked after by a local authority

10.6 A child is 'looked after' by a local authority if the local authority is providing him with accommodation in the exercise of any functions of their social services committee under the Local Authority Social Services Act 1970, and in particular functions under the Children Act 1989 (section 22(1)(b)). This has replaced the former concept of 'voluntary care'. A child placed in the care of a local authority by an order under section 31 is also 'looked after' for the purposes of the Children Act 1989 (section 22(1)(a)). Any local authority looking after a child must make arrangements for him to live with a person who is a local authority foster parent, or a relative, friend or other person connected with him, unless this is not reasonably practicable or consistent with his welfare, and subject to the Arrangements for Placement of Children (General) Regulations 1991 (SI 1991 No 890) and the Foster Placement (Children) Regulations 1991 (SI 1991 No 910). Where the child is in care, only if the placement is made in accordance with the Placement of Chidren with Parents Etc Regulations 1991 (SI 1991 No 893) may he be placed with one of the following:

- a parent
- a person with parental responsibility for him
- a person in whose favour there was a residence order immediately before the care order was made.

A child who is being looked after by a local authority may be placed in secure accommodation if he has a history of absconding and is likely to abscond from other accommodation, and if he does so is likely to suffer harm. Secure accommodation may also be used for a child who is likely to injure himself or others if he is kept in any other kind of accommodation. The Children Act 1989 (Secure Accommodation) Regulations 1991 (SI 1991 No 1505) restrict the use of secure accommodation to an aggregate of 72 hours within any 28 day period, without a court order under section 25 of the Children Act 1989. Unless he is in care, a child who has been placed in secure accommodationmay be removed by a person with parental responsibility for him, even when he is there by virtue of a court order under section 25(4). It is the duty of the local authority looking after a child to safeguard and promote his welfare, and to make use of services available for children who are being cared for by their own parents as seems reasonable to the authority in his case. The local authority may not make a decision about a child they are looking after, or proposing to look after, without consulting (so far as reasonably practicable) the child, his parents, any other person with parental responsibility for him, and any other person whose wishes and feelings the local authority consider to be relevant (section 23(4)). Having consulted, they must take into account the wishes and feelings of the child, having regard to his age and understanding, and the other persons they have consulted, and the child's religion, race, cultural and linguistic background before making any decision. These requirements to consult apply to a child in care as well as a child otherwise being looked after. A local authority may exercise its powers with respect to a child they are looking after in a manner consistent with their duties to safeguard and promote the welfare of the child, to make use of services for him and to consult, for the purpose of protecting members of the public from serious injury if it appears to them to be necessary to do so. The Secretary of State may also direct a local authority to act in that manner if he considers it necessary in order to protect members of the public from serious injury. The case of every child being looked after must be reviewed by the local authority within 4 weeks of the date when they first began to look after him, again 3 months after that date and subsequently every 6 months, in compliance with the Review of Children Cases Regulations 1991 (SI 1991 No 985). The prime objective of the reviews is to ensure that the child's upbringing is not suffering unreasonably because he is being looked after by the local authority, and that a satisfactory plan exists for his future and that it is being implemented effectively. Each local authority must establish a procedure for representations, including complaints, to be made to it about children who are being looked after by them, or who are not being looked after by them but are in need. When a child who is being looked after dies, the local authority must notify the Secretary of State and, so far as is practicable, the parents of the child and any other person who had parental responsibility for him. They may arrange for the burial or cremation of the child's body with the consent (where it is reasonably practicable to obtain it) of every person who had parental responsibility for the child. If the circumstances warrant it, and a parent or other person connected with the child cannot afford to attend the funeral without undue financial hardship, they may pay the person travelling and other expenses to attend the funeral.

Advice and assistance for children

10.7 It is the duty of a local authority which is looking after a child to advise, assist and befriend him with a view to promoting his welfare when he ceases to be looked after by them (section 24(1)). The local authority may assist a child by giving him benefits in kind or, in exceptional circumstances, in cash and the assistance may be unconditional or subject to conditions about repayment of the assistance or of its value, in whole or in part. Before giving the assistance, or imposing any conditions, the local authority must have regard to the means of the child and of each of his parents. The assistance may include, in particular, under Part II of Schedule 2:

- expenses for visits to or by a child - paragraph 16
- the appointment of a visitor if a child is out of touch with family and friends or has not been visited - paragraph 17
- guaranteeing an apprenticeship deed or articles of clerkship - paragraph 18
- arranging for a child to live outside England and Wales - paragraph 19

The expenses of a visit may only be met where it appears that it could not otherwise take place without undue financial hardship and the circumstances warrant the making of the visit. The local authority may make payments for the travelling, subsistence and other expenses incurred in making the visit, to those who visit the child, or to the child or a person on his behalf when she is making the visit. These visits may be to, or from:

- a parent of the child
- any other person with parental responsibility for the child
- any relative, friend or other person connected with him.

If communication between a child and his parents or any other person who has parental responsibility for his has been infrequent, or he has not been visited by or lived with any of them for 12 months, the local authority must appoint an independent person as visitor if this would be in the child's best interests. The visitor must visit, assist and befriend the child, and the local authority must pay him his reasonable expenses for doing so. Provided that the child has sufficient understanding to make an informed decision, he may object to the appointment of a visitor (in which case it may not be made) or the continuation of an appointment (in which case it must be terminated). The local authority may also arrange, or assist in arranging, for a child to live outside England and Wales. If the child is in care, the local authority must obtain a court order (see para **3.19**); otherwise the approval of every person who has parental responsibility for the child must be obtained. There seems to be an odd omission in the relevant provision (sub-paragraph (2) of paragraph 19), because the Act is silent on the question of the consent of the child to such an arrangement, whereas before a court can approve arrangements for a child in care to live outside England and Wales it must be satisfied that the child consents. The local authority, of course, has a duty to ascertain the wishes and feelings of the child by virtue of section 22(4)(a), and must have regard to them before coming to a decision (section 22(5)(a)); but it does not need the *consent* of the child. It is not only children who are being looked after that a local authority has a duty to advise and befriend; they owe such a duty to 'a person qualifying for advice and assistance', that is a person who is under 21 but who was, while still a child but over the age of 16, but no longer is:

- looked after by the local authority
- accommodated by or on behalf of a voluntary organisation
- accommodated in a registered children's home
- accommodated for a consecutive period of at least three months by a health authority, local education authority or in any residential care home, nursing home or mental nursing home
- privately fostered.

If 'a person qualifying for advice and assistance' within their area asks a local authority for help, and it appears that he is in need of advice or being befriended they must advise and befriend him. If he was not being looked after by a local authority and the person by whom he was being looked after does not have the necessary facilities to do so, they may advise and befriend him (but do not have to do so). They may also give 'a person qualifying for advice and assistance' assistance, but this is at the discretion of the local authority, and it may be in kind or, in exceptional circumstances, in cash. The assistance may be unconditional or subject to conditions about repayment of the assistance or of its value, in whole or in part. Before giving the assistance, or imposing any conditions, the local authority must have regard to the means of the child and of each of his parents. Mention has already been made in para **10.1** of the duty of each local authority to provide advice and assistance to children in need, and their families. Schedule 2 specifically gives a local authority power to assist a child in need by providing him and his family with:

- advice, guidance, counselling
- occupational, social, cultural or recreational activities
- home help
- facilities for, or assistance with, travelling to and from home to take advantage of services
- assistance to have a holiday.

Some of these activities may be undertaken, for example, at a family centre (see para **10.3**).

Promotion and maintenance of child/family contact

10.8 Section 17(1)(b) of the Children Act 1989 requires local authorities to promote the upbringing of children in need by their families, so far as is consistent with their duty to safeguard and promote the welfare of such children. Where they accommodate children, so far as is reasonably practicable and consistent with the children's welfare, they must ensure that the accommodation is near their homes, and that if they are accommodating children from the same family that they are kept together. The policy implemented by the Act, and which each local authority must follow, is to ensure that so far as possible a child remains with his family, and where this is not possible that he is kept as close to his family as is practicable in order to foster and maintain his links with it. Apart from the advice and assistance which a local authority must provide for children in need living with their families, under paragraph 8 of Schedule 2 (see para **10.7**), they must take such steps as are reasonably practicable, where a child in need is living apart from his family, to enable him to live with his family or to promote contact between him and his family. This must be done if in the opinion of the local authority it is necessary to do so in order to safeguard or promote his welfare. If a child is being looked after by a local authority, unless it is not reasonably practicable or consistent with the child's welfare, they must endeavour to promote contact between the child and:

- his parents
- any other person who has parental responsibility for him
- any relative, friend or person connected with him.

They must also keep parents and persons with parental responsibility for the child informed of where the child is being accommodated, and in turn each of those persons must keep the local authority informed of their address. If a child is transferred from one local authority to another, then each local authority involved in the transfer must inform those persons, and their duty is not discharged until at least one of them has been informed. The local authority need not inform anybody of the whereabouts of a child in their care if they have reasonable cause to believe that informing a person would prejudice the child's welfare.

Contributions to the cost of services and maintenance of a child

10.9 Services, other then advice, guidance or counselling, provided by a local authority under sections 17 and 18 of the Children Act 1989 may be charged at a price which the local authority considers reasonable, but a person of insufficient means to pay the full charge may not be asked to pay more than he can reasonably be expected to pay. The person who can be asked to pay for such services are the parents of a child under 16, a child over 16 and any member of the child's family for whom a service has been provided (section 29(1), (2) and (4)). The recovery of contributions to the maintenance of a child looked after by a local authority is dealt with in Part III of Schedule 2. Paragraph 21 requires a local authority who are looking after a child (except one in police protection, being detained or on remand etc, under an interim care order or where the child has been sentenced for serious crime) to consider whether they should seek contributions to his maintenance from any person liable to contribute. Those persons (the contributors) are each of the parents of a child under 16, and the child if he is 16 or more, but they cannot be required to contribute while the child is allowed by the local authority to live with a parent. The local authority will in the first place try to arrive at an agreed contribution with the contributor and serve a contribution notice on the contributor, but if the contributor will not agree to the sum specified in the contribution notice, or withdraws his agreement, the local authority must apply to a magistrates' court for a contribution order (Schedule 2, paragraph 23 and article 3(1)(p) of the Children (Allocation of Proceedings) Order 1991). A contribution order may not exceed the weekly sum specified in the contribution notice, nor may it take effect from before the date of that notice, and it will be discharged by an agreement reached with the contributor following any later contribution notice which the local authority serve on him. A contribution order may be varied or revoked on the application of the contributor or the local authority, and although it is not specified in the rules it would appear appropriate and necessary for a contributor seeking a variation or discharge to model his application on pages 1 and 2 of Form CHA15, and to provide a statement of means in Form CHA14. A contribution order may be enforced as a magistrates' court maintenance order under section 150 of the Magistrates' Courts Act 1980. In enforcement proceedings:

- a document which purports to be a copy of an order made by a court under paragraph 23, and which is certified as a true copy by the clerk of the court, is evidence of the order
- a certificate which purports to be signed by the clerk or some other duly authorised officer of the local authority which obtained the contribution order and which states that any sum due to the authority under the order is overdue and unpaid, is evidence of that fact.

APPENDIX 1

The Family Proceedings Courts (Children Act 1989) Rules 1991
(SI 1991 No 1395)

PART I

Introductory

PART II

General

PART III

Miscellaneous

SCHEDULES

PART I

INTRODUCTORY

Citation, commencement and interpretation

1.—(1) These Rules may be cited as the Family Proceedings Courts (Children Act 1989) Rules 1991 and shall come into force on 14th October 1991.

(2) Unless a contrary intention appears-
a section or schedule referred to means the section or schedule in the Act of 1989,
   'application' means an application made under or by virtue of the Act of 1989 or under these Rules, and 'applicant' shall be construed accordingly,
   'business day' means any day other than-
   (a) a Saturday, Sunday, Christmas Day or Good Friday; or
   (b) a bank holiday, that is to say, a day which is, or is to be observed as, a bank holiday, or a holiday, under the Banking and Financial Dealings Act 1971(a), in England and Wales,
   'child'-

(a) 1971 c 80.

    (a)   means, in relation to any relevant proceedings, subject to sub-paragraph (b), a person under the age of 18 with respect to whom the proceedings are brought, and

    (b)   where paragraph 16(1) of Schedule 1 applies, also includes a person who has reached the age of 18;

'contribution order' has the meaning, assigned to it by paragraph 23(2) of Schedule 2,

'court' means a family proceedings court constituted in accordance with sections 86 and 67 of the Magistrates' Courts Act 1980 or, in respect of those proceedings prescribed in rule 2(5), a single justice who is a member of a family panel,

'directions appointment' means a hearing for directions under rule 14(2),

'emergency protection order' means an order under section 44,

'file' means deposit with the justices' clerk,

'form' means a form in Schedule 1 to these Rules with such variation as the circumstances of the particular case may require,

'guardian ad litem' means a guardian at litem appointed under section 41, of the child with respect to whom the proceedings are brought,

'justices' clerk' has the meaning assigned to it by section 70 of the Justices of the Peace Act 1979 and includes any person who performs a justices' clerk's functions by virtue of rule 32,

'leave' includes approval,

'note' includes a record made by mechanical means,

'parental responsibility' has the meaning assigned to it by section 3.

'parties' in relation to any relevant proceedings means the respondents specified for those proceedings in the third column of Schedule 2 to these Rules, and the applicant,

'recovery order' means an order under section 50,

'relevant proceedings' has the meaning assigned to it by section 93(3),

'section 8 order' has the meaning assigned to it by section 8(2),

'specified proceedings' has the meaning assigned to it by section 41(6) and rule 2(2),

'the 1981 rules' means the Magistrates' Courts Rules 1981(a),

'the Act of 1989' means the Children Act 1989(b),

'welfare officer' means a person who has been asked to prepare a welfare report under section 7.

Matters prescribed for the purposes of the Act of 1989

2.—(1) The parties to proceedings in which directions are given under section 38(6), and any person named in such a direction, form the

---

(a)   SI 1981/552, amended by 1982/245, 1983/523, 1984/1552, 1985/1695 and 1944, 1986/1332, 1988/2132, 1989/300 and 384; 1990/336, 1190 and 2260.

(b)   1989 c 41.

prescribed class for the purposes of section 38(8)(b) (application to vary directions made with interim care or interim supervision order).

(2) The following proceedings are specified for the purposes of section 41 in accordance with subsection (6)(i) thereof-
  (a) proceedings under section 25;
  (b) applications under section 33(7);
  (c) proceedings under paragraph 19(1) of Schedule 2;
  (d) applications under paragraph 6(3) of Schedule 3.

(3) The applicant for an order that has been made under section 43(1) and the persons referred to in section 43(11) may, in any circumstances, apply under section 43(12) for a child assessment order to be varied or discharged.

(4) The following persons form the prescribed class for the purposes of section 44(9)(b) (application to vary directions)-
  (a) the parties to the application for the order in respect of which it is sought to vary the directions;
  (b) the guardian ad litem;
  (a) the local authority in whose area the child concerned is ordinarily resident;
  (d) any person who is named in the directions.

(5) The following proceedings are prescribed for the purposes of section 93(2)(i) as being proceedings with respect to which a single justice may discharge the functions of a family proceedings court, that is to say, proceedings-
  (a) where an ex parte application is made under sections 10, 44(1), 48(9), 50(1), 75(1) or 102(1),
  (b) subject to rule 28, under sections 11(3) or 38(1),
  (c) under sections 4(3)(b), 7, 14, 34(3)(b), 37, 41, 44(9)(b) and (11)(b)(iii), 48(4), 91(15) or (17), or paragraph 11(4) of Schedule 14,
  (d) in accordance with any Order made by the Lord Chancellor under Part 1 of Schedule 11, and
  (e) in accordance with rules 3 to 8, 10 to 19, 21, 22, or 27.

PART II
GENERAL
Application for leave to commence proceedings

3.—(1) Where the leave of the court is required to bring any relevant proceedings, the person seeking leave shall file-
  (a) a written request for leave setting out the reasons for the application; and
  (b) a draft of the application for the making of which leave is sought in the appropriate form in Schedule 1 to these Rules or, where

there is no such form, in writing, together with sufficient copies for one to be served on each respondent.

(2) On considering a request for leave filed under paragraph (1), the court shall-
  (a) grant the request, whereupon the justices' clerk shall inform the person making the request of the decision, or
  (b) direct that a date be fixed for a hearing of the request, whereupon the justices' clerk shall fix such a date and give such notice as the court directs to the person making the request and to such other persons as the court requires to be notified, of the date so fixed.

(3) Where leave is granted to bring any relevant proceedings, the application shall proceed in accordance with rule 4; but paragraph (1)(a) of that rule shall not apply.

Application

4.—(1) Subject to paragaph (4), an applicant shall-
  (a) file the application in respect of each child in the appropriate form in Schedule 1 to these Rules or where there is no such form, in writing, together with sufficient copies for one to be served on each respondent, and
  (b) serve a copy of the application, endorsed in accordance with paragraph (2)(b), on each respondent such minimum number of days prior to the date fixed under paragraph (2)(a) as is specified in relation to that application in column (ii) of Schedule 2 to these Rules.

(2) On receipt of the documents filed under paragraph (1)(a), the justices' clerk shall-
  (a) fix the date, time and place for a hearing or a directions appointment, allowing sufficient time for the applicant to comply with paragraph (1)(b),
  (b) endorse the date, time and place so fixed upon the copies of the application filed by the applicant, and
  (c) return the copies to the applicant forthwith.

(3) The applicant shall, at the same time as complying with paragraph (1)(b), give written notice of the proceedings, and of the date, time and place of the hearing or appointment fixed under paragraph (2)(a) to the persons set out in relation to the relevant class of proceedings in column (iv) of Schedule 2 to these Rules.

(4) An application for-
  (a) a prohibited steps order, or a specific issue order, under section 8,
  (b) an emergency protection order,
  (c) a warrant under section 48(9),
  (d) a recovery order, or
  (e) a warrant under section 102(1),

Appendix 1

may, with leave of the justices' clerk, be made ex parte in which case
the applicant shall-

> (i) file with the justices' clerk or the court the application
> in respect of each child in the appropriate form in Schedule
> 1 to these Rules at the time when the application is made
> or as directed by the justices' clerk, and
>
> (ii) in the case of an application for a prohibited steps order,
> or a specific issue order, under section 8 or an emergency
> protection order, and also in the case of an application
> for an order under section 75(1) where the application is
> ex parte, serve a copy of the application on each respondent
> within 48 hours after the making of the order.

(5) Where the court refuses to make an order on an ex parte application
it may direct that the application be made inter partes.

(6) In the case of proceedings under Schedule 1, the application under
paragraph (1) shall be accompanied by a statement setting out the
financial details which the applicant believes to be relevant to the
application and containing a declaration that it is true to the maker's
best knowledge and belief, together with sufficient copies for one to
be served on each respondent.

Withdrawal of application

5.—(1) An aplication may be withdrawn only with leave of the court.

(2) Subject to paragraph (3), a person seeking leave to withdraw an
application shall file and serve on the parties a written request for leave
setting out the reasons for the request.

(3) The request under paragraph (2) may be made orally to the court
if the parties and, if appointed, the guardian ad litem or the welfare
officer are present.

(4) Upon receipt of a written request under paragraph (2), the court
shall-

> (a) if-
> > (i) the parties consent in writing.
> > (ii) any guardian ad litem has had an opportunity to make
> > representations, and
> > (iii) the court thinks fit,

grant the request; in which case the justices' clerk shall notify the parties,
the guardian ad litem and the welfare officer of the granting of the
request; or

> (b) the justices' clerk shall fix a date for the hearing of the request
> and give at least 7 days' notice to the parties, the guardian ad
> litem and the welfare officer of the date fixed.

Transfer of proceedings

6.—(1) Where, in any relevant proceedings, the justices' clerk or the
court receives a request in writing from a party that the proceedings

be transferred to another family proceedings court or to a county court, the justices' clerk or court shall issue a certificate in the appropriate form in Schedule 1 to these Rules, granting or refusing the request in accordance with any Order made by the Lord Chancellor under Part I of Schedule 11(**a**).

(2) Where a request is granted under paragraph (1), the justices' clerk shall send a copy of the certificate-
- (a) to the parties,
- (b) to any guardian ad litem, and
- (c) to the family proceedings court or to the county court to which the proceedings are to be transferred.

(3) Any consent given or refused by a justices' clerk in accordance with any Order made by the Lord Chancellor under Part I of Schedule 11 shall be recorded in writing by the justices' clerk at the time it is given or refused or as soon as practicable thereafter.

(4) Where a request to transfer proceedings to a county court is refused under paragraph (1), the person who made the request may apply in accordance with rule 4.6 of the Family Proceedings Rules 1991(**b**) for an order under any Order made by the Lord Chancellor under Part I of Schedule 11.

Parties

7.—(1) The respondents to relevant proceedings shall be those persons set out in the relevant entry in column (iii) of Schedule 2 to these Rules.

(2) In any relevant proceedings a person may file a request in writing that he or another person-
- (a) be joined as a party, or
- (b) cease to be a party.

(3) On considering a request under paragraph (2) the court shall, subject to paragraph (4)-
- (a) grant it without a hearing or representations, save that this shall be done only in the case of a request under paragraph (2)(a), whereupon the justices' clerk shall inform the parties and the person making the request of that decision, or
- (b) order that a date be fixed for the consideration of the request, whereupon the justices' clerk shall give notice of the date so fixed together with a copy of the request-
  - (i) in the case of a request under paragraph (2)(a), to the applicant, and
  - (ii) in the case of a request under paragraph (2)(b), to the parties, or

(**a**) The Children (Allocation of Proceedings) Order 1991 (SI 1991 No 1677).
(**b**) SI 1991/1247.

(c) invite the parties or any of them to make written representations, within a specified period, as to whether the request should be granted; and upon the expiry of the period the court shall act in accordance with sub-paragraph (a) or (b).

(4) Where a person with parental responsibility requests that he be joined under paragraph (2)(a), the court shall grant his request.

(5) In any relevant proceedings the court may direct–
   (a) that a person who would not otherwise be a respondent under these Rules be joined as a party to the proceedings, or
   (b) that a party to the proceedings cease to be a party.

Service

8.—(1) Where service of a document is required by these Rules (and not by a provision to which section 105(8) (service of notice or other document under the Act) applies) it may be effected–
   (a) if the person to be served is not known by the person serving to be acting by solicitor–
      (i) by delivering it to him personally, or
      (ii) by delivering it at, or by sending it by first-class post to, his residence or his last known residence, or
   (b) if the person to be served is known by the person serving to be acting by solicitor–
      (i) by delivering the document at, or sending it by first-class post to, the solicitor's address for service,
      (ii) where the solicitor's address for service includes a numbered box at a document exchange, by leaving the document at that document exchange or at a document exchange which transmits documents on every business day to that document exchange, or
      (iii) by sending a legible copy of the document by facsimile transmission to the solicitor's office.

(2) In this rule, 'first-class post' means first-class post which has been pre-paid or in respect of which pre-payment is not required.

(3) Where a child who is a party to any relevant proceedings is required by these Rules to serve a document, service shall be effected by–
   (a) the solicitor acting for the child,
   (b) where there is no such solicitor, the guardian ad litem, or
   (c) where there is neither such a solicitor nor a guardian ad litem, the justices' clerk.

(4) Service of any document on a child shall, subject to any direction of the justices' clerk or the court, be effected by service on–
   (a) the solicitor acting for the child,
   (b) where there is no such solicitor, the guardian ad litem, or
   (c) where there is neither such a solicitor nor a guardian ad litem, with leave of the justices' clerk or the court, the child.

(5) Where the justices' clerk or the court refuses leave under paragraph (4)(c), a direction shall be given under paragraph (8).

(6) A document shall, unless the contrary is proved, be deemed to have been served–
- (a) in the case of service by first-class post, on the second business day after posting, and
- (b) in the case of service in accordance with paragraph (1)(b)(ii), on the second business day after the day on which it is left at the document exchange.

(7) At or before the first directions appointment in, or hearing of; relevant proceedings, whichever occurs first, the applicant shall file a statement that service of–
- (a) a copy of the application has been effected on each respondent, and
- (b) notice of the proceedings has been effected under rule 4(3);

and the statement shall indicate
- (i) the manner, date, time and place of service, or
- (ii) where service was effected by pose, the date, time and place of posting.

(8) In any relevant proceedings, the justices' clerk or the court may direct that a requirement of these Rules to serve a document shall not apply or shall be effected in such manner as the justices' clerk or court directs.

Answer to application

9.—(1) Within 14 days of service of an application for a section 8 order, each respondent shall file and serve on the parties an answer to the application in the appropriate form in Schedule 1 to these Rules.

(2) Within 14 days of service of an application under Schedule 1, each respondent shall file and serve on the parties an answer to the application in the appropriate form in Schedule 1 to these Rules.

Appointment of guardian ad litem

10.—(1) As soon as practicable after the commencement of specified proceedings or the transfer of such proceedings to the court, the justices' clerk or the court shall appoint a guardian ad litem unless–
- (a) such an appointment has already been made by the court which made the transfer and is subsisting, or
- (b) the justices' clerk or the court considers that such an appointment is not necessary to safeguard the interests of the child.

(2) At any stage in specified proceedings a party may apply, without notice to the other parties unless the justices' clerk or the court otherwise directs, for the appointment of a guardian ad litem.

(3) The justices' clerk or the court shall grant an application under paragraph (2) unless it is considered that such an appointment is not

necessary to safeguard the interests of the child, in which case reasons shall be given; and a note of such reasons shall be taken by the justices' clerk.

(4) At any stage in specified proceedings the justices' clerk or the court may appoint a guardian ad litem even though no application is made for such an appointment.

(5) The justices' clerk shall, as soon as practicable, notify the parties and any welfare officer of an appointment under this rule or, as the case may, be of a decision not to make such an appointment.

(6) Upon the appointment of a guardian ad litem the justices' clerk shall, as soon as practicable, notify him of the appointment and serve on him copies of the application and of documents filed under rule 17(1).

(7) A guardian ad litem appointed from a panel established by regulations made under section 41(7) shall not-
  (a) be a member, officer or servant of a local authority which, or an authorised person (within the meaning of section 31(9)) who, is a party to the proceedings unless he is employed by such an authority solely as a member of a panel of guardians ad litem and reporting officers;
  (b) be, or have been, a member, officer or servant of a local authority or voluntary organisation (within the meaning of section 105(1)) who has been directly concerned in that capacity in arrangements relating to the care, accommodation or welfare of the child during the five years prior to the commencement of the proceedings;
  (c) be a serving probation officer (except that a probation officer who has not in that capacity been previously concerned with the child or his family and who is employed part-time may, when not engaged in his duties as a probation officer, act as a guardian ad litem).

(8) When appointing a guardian ad litem, the justices' clerk or the court shall consider the appointment of anyone who has previously acted as guardian ad litem of the same child.

(9) The appiontment of a guardian ad litem under this rule shall continue for such time as is specified in the appointment or until terminated by the court.

(10) When terminating an appointment in accordance with paragraph (9), the court shall give reasons in writing for so doing, a note of which shall be taken by the justices' clerk.

(11) Where the justices' clerk or the court appoints a guardian ad litem in accordance with this rule or refuses to make such an appointment, the justices' clerk shall record the appointment or refusal in the appropriate form in Schedule 1 to these Rules.

Powers and duties of guardian ad litem

11.—(1) In carrying out his duty under section 41(2), the guardian ad litem shall have regard to the principle set out in section 1(2) and the matters set out in section 1(3)(a) to (f) as if for the word 'court' in that section there were substituted the words 'guardian ad litem'.

(2) The guardian ad litem shall–
- (a) appoint a solicitor to represent the child, unless such a solicitor has already been appointed, and
- (b) give such advice to the child as is appropriate having regard to his understanding and, subject to rule 12(1)(a), instruct the solicitor representing the child on all matters relevant to the interests of the child, including possibilities for appeal, arising in the course of the proceedings.

(3) Where it appears to the guardian ad litem that the child–
- (a) is instructing his solicitor direct, or
- (b) intends to, and is capable of, conducting the proceedings on his own behalf, he shall so inform the court through the justices' clerk and thereafter–
    - (i) shall perform all of his duties set out in this rule, other than duties under paragraph (2)(a) and such other duties as the justices' clerk or the court may direct,
    - (ii) shall take such part in the proceedings as the justices' clerk or the court may direct, and
    - (iii) may, with leave of the justices' clerk or the court, have legal representation in his conduct of those duties.

(4) The guardian ad litem shall, unless excused by the justices' clerk or the court attend all directions appointments in, and hearings of, the proceedings and shall advise the justices' clerk or the court on the following matters–
- (a) whether the child is of sufficient understanding for any purpose including the child's refusal to submit to a medical or psychiatric examination or other assessment that the court has power to require, direct or order;
- (b) the wishes of the child in respect of any matter relevant to the proceedings, including his attendance at court;
- (c) the appropriate forum for the proceedings;
- (d) the appropriate timing of the proceedings or any part of them;
- (e) the options available to it in respect of the child and the suitability of each such option including what order should be made in determining the application;
- (f) any other matter concerning which the justices' clerk or the court seeks his advice or concerning which he considers that the justices' clerk or the court should be informed.

(5) The advice given under paragraph (4) may, subject to any order

of the court, be given orally or in writing, and if the advice be given orally, a note of it shall be taken by the justices' clerk or the court.

(6) The guardian ad litem shall, where practicable, notify any person whose joinder as a party to those proceedings would be likely, in the guardian ad litem's opinion, to safeguard the interests of the child of that person's right to apply to be joined under rule 7(2) and shall inform the justices' clerk or the court-

    (a) of any such notification given,

    (b) of anyone whom he attempted to notify under this paragraph but was unable to contact, and

    (c) of anyone whom he believes may wish to be joined to the proceedings.

(7) The guardian ad litem shall, unless the justices' clerk or the court otherwise directs, not less than 7 days before the date fixed for the final hearing of the proceedings, file a written report advising on the interests of the child and the justices' clerk shall, as soon as practicable, serve a copy of the report on the parties.

(8) The guardian ad litem shall serve and accept service of documents on behalf of the child in accordance with rule 8(3)(b) and (4)(b) and, where the child has not himself been served, and has sufficient understanding, advise the child of the contents of any documents so served.

(9) The guardian ad litem shall make such investigations as may be necessary for him to carry out his duties and shall, in particular-

    (a) contact or seek to interview such persons as he thinks appropriate or as the court directs,

    (b) if he inspects records of the kinds referred to in section 42, bring to the attention of the court, through the justices' clerk, and such other persons as the justices' clerk or the court may direct, all such records and documents which may, in his opinion, assist in the proper determination of the proceedings, and

    (c) obtain such professional assistance as is available to him which he thinks appropriate or which the justices' clerk or the court directs him to obtain.

(10) In addition to his duties under other paragraphs of this rule, the guardian ad litem shall provide to the justices' clerk and the court such other assistance as may be required.

(11) A party may question the guardian ad litem about oral or written advice tendered by him to the justices' clerk or the court under this rule.

Solicitor for child

12.—(1) A solicitor appointed under section 41(3) or in accordance with rule 11(2)(a) shall represent the child-

(a) in accordance with instructions received from the guardian ad litem (unless the solicitor considers, having taken into account the views of the guardian ad litem and any direction of the court under rule 11(3), that the child wishes to give instructions which conflict with those of the guardian ad litem and that he is able, having regard to his understanding, to give such instructions on his own behalf in which case he shall conduct the proceedings in accordance with instructions received from the child), or

(b) where no guardian ad litem has been appointed for the child and the condition in section 41(4)(b) is satisfied, in accordance with instructions received from the child, or

(c) in default of instructions under (a) or (b), in furtherance of the best interests of the child.

(2) A solicitor appointed under section 41(3) or in accordance with rule 11(2)(a) shall serve and accept service of documents on behalf of the child in accordance with rule 8(3)(a) and (4)(a) and, where the child has not himself been served and has sufficient understanding, advise the child of the contents of any document so served.

(3) Where the child wishes an appointment of a solicitor under section 41(3) or in accordance with rule 11(2)(a) to be terminated, he may apply to the court for an order terminating the appointment; and the solicitor and the guardian ad litem shall be given an opportunity to make representations.

(4) Where the guardian ad litem wishes an appointment of a solicitor under section 41(3) to be terminated, he may apply to the court for an order terminating the appointment, and the solicitor and, if he is of sufficient understanding, the child, shall be given an opportunity to make representations.

(5) When terminating an appointment in accordance with paragraph (3) or (4), the court shall give reasons for so doing, a note of which shall be taken by the justices' clerk.

(6) Where the justices' clerk or the court appoints a solicitor under section 41(3) or refuses to make such an appointment, the justices' clerk shall record the appointment or refusal in the appropriate form in Schedule 1 to these Rules and serve a copy on, the parties and, where he is appointed, on the solicitor.

Welfare officer

13.—(1) The welfare officer shall, unless excused by the court or the justices' clerk, attend a hearing if the justices' clerk gives him notice that his report will be given or considered at that hearing; and any party may question the welfare officer about his report at such a hearing.

(2) A welfare officer shall file a copy of any written report at or by such time as the justices' clerk or the court directs or, in the absence

of a direction, at least 5 days before a hearing of which he is given notice under paragraph (1); and the justices' clerk shall, as soon as practicable, serve a copy of the report on the parties and any guardian ad litem.

Directions

14.—(1) In this rule 'party' includes the guardian ad litem and, where a request or direction concerns a report under section 7, the welfare officer.

(2) In any relevant proceedings the justices' clerk or the court may, subject to paragraph (5), give, vary or revoke directions for the conduct of the proceedings including–
- (a) the timetable for the proceedings;
- (b) varying the time within which or by which an act required, by these Rules, to be done;
- (c) the attendance of the child;
- (d) the appointment of a guardian ad litem whether under section 41 or otherwise, or of a solicitor under section 41(3);
- (e) the service of documents;
- (f) the submission of evidence including experts' reports;
- (g) the preparation of welfare reports under section 7;
- (h) the transfer of the proceedings to another court in accordance with any Order made by the Lord Chancellor under Part I of Schedule 11;
- (i) consolidation with other proceedings;

and the justices' clerk shall, on receipt of an application, or where proceedings have been transferred to his court, consider whether such directions need to be given.

(3) Where the justices' clerk or a single justice who is holding a directions appointment considers, for whatever reason, that it is inappropriate to give directions on a particular matter, he shall refer the matter to the court which may give any appropriate direction.

(4) Where a direction is given under paragraph (2)(h), a certificate shall be issued in the appropriate form in Schedule 1 to these Rules and the justices' clerk shall follow the procedure set out in rule 6(2).

(5) Directions under paragraph (2) may be given, varied or revoked either–
- (a) of the justices' clerk or the court's own motion having given the parties notice of the intention to do so and an opportunity to attend and be heard or to make written representations,
- (b) on the written request of a party specifying the direction which is sought, filed and served on the other parties, or
- (c) on the written request of a party specifying the direction which is sought, to which the other parties consent and which they or their representatives have signed.

(6) In an urgent case, the request under paragraph (5)(b) may, with the leave of the justices' clerk or the court, be made-

(a) orally

(b) without notice to the parties, or

(c) both as in sub-paragraph (a) and as in sub-paragraph (b).

(7) On receipt of a request under paragraph (5)(b) the justices' clerk shall fix a date for the hearing of the request and give not less than 2 days' notice to the parties of the date so fixed.

(8) On considering a request under paragraph (5)(c) the justices' clerk or the court shall either-

(a) grant the request, whereupon the justices' clerk shall inform the parties of the decision, or

(b) direct that a date be fixed for the hearing of the request, whereupon the justices' clerk shall fix such a date and give not less than 2 days' notice to the parties of the date so fixed.

(9) Subject to rule 28, a party may request, in accordance with paragraph 5(b) or (c), that an order be made under section 11(3) or, if he is entitled to apply for such an order, under section 38(1), and paragraphs (6), (7) and (8) shall apply accordingly.

(10) Where, in any relevant proceedings, the court has power to make an order of its own motion, the power to give directions under paragraph (2) shall apply.

(11) Directions of the justices' clerk or a court which are still in force immediately prior to the transfer of relevant proceedings to another court shall continue to apply following the transfer, subject to any changes of terminology which are required to apply those directions to the court to which the proceedings are transferred, unless varied or discharged by directions under paragraph (2).

(12) The justices' clerk or the court shall take a note of the giving, variation or revocation of a direction under this rule and serve, as soon as practicable, a copy of the note on any party who was not present at the giving variation or revocation.

Timing of proceedings

15.—(1) Any period of time fixed by these Rules, or by any order or direction, for doing any act shall be reckoned in accordance with this rule.

(2) Where the period, being a period of 7 days or less, would include a day which is not a business day, that day shall be excluded.

(3) Where the time fixed for filing a document with the justices' clerk expires on a day on which the justices' clerk's office is closed, and for that reason the document cannot be filed on that day, the document

213

Appendix 1

shall be filed in time if it is filed on the next day on which the justices' clerk's office is open.

(4) Where these Rules provide a period of time within which or by which a certain act is to be performed in the course of relevant proceedings, that period may not be extended otherwise than by a direction of the justices' clerk or the court under rule 14.

(5) At the-
- (a) transfer to a court of relevant proceedings,
- (b) postponement or adjournment of any hearing or directions appointment in the course of relevant proceedings, or
- (c) conclusion of any such hearing or directions appointment other than one at which the proceedings are determined, or so soon thereafter as is practicable,

the justices' clerk or the court shall-
- (i) fix a date upon which the proceedings shall come before the justices' clerk or the court again for such purposes as the justices' clerk or the court directs, which date shall, where paragraph (a) applies, be as soon as possible after the transfer, and
- (ii) give notice to the parties and to the guardian ad litem or the welfare officer of the date so fixed.

Attendance at directions appointment and hearing

16.—(1) Subject to paragraph (2), a party shall attend a directions appointment of which he has been given notice in accordance with rule 14(5) unless the justices' clerk or the court otherwise directs.

(2) Relevant proceedings shall take place in the absence of any party including the child if-
- (a) the court considers it in the interests of the child having regard to the matters to be discussed or the evidence likely to be given, and
- (b) the party is represented by a guardian ad litem or solicitor;

and when considering the interests of the child under sub-paragraph (a) the court shall give the guardian ad litem, solicitor for the child and, if he is of sufficient understanding, the child, an opportunity to make representations.

(3) Subject to paragraph (4) below, where at the time and place appointed for a hearing or directions appointment the applicant appears but one or more of the respondents do not, the justices' clerk or the court may proceed with the hearing or appointment.

(4) The court shall not begin to hear an application in the absence of a respondent unless-
- (a) it is proved to the satisfaction of the court that he received reasonable notice of the date of the hearing; or
- (b) the court is satisfied that the circumstances of the case justify proceeding with the hearing.

(5) Where, at the time and place appointed for a hearing or directions appointment, one or more respondents appear but the applicant does not, the court may refuse the application or, if sufficient evidence has previously been received, proceed in the absence of the applicant.

(6) Where at the time and place appointed for a hearing or directions appointment neither the applicant nor any respondent appears, the court may refuse the application.

(7) If the court considers it expedient in the interests of the child, it shall hear any relevant proceedings in private when only the officers of the court, the parties, their legal representatives and such other persons as specified by the court may attend.

Documentary evidence

17.—(1) Subject to paragraphs (4) and (5), in any relevant proceedings a party shall file and serve on the parties, any welfare officer and any guardian ad litem of whose appointment he has been given notice under rule 10(5)-
- (a) written statements of the substance of the oral evidence which the party intends to adduce at a hearing of, or a directions appointment in, those proceedings, which shall-
  - (i) be dated,
  - (ii) be signed by the person making the statement, and
  - (iii) contain a declaration that the maker of the statement believes it to be true and understands that it may be placed before the court, and
- (b) copies of any documents, including, subject to rule 18(3), experts' reports, upon which the party intends to rely, at a hearing of, or a directions appointment in, those proceedings,

at or by such time as the justices' clerk or the court directs or, in the absence of a direction, before the hearing or appointment.

(2) A party may, subject to any direction of the justices' clerk or the court about the timing of statements under this rule, file and serve on the parties a statement which is supplementary to a statement served under paragraph (1).

(3) At a hearing or directions appointment a party may not, without the leave of the justices' clerk, in the case of a directions appointment, or the court-
- (a) adduce evidence, or
- (b) seek to rely on a document,

in respect of which he has failed to comply with the requirements of paragraph (1).

(4) In proceedings for a section 8 order a party shall-
- (a) neither file nor serve any document other than as required or authorised by these Rules, and
- (b) in completing a form prescribed by these Rules, neither give

Appendix 1

information, nor make a statement, which is not required or
authorised by that form,
without the leave of the justices' clerk or the court.

(5) In proceedings for a section 8 order, no statement or copy may
be filed under paragraph (1) until such time as the justices' clerk or
the court directs.

Expert evidence – examination of child

18.—(1) No person may, without the leave of the justices' clerk or
the court, cause the child to be medically or psychiatrically examined,
or otherwise assessed, for the purpose of the preparation of expert
evidence for use in the proceedings.

(2) An application for leave under paragraph (1) shall, unless the
justices' clerk or the court otherwise directs, be served on all the parties
to the proceedings and on the guardian ad litem.

(3) Where the leave of the justices' cierk or the court has not been
given under paragraph (1), no evidence arising out of an examination
or assessment to which that paragraph applies may be adduced without
the leave of the court.

Amendment

19.—(1) Subject to rule 17(2), a document which has been filed or
served in any relevant proceedings may not be amended without the
leave of the justices' clerk or the court which shall, unless the justices'
clerk or the court otherwise directs, be requested in writing.

(2) On considering a request for leave to amend a document the justices'
clerk or the court shall either–
  (a) grant the request, whereupon the justices' clerk shall inform
       the person making the request of that decision, or
  (b) invite the parties or any of them to make representations, within
       a specified period, as to whether such an order should be made.

(3) A person amending a document shall file it with the justices'
clerk and serve it on those persons on whom it was served prior to
amendment; and the amendments shall be identified.

Oral evidence

20. The justices' clerk or the court shall keep a note of the substance
of the oral evidence given at a hearing of, or directions appointment
in, relevant proceedings.

Hearing

21.—(1) Before the hearing, the justice or justices who will be dealing with the case shall read any documents which have been filed under rule 17 in respect of the hearing.

(2) The justices' clerk at a directions appointment, or the court at a hearing or directions appointment, may give directions as to the order of speeches and evidence.

(3) Subject to directions under paragraph (2), at a hearing of, or directions appointment in, relevant proceedings, the parties and the guardian ad litem shall adduce their evidence in the following order-
   (a) the applicant,
   (b) any party with parental responsibility for the child,
   (c) other respondents,
   (d) the guardian ad litem,
   (e) the child if he is a party to the proceedings and there is no guardian ad litem.

(4) After the final hearing of relevant proceedings, the court shall make its decision as soon as is practicable.

(5) Before the court makes an order or refuses an application or request, the justices' clerk shall record in writing-
   (a) the names of the justice or justices constituting the court by which the decision is made, and
   (b) in consultation with the justice or justices, the reasons for the court's decision and any findings of fact.

(6) When making an order or when refusing an application, the court or one of the justices constituting the court by which the decision is made, shall state any findings of fact and the reasons for the court's decision.

(7) After the court announces its decision, the justices' clerk shall as soon as practicable-
   (a) make a record of any order made in the appropriate form in Schedule 1 to these Rules or, where there is no such form, in writing; and
   (b) subject to paragraph (8), serve a copy of any order made on the parties to the proceedings and on any person with whom the child is living.

(8) Within 48 hours after the making of an order under section 48(4) or the making, ex parte, of-
   (a) a prohibited steps order, or a specific issue order, under section 8, or
   (b) an order under section 44, 48(9), 50, 75(1) or 102(1),
the applicant shall serve a copy of the order in the appropriate form in Schedule 1 to these Rules on-
   (i) each party,
   (ii) any person who has actual care of the child, or who had such care immediately prior to the making of the order, and

217

     (iii)   in the case of an order referred to in sub-paragraph (b), the local authority in whose area the child lives or is found.

PART III
MISCELLANEOUS

Costs

22.—(1) In any relevant proceedings, the court may, at any time during the proceedings in that court, make an order that a party pay the whole or any part of the costs of any other party.

(2) A party against whom the court is considering making a costs order shall have an opportunity to make representations as to why the order should not be made.

Confidentiality of documents

23.—(1) No document, other than a record of an order, held by the court and relating to relevant proceedings shall be disclosed, other than to–

    (a) a party,
    (b) the legal representative of a party,
    (c) the guardian ad litem,
    (d) the Legal Aid Board, or
    (e) a welfare officer,

without leave of the justices' clerk or the court.

(2) Nothing in this rule shall prevent the notification by the court or the justices' clerk of a direction under section 37(1) to the authority concerned.

Enforcement of residence order

24. Where a person in whose favour a residence order is in force wishes to enforce it he shall file a written statement describing the alleged breach of the arrangements settled by the order whereupon the justices' clerk 'shall fix a date, time and place for a hearing of the proceedings and give notice, as soon as practicable to the person wishing to enforce the residence order and any person whom it is alleged is in breach of the arrangements settled by that order, of the date fixed.

Notification of consent

25. Consent for the purposes of–

    (a) section 16(3),
    (b) section 33(7), or
    (c) paragraph 19(1) of Schedule 2,

shall be given either–

      (i) orally in court, or

    (ii)   writing to the justices' clerk or the court and signed by the person giving his consent.

Secure accommodation

26. In proceedings under seetion 25, the justices' clerk shall, if practicable, arrange for copies of all written reports before the court to be made available before the hearing to-
- (a) the applicant,
- (b) the parent or guardian of the child,
- (c) any legal representative of the child,
- (d) the guardian ad litem, and
- (e) the child, unless the justices' clerk or the court otherwise directs;

and copies of such reports may, if the court considers it desirable, be shown to any person who is entitled to notice of the proceedings in accordance with these Rules.

Investigation under section 37

27.—(1) This rule applies where a direction is given to an appropriate authority by a family proceedings court under section 37(1).

(2) On giving a direction the court shall adjourn the proceedings and the justices' clerk or the court shall record the direction in writing.

(3) A copy of the direction recorded under paragraph (2) shall, as soon as practicable after the direction is given, be served by the justices' clerk on the parties to the proceedings in which the direction is given and, where the appropriate authority is not a party, on that authority.

(4) When serving the copy of the direction on the appropriate authority the justices' clerk shall also serve copies of such of the documentary evidence which has been, or is to be, adduced in the proceedings as the court may direct.

(5) Where a local authority informs the court of any of the matters set out in section 37(3)(a) to (c) it shall do so in writing.

Limits on the power of a justices' clerk or a single justice to make an order under section 11(3) or section 38(1)

28. A justices' clerk or single justice shall not make an order under section 11(3) or section 38(1) unless-
- (a) a written request for such an order has been made to which the other parties and any guardian ad litem consent and which they or their representatives have signed,
- (b) a previous such order has been made in the same proceedings, and
- (c) the terms of the order sought are the same as those of the last such order made.

Appeals to a family proceedings court under section 77(6) and paragraph 8(1) of Schedule 8

29.—(1) An appeal under section 77(6) or paragraph 8(1) of Schedule 8 shall be by application in accordance with rule 4.

(2) An appeal under section 77(6) shall be brought within 21 days from the date of the step to which the appeal relates.

Contribution orders

30.—(1) An application for a contribution order under paragraph 23(1) of Schedule 2 shall be accompanied by a copy of the contribution notice served in accordance with paragraph 22(1) of that Schedule and a copy of any notice served by the contributor under paragraph 22(8) of that Schedule.

(2) Where a local authority notifies the court of an agreement reached under paragraph 23(6) of Schedule 2, it shall do so in writing through the justices' clerk.

(3) An application for the variation or revocation of a contribution order under paragraph 23(8) of Schedule 2 shall be accompanied by a copy of the contribution order which it is sought to vary or revoke.

Direction to local education authority to apply for education supervision order

31.—(1) For the purposes of section 40(3) and (4) of the Education Act 1944(**a**), a direction by a magistrates' court to a local education authority to apply for an education supervision order shall be given in writing.

(2) Where, following such a direction, a local education authority informs the court that they have decided not to apply for an education supervision order, they shall do so in writing.

Delegation by justices' clerk

32.—(1) In this rule, 'employed as a clerk in court' has the same meaning as in rule 2(1) of the Justices' Clerks (Qualifications of Assistants) Rules 1979(**b**).

(2) Anything authorised to be done by, to or before a justices' Clerk under these Rules, or under paragraphs 13 to 15C of the Schedule to the Justices' Clerks Rules 1970(**c**) as amended by Schedule 3 to these Rules, may be done instead by, to or before a person employed as a

---

(a) 1944 c 31 (7 and 8 Geo 6); relevant amendments are made by paragraphs 8 to 10 of Schedule 13 to the Children Act 1989.
(b) SI 1979/570, amended by 1980/1897.
(c) SI 1970/231, amended by 1975/300, 1976/1767, 1978/754 and 1983/527.

clerk in court where that person is appointed by the magistrates' courts committee to assist him and where that person has been specifically authorised by the justices' clerk for that purpose.

(3) Any authorisation by the justices' clerk under paragraph (2) shall be recorded in writing at the time the authority is given or as soon as practicable thereafter.

Application of section 97 of the Magistrates' Courts Act 1980

33. Section 97 of the Magistrates' Courts Act 1980 shall apply to relevant proceedings in a family proceedings court as it applies to a hearing of a complaint under that section.

Consequential and minor amendments, savings and transitionals

34.—(1) Subject to paragraph (3) the consequential and minor amendments in Schedule 3 to these Rules shall have effect.

(2) Subject to paragraph (3), the provisions of the 1981 rules shall have effect subject to these Rules.

(3) Nothing in these Rules shall affect any proceedings which are pending (within the meaning of paragraph 1 of Schedule 14 to the Act of 1989) immediately before these Rules come into force.

25th May 1991   *Mackay of Clashfern C*

SCHEDULE 1

FORMS

CHA 1. Application for a Parental Responsibility Order.
     2. Parental Responsibility Order.
     3. Application for the appointment of a guardian.
     4. Order for the appointment of a guardian.
     5. Application for the termination of an appointment of a guardian.
     6. Order terminating the appointment of a guardian.
     7. Contact/Residence Order.
     8. Prohibited Steps Order.
     9   Specific Issue Order.
    10. Application for a Contact Order, Prohibited Steps Order, Residence Order or Specific Issue Order,
   10A. Respondent's Answer to Section 10 Application.
    11. Application to change child's surname.

11A. Application to remove child from the jurisdiction of the UK.

12. Order authorising change of child's surname/removal of child from the jurisdiction of the UK.

13. Application for Financial Provision.

13A. Respondent's Answer to Application for Financial Provision.

14. Statement of Means.

15. Application for variation/discharge of an order for financial provision.

16. Family Assistance Order.

17. Application for authority to hold a child in secure accommodation.

18. Order authorising child to be held in secure accommodation.

19. Application for a Care/Supervision Order.

20. Order for the care/supervision of a child.

21. Application for contact with a child in care.

22. Order allowing contact with a child in care.

23. Application for permission to refuse contact with a child in care.

24. Order refusing contact with a child in care.

25. Application for an Education Supervision Order.

26. Education Supervision Order.

27. Interim Care/Supervision Order.

28. Application to discharge Care/Supervision Order vary Supervision Order or substitute Supervision Order for a Care Order.

29. Order discharging Care/Supervision Order, varying Supervision Order or substituting Supervision Order for a Care Order.

30. Order making or refusing the appointment of a guardian ad litem.

31. Order making or refusing the appointment of solicitor.

32. Application for a Child Assessment Order.

33. Child Assessment Order.

34. Application for an Emergency Protection Order.

35. Emergency Protection Order.

36. Application to vary Emergency Protection Order directions.

37. Order varying Emergency Protection Order directions.

38. Application to extend Emergency Protection Order.

39. Order extending an Emergency Protection Order.

40. Application to discharge an Emergency Protection Order.

41. Order discharging an Emergency Protection Order.

42. Order authorising search for another child.

43. Application for a Warrant under Section 48.

44. Application for a Warrant under Section 48.

45. Application for Recovery Order.

46. Recovery Order.

SCHEDULE 2
Rules 4 and 7
RESPONDENTS AND NOTICE

(i)	(ii)	(iii)	(iv)
Provisions under which proceedings brought	*Minimum number of days prior to hearing or directions appointment for service under rule 4(1)(b)*	*Respondents*	*Persons to whom notice is to be given*
All applications.	See separate entries below	Subject to separate entries below,	Subject to separate entries below,
		every person whom the applicant believes to have parental responsibility for the child;	the local authority providing accommodation for the child;

Appendix 1

(i)	(ii)	(iii)	(iv)
Provisions under which proceedings brought	*Minimum number of days prior to hearing or directions appointment for service under rule 4(1)(b)*	*Respondents*	*Persons to whom notice is to be given*
		where the child is the subject of a care order, every person whom the applicant believes to have had parental responsibility immediately prior to the making of the care order;	persons who are caring for the child at the time when the proceedings are commenced;
		in the case of an application to extend, vary or discharge an order, the parties to the proceedings leading to the order which it is sought to have extended, varied or discharged;	in the case of proceedings brought in respect of a child who is alleged to be staying in a refuge which is certificated under section 51(1) or (2) the person who is providing the refuge
		in the case of specified proceedings, the child.	
Section 8 or Schedule 1.	21 days	As for 'all applications' above, and:	As for 'all applications' above, and:
		in the case of proceedings under Schedule 1, those persons whom the applicant believes to be interested in or affected by the proceedings.	in the case of an application for a section 8 order, every person whom the applicant believes- (i) to be named in a court order with respect to the same child, which has not ceased to have effect, (ii) to be a party to pending proceedings in respect of the same child, or

(i)	(ii)	(iii)	(iv)
Provisions under which proceedings brought	*Minimum number of days prior to hearing or directions appointment for service under rule 4(1)(b)*	*Respondents*	*Persons to whom notice is to be given*
			(iii) to be a person with whom the child has lived for at least 3 years prior to the application, unless, in a case to which (i) or (ii) applies, the applicant believes that the court order or pending proceedings are not relevant to the application.
Section 4(1)(a), 4(3), 5(1), 6(7), 13(1), 16(6), 33(7), 77(6), paragraph 19(1), 23(1) or 23(8) of Schedule 2, paragraph 8(1) of Schedule 8, or paragraph 11(3) or 16(5) of Schedule 14.	14 days	Except for proceedings under section 77(6), Schedule 2, or paragraph 8(1) of Schedule 8, as for 'all applications' above, and: in the case of an application under paragraph 11(3)(b) or 16(5) of Schedule 14, any person, other than the child, named in the order or directions which it is sought to discharge or vary; in the case of proceedings under section 77(6), the local authority against whose decision the appeal is made;	As for 'all applications' above, and: in the case of an application under paragraph 19(1) of Schedule 2, the parties to the proceedings leading to the care order; in the case of an application under section 5(1), the father of the child if he does not have parental responsibility.

Appendix 1

(i)	(ii)	(iii)	(iv)
Provisions under which proceedings brought	*Minimum number of days prior to hearing or directions appointment for service under rule 4(1)(b)*	*Respondents*	*Persons to whom notice is to be given*
		in the case of an application under paragraph 23(1) of Schedule 2, the contributor, in the case of an application under paragraph 23(8) of Schedule 2- (i) if the applicant is the local authority, the contributor, and (ii) if the applicant is the contributor, the local authority. In the case of an application under paragraph 8(1) of Schedule 8, the local authority against whose decision the appeal is made.	
Section 36(1), 39(1), 39(2), 39(3), 39(4), 43(1), or paragraph 6(3), 15(2) or 17(1) of Schedule 3.	7 days	As for 'all applications' above, and: in the case of an application under section 39(2) or (3), the supervisor, in the case of proceedings under paragraph 17(1) of Schedule 3, the local education authority concerned;	As for 'all applications' above, and: in the case of an application for an order under section 43(1)- (i) every person whom the applicant believes to be a parent of the child, (ii) every person whom the applicant believes to be caring for the child,

(i)	(ii)	(iii)	(iv)
Provisions under which proceedings brought	*Minimum number of days prior to hearing or directions appointment for service under rule 4(1)(b)*	*Respondents*	*Persons to whom notice is to be given*
		in the case of proceedings under section 36 or paragraph 15(2) or 17(1) of Schedule 3, the child.	(iii) every person in whose favour a contact order is in force with respect to the child, and (iv) every person who is allowed to have contact with the child by virtue of an order under section 34.
Section 31, 34(2), 34(3), 34(4), 34(9) or 38(8)(b).	3 days	As for 'all applications' above, and: in the case of an application under section 34, the person whose contact with the child is the subject of the application.	As for 'all applications' above, and: in the case of an application under section 31- (i) every person whom the applicant believes to be a party to pending relevant proceedings in respect of the same child, and (ii) every person whom the applicant believes to be a parent without parental responsibility for the child.
Section 43(12).	2 days	As for 'all applications' above	Those of the persons referred to in section 43(11)(a) to (e) who were not party to the application for the order which it is sought to have varied or discharged.

227

(i)	(ii)	(iii)	(iv)
Provisions under which proceedings brought	*Minimum number of days prior to hearing or directions appointment for service under rule 4(1)(b)*	*Respondents*	*Persons to whom notice is to be given*
Section 25, 44(1), 44(9)(b), 45(4), 45(8), 46(7), 48(9), 50(1), 75(1) or 102(1).	1 day	Except for applications under section 75(1) or 102(1), as for 'all applications' above, and: in the case of an application under section 44(9)(b) (i) the parties to the application for the order in respect of which it is sought to vary the directions; (ii) any person who was caring for the child prior to the making of the order; and (iii) any person whose contact with the child is affected by the direction which it is sought to have varied; in the case of an application under section 50, the person whom the applicant alleges to have effected or to have been or to be responsible for the taking or keeping of the child;	As for 'all applications' above, and: in the case of an application under section 44(1), every person whom the applicant believes to be a parent of the child; in the case of an application under section 44(9)(b)- (i) the local authority in whose area the child is living, and (ii) any person whom the applicant believes to be affected by the direction which it is sought to have varied.

(i)	(ii)	(iii)	(iv)
Provisions under which proceedings brought	*Minimum number of days prior to hearing or directions appointment for service under rule 4(1)(b)*	*Respondents*	*Persons to whom notice is to be given*
		in the case of an application under section 75(1) the registered person; in the case of an application under section 102(1) the person referred to in section 102(1) and any person preventing or likely to prevent such a person from exercising powers under enactments mentioned in subsection (6) of that section.	

SCHEDULE 3

Rule 34(1)

CONSEQUENTIAL AND MINOR AMENDMENTS

In the Justices' Clerks Rules 1970(a) for paragraphs 13, 14 and 15 of the Schedule there shall be substituted the following paragraphs:

'**13.** The transfer of proceedings in accordance with any order made by the Lord Chancellor under Part I of Schedule 11.

14. The appointing of a guardian ad litem or solicitor for a child under section 41 of the Children Act 1989.

15. The giving variation or revocation of directions in accordance with rule 14 of the Family Proceedings Courts (Children Act 1989) Rules 1991.

(a) SI 1970/231 amended by SI 1975/300, 1976/1767, 1978/754 and 1983/527.

15A. The making of an order in accordance with rule 28 of the Family Proceedings Courts (Children Act 1989) Rules 1991 under sections 11(3) or 38(1) of the Children Act 1989.

15B. By virtue of rule 33 of the Family Proceedings Courts (Children Act 1989) Rules 1991, the issuing of a witness summons under section 97 of the Magistrates' Courts Act 1980 in relevant proceedings within the meaning of section 93(3) of the Children Act 1989.

15C. The requesting of a welfare report under section 7 of the Children Act 1989.'.

APPENDIX 2

The Family Proceedings Rules 1991[1]
(SI 1991 No 1247)

---

[1] As amended by the Family Proceedings (Amendment) Rules 1991 (SI 1991 No 2113): amendments are indicated by the year of the amending instrument in square brackets at the end of the relevant passage in the text, eg [1991].

PART I
PRELIMINARY

Citation and commencement

1.1 These rules may be cited as the Family Proceedings Rules 1991 and shall come into force on 14th October 1991.

Interpretation

1.2—(1) In these rules, unless the context otherwise requires-
'the Act of 1973' means the Matrimonial Causes Act 1973(**a**);
'the Act of 1984' means the Matrimonial and Family Proceedings Act 1984(**b**);
'the Act of 1986' means the Family Law Act 1986(**c**);
'the Act of 1989' means the Children Act 1989(**d**);
'ancillary relief' means-
  (a) an avoidance of disposition order,
  (b) a financial provision order,
  (c) an order for maintenance pending suit,
  (d) a property adjustment order, or
  (e) a variation order,
'avoidance of disposition order' means an order under section 37(2)(b) or (c) of the Act of 1973;

(**a**) 1973 c 18.
(**b**) 1984 c 42. Section 40 was amended by the Courts and Legal Services Act 1990 (c 41), Schedule 18, paragraph 50.
(**c**) 1986 c 55.
(**d**) 1989 c 41.

'business day' has the meaning assigned to it by rule 1.5(6);
'cause' means a matrimonial cause as defined by section 32 of the
Act of 1984 or proceedings under section 19 of the Act of 1973(a)
(presumption of death and dissolution of marriage);
'child' and 'child of the family' have, except in Part IV, the meanings
respectively assigned to them by section 52(1) of the Act of 1973(b);
'consent order' means an order under section 33A of the Act of 1973(c);
'court' means a judge or the district judge;
'court of trial' means a divorce county court designated by the Lord
Chancellor as a court of trial pursuant to section 33(1) of the Act
of 1984 and, in relation to matrimonial proceedings pending in a
divorce county court, the principal registry shall be treated as a court
of trial having its place of sitting at the Royal Courts of Justice;
'defended cause' means a cause not being an undefended cause;
'district judge', in relation to proceedings in the principal registry, a
district registry or a county court, means the district judge or one of
the district judges of that registry or county court, as the case may be;
'district registry' means any district registry having a divorce county
court within its district;
'divorce county court' means a county court so designated by the
Lord Chancellor pursuant to section 33(1) of the Act of 1984;
'divorce town', in relation to any matrimonial proceedings, means
a place at which sittings of the High Court are authorised to be
held outside the Royal Courts of Justice for the hearing of such
proceedings or proceedings of the class to which they belong;
'document exchange' means any document exchange for the time
being approved by the Lord Chancellor,
'family proceedings' has the meaning assigned to it by section 32
of the Act of 1984;
'financial provision order' means any of the orders mentioned in
section 21(1) of the Act of 1973 except an order under section 27(6)
of that Act(d);
'financial relief' has the same meaning as in section 37 of the Act
of 1973;
'judge' does not include a district judge;
'notice of intention to defend' has the meaning assigned to it by
rule 10.8;
'order for maintenance pending suit' means an order under section

(a) Section 19 was repealed in part by the Domicile and Matrimonial Proceedings
Act 1973 (c 45), section 17(2) and Schedule 6.
(b) Section 52(1) was applied by section 27 of the Matrimonial and Family
Proceedings Act 1984 (c 42). No other applications, or any other repeals
or amendments are relevant to these rules.
(c) Section 33A was inserted by section 7 of the Matrimonial and Family
Proceedings Act 1984 (c 42).
(d) The only relevant amendment is made by section 63(3) of the Domestic
Proceedings and Magistrates' Courts Act 1978 (c 22).

22 of the Act of 1973;

'person named' includes a person described as 'passing under the name of A.B.';

'the President' means the President of the Family Division or, in the case of his absence or incapacity through illness or otherwise or of a vacancy in the office of President, the senior puisne judge of that Division;

'principal registry' means the Principal Registry of the Family Division;

'proper officer' means-

(a) in relation to the principal registry, the chief clerk of the family proceedings department, and

(b) in relation to any other court or registry, the chief clerk,

or other officer of the court or registry acting on his behalf in accordance with directions given by the Lord Chancellor;

'property adjustment order' means any of the orders mentioned in section 21(2) of the Act of 1973;

'registry for the divorce town' shall be construed in accordance with rule 2.32(6);

'Royal Courts of Justice', in relation to matrimonial proceedings pending in a divorce county court, means such place, being the Royal Courts of Justice or elsewhere, as may be specified in directions given by the Lord Chancellor pursuant to section 42(2)(a) of the Act of 1984;

'senior district judge' means the senior district judge of the Family Division or, in his absence from the principal registry, the senior of the district judges in attendance at the registry;

'special procedure list' has the meaning assigned to it by rule 2.24(3);

'undefended cause' means-

(i) a cause in which no answer has been filed or any answer filed has been struck out, or

(ii) a cause which is proceeding only on the respondent's answer and in which no reply or answer to the respondent's answer has been filed or any such reply or answer has been struck out, or

(iii) a cause to which rule 2.12(4) applies and in which no notice has been given under that rule or any notice so given has been withdrawn, or

(iv) a cause in which an answer has been filed claiming relief but in which no pleading has been filed opposing the grant of a decree on the petition or answer or any pleading or part of a pleading opposing the grant of such relief has been struck out, or

(v) any cause not within (i) to (iv) above in which a decree has been pronounced;

'variation order' means an order under section 31 of the Act of 1973(a).

(2) Unless the context otherwise requires, a cause begun by petition shall be treated as pending for the purposes of these rules notwithstanding that a final decree or order has been made on the petition.

(3) Unless the context otherwise requires, a rule or Part referred to by number means the rule or Part so numbered in these rules.

(4) In these rules a form referred to by number means the form so numbered in Appendix 1(b) to these rules with such variation as the circumstances of the particular case may require.

(5) In these rules any reference to an Order and rule is–
  (a) if prefixed by the letters 'CCR', a reference to that Order and rule in the County Court Rules 1981(c), and
  (b) if prefixed by the letters 'RSC', a reference to that Order and rule in the Rules of the Supreme Court 1965(d).

(6) References in these rules to a county court shall, in relation to matrimonial proceedings, be construed as references to a divorce county court.

(7) In this rule and in rule 1.4, 'matrimonial proceedings' means proceedings of a kind with respect to which divorce county courts have jurisdiction by or under section 33, 34 or 35 of the Act of 1984.

Application of other rules

1.3—(1) Subject to the provisions of these rules and of any enactment the County Court Rules 1981 and the Rules of the Supreme Court 1965 shall apply, with the necessary modifications, to family proceedings in a county court and the High Court respectively.

(2) For the purposes of paragraph (1) any provision of these rules authorising or requiring anything to be done in family proceedings shall be treated as if it were, in the case of proceedings pending in a county court, a provision of the County Court Rules 1981 and, in the case of proceedings pending in the High Court, a provision of the Rules of the Supreme Court 1965.

County court proceedings in principal registry

1.4—(1) Subject to the provisions of these rules, matrimonial

(a) Section 31: amended by section 8(2) of the Matrimonial Homes and Property Act 1981 (c 24), section 51 of the Administration of Justice Act 1982 (c 53), section 6 of the Matrimonial and Family Proceedings Act 1984 (c 42).
(b) Appendix 1 was amended by The Family Proceedings (Amendment) Rules 1991 (SI 1991 No 2193), which revised Forms CHA15, 17, 31 and 57 and added Forms CHA66 to 69.
(c) SI 1981/1687.
(d) SI 1965/1776.

proceedings pending at any time in the principal registry which, if they had been begun in a divorce county court, would be pending at that time in such a court, shall be treated, for the purposes of these rules and of any provision of the County Court Rules 1981 and the County Courts Act 1984(**a**), as pending in a divorce county court and not in the High Court.

(2) Unless the context otherwise requires, any reference to a divorce county court in any provision of these rules which relates to the commencement or prosecution of proceedings in a divorce county court, or the transfer of proceedings to or from such a court, includes a reference to the principal registry.

Computation of time

1.5—(1) Any period of time fixed by these rules, or by any rules applied by these rules, or by any decree, judgment, order or direction for doing any act shall be reckoned in accordance with the following provisions of this rule.

(2) Where the act is required to be done not less than a specified period before a specified date, the period starts immediately after the date on which the act is done and ends immediately before the specified date.

(3) Where the act is required to be done within a specified period after or from a specified date, the period starts immediately after that date.

(4) Where, apart from this paragraph, the period in question, being a period of seven days or less, would include a day which is not a business day, that day shall be excluded.

(5) Where the time so fixed for doing an act in the court office expires on a day on which the office is closed, and for that reason the act cannot be done on that day, the act shall be in time if done on the next day on which the office is open.

(6) In these rules 'business day' means any day other than-
  (a) a Saturday, Sunday, Christmas Day or Good Friday; or
  (b) a bank holiday under the Banking and Financial Dealings Act 1971(**b**), in England and Wales.

* * * * *

PART IV
PROCEEDINGS UNDER THE CHILDREN ACT 1989
Interpretation and application

4.1—(1) In this Part of these rules, unless a contrary intention appears-

---

(**a**) 1984 c 28.
(**b**) 1971 c 80.

a section or schedule referred to means the section or schedule so numbered in the Act of 1989;

'a section 8 order' has the meaning assigned to it by section 8(2);

'application' means an application made under or by virtue of the Act of 1989 or under these rules, and 'applicant' shall be construed accordingly;

'child', in relation to proceedings to which this Part applies-

(a) means, subject to sub-paragraph (b), a person under the age of 18 with respect to whom the proceedings are brought, and

(b) where the proceedings are under Schedule 1, also includes a person who has reached the age of 18;

'directions appointment' means a hearing for directions under rule 4.14(2);

'emergency protection order' means an order under section 44;

'guardian ad litem' means a guardian ad litem, appointed under section 41, of the child with respect to whom the proceedings are brought;

'leave' includes permission and approval;

'note' includes a record made by mechanical means;

'parental responsibility' has the meaning assigned to it by section 3;

'recovery order' means an order under section 50;

'specified proceedings' has the meaning assigned to it by section 41(6) and rule 4.2(2); and

'welfare officer' means a person who has been asked to prepare a welfare report under section 7.

(2) Except where the contrary intention appears, the provisions of this Part apply to proceedings in the High Court and the county courts-

(a) on an application for a section 8 order;

(b) on an application for a care order or a supervision order;

(c) on an application under section 4(1)(a), 4(3), 5(1), 6(7), 13(1), 16(6), 33(7), 34(2), 34(3), 34(4), 34(9), 36(1), 38(8)(b), 39(1), 39(2), 39(3), 39(4), 43(1), 43(12), 44, 45, 46(7), 48(9), 50(1) or 102(1); [1991]

(d) under Schedule 1, except where financial relief is also sought by or on behalf of an adult;

(e) on an application under paragraph 19(1) of Schedule 2;

(f) on an application under paragraph 6(3), 15(2) or 17(1) of Schedule 3:

(g) on an application under paragraph 11(3) or 16(5) of Schedule 14; or

(h) under section 25.

Matters prescribed for the purposes of the Act of 1989

4.2—(1) The parties to proceedings in which directions are given under section 38(6), and any person named in such a direction, form the prescribed class for the purposes of section 38(8) (application to vary directions made with interim care or interim supervision order).

(2) The following proceedings are specified for the purposes of section 41 in accordance with subsection (6)(i) thereof–
- (a) proceedings under section 25;
- (b) applications under section 33(7);
- (c) proceedings under paragraph 19(1) of Schedule 2;
- (d) applications under paragraph 6(3) of Schedule 3.
- (e) appeals against the determination of proceedings of a kind set out in sub paragraphs (a) to (d) [1991].

(3) The applicant for an order that has been made under section 43(1) and the persons referred to in section 43(11) may, in any circumstances, apply under section 43(12) for a child assessment order to be varied or discharged.

(4) The following persons form the prescribed class for the purposes of section 44(9) (application to vary directions)–
- (a) the parties to the application for the order in respect of which it is sought to vary the directions;
- (b) the guardian ad litem;
- (c) the local authority in whose area the child concerned is ordinarily resident;
- (d) any person who is named in the directions.

Application for leave to commence proceedings

4.3—(1) Where the leave of the court is required to bring any proceedings to which this Part applies, the person seeking leave shall file–
- (a) a written request for leave setting out the reasons for the application; and
- (b) a draft of the application for the making of which leave is sought in the appropriate form in Appendix 1 to these rules or, where there is no such form, in writing, together with sufficient copies for one to be served on each respondent.

(2) On considering a request for leave filed under paragraph (1), the court shall–
- (a) grant the request, whereupon the proper officer shall inform the person making the request of the decision, or
- (b) direct that a date be fixed for the hearing of the request, whereupon the proper officer shall fix such a date and give such notice as the court directs to the person making the request and to such other persons as the court requires to be notified, of the date so fixed.

(3) Where leave is granted to bring proceedings to which this Part applies the application shall proceed in accordance with rule 4.4; but paragraph (1)(a) of that rule shall not apply.

(4) In the case of a request for leave to bring proceedings under Schedule 1, the draft application under paragraph (1) shall be accompanied by a statement setting out the financial details which the person seeking leave believes to be relevant to the request and containing a declaration

that it is true to the maker's best knowledge and belief, together with sufficient copies for one to be served on each respondent.

Application

4.4—(1) Subject to paragraph (4), an applicant shall–
  (a) file the application in respect of each child in the appropriate form in Appendix 1 to these rules or, where there is no such form, in writing, together with sufficient copies for one to be served on each respondent, and
 (b) serve a copy of the application, endorsed in accordance with paragraph (2)(b), on each respondent such number of days prior to the date fixed under paragraph (2)(a) as is specified for that application in column (ii) of Appendix 3 to these rules.

(2) On receipt of the documents filed under paragraph (1)(a) the proper officer shall–
  (a) fix the date for a hearing or a directions appointment, allowing sufficient time for the applicant to comply with paragraph (1)(b),
  (b) endorse the date so fixed upon the copies of the application filed by the applicant, and
  (c) return the copies to the applicant forthwith.

(3) The applicant shall, at the same time as complying with paragraph (1)(b), give written notice of the proceedings, and of the date and place of the hearing or appointment fixed under paragraph (2)(a), to the persons set out for the relevant class of proceedings in column (iii) of Appendix 3 to these rules.

(4) An application for–
  (a) a prohibited steps order, or a specific issue order, under section 8,
  (b) an emergency protection order,
  (c) a warrant under section 48(9),
  (d) a recovery order, or
  (e) a warrant under section 102(1). [1991]
may be made ex parte in which case the applicant shall–
        (i) file the application in respect of each child in the appropriate form in Appendix 1 to these rules–
            (a) where the application is made by telephone, within 24 hours after the making of the application, or
            (b) in any other case, at the time when the application is made, and
       (ii) in the case of an application for a prohibited steps order, or a specific issue order, under section 8 or an emergency protection order, serve a copy of the application on each respondent within 48 hours after the making of the order.

(5) Where the court refuses to make an order on an ex parte application it may direct that the application be made inter partes.

(6) In the case of proceedings under Schedule 1, the application under paragraph (1) shall be accompanied by a statement setting out the

financial details which the applicant believes to be relevant to the application and containing a declaration that it is true to the maker's best knowledge and belief, together with sufficient copies for one to be served on each respondent.

Withdrawal of application

4.5—(1) An application may be withdrawn only with leave of the court.

(2) Subject to paragraph (3), a person seeking leave to withdraw an application shall file and serve on the parties a written request for leave setting out the reasons for the request.

(3) The request under paragraph (2) may be made orally to the court if the parties and either the guardian ad litem or the welfare officer are present.

(4) Upon receipt of a written request under paragraph (2) the court shall-

  (a) if-
      (i)   the parties consent in writing,
     (ii) the guardian ad litem has had an opportunity to make representations, and
    (iii) the court thinks fit,
      grant the request, in which case the proper officer shall notify the parties, the guardian ad litem and the welfare officer of the granting of the request, or
  (b) direct that a date be fixed for the hearing of the request in which case the proper officer shall give at least 7 days' notice to the parties, the guardian ad litem and the welfare officer, of the date fixed.

Transfer [1991]

4.6—(1) Where an application is made, in accordance with the provisions of the Allocation Order, to a county court for an order transferring proceedings from a magistrates' court following the refusal of the magistrates' court to order such a transfer, the applicant shall-

  (a) file the application in Form CHA58, together with a copy of the certificate issued by the magistrates' court, and
  (b) serve a copy of the documents mentioned in sub-paragraph (a) personally on all parties to the proceedings which it is sought to have transferred,

within 2 days after receipt by the applicant of the certificate. [1991]

(2) Within 2 days after receipt of the documents served under paragraph (1)(b), any party other than the applicant may file written representations.

(3) The court shall, not before the fourth day after the filing of the application under paragraph (1), unless the parties consent to earlier consideration, consider the application and either-

- (a) grant the application, whereupon the proper officer shall inform the parties of that decision, or
- (b) direct that a date be fixed for the hearing of the application, whereupon the proper officer shall fix such a date and give not less than 1 day's notice to the parties of the date so fixed.

(4) Where proceedings are transferred from a magistrates' court to a county court in accordance with the provisions of the Allocation Order, the county court shall consider whether to transfer those proceedings to the High Court in accordance with that Order and either-

- (a) determine that such an order need not be made,
- (b) make such an order,
- (c) order that a date be fixed for the hearing of the question whether such an order should be made, whereupon the proper officer shall give such notice to the parties as the court directs of the date so fixed, or
- (d) invite the parties to make written representations, within a specified period, as to whether such an order should be made; and upon receipt of the representations the court shall act in accordance with sub-paragraph (a), (b) or (c). [1991]

(5) The proper officer shall notify the parties of an order transferring the proceedings from a county court or from the High Court made in accordance with the provisions of the Allocation Order. [1991]

(6) Before ordering the transfer of proceedings from a county court to a magistrates' court in accordance with the Allocation Order, the county court shall notify the magistrates' court of its intention to make such an order and invite the views of the clerk to the justices on whether such an order should be made. [1991]

(7) An order transferring proceedings from a county court to a magistrates' court in accordance with the Allocation Order shall-

- (a) be in form CHA66, and
- (b) be served by the court on the parties. [1991]

(8) In this rule 'the Allocation Order' means the Children (Allocation of Proceedings) Order 1991(a) or any Order replacing that Order. [1991]

Parties

4.7—(1) The respondents to proceedings to which this Part applies shall be those persons set out in the relevant entry in column (iv) of Appendix 3 to these rules.

(2) In proceedings to which this Part applies, a person may file a request in writing that he or another person-

- (a) be joined as a party, or
- (b) cease to be a party.

(a) SI 1991/1677.

(3) On considering a request under paragraph (2) the court shall, subject to paragraph (4)-
- (a) grant it without a hearing or representations, save that this shall be done only in the case of a request under paragraph (2)(a), whereupon the proper officer shall inform the parties and the person making the request of that decision, or
- (b) order that a date be fixed for the consideration of the request, whereupon the proper officer shall give notice of the date so fixed, together with a copy of the request-
  - (i) in the case of a request under paragraph (2)(a), to the applicant, and
  - (ii) in the case of a request under paragraph (2)(b), to the parties, or
- (c) invite the parties or any of them to make written representations, within a specified period, as to whether the request should be granted; and upon the expiry of the period the court shall act in accordance with sub-paragraph (a) or (b).

(4) Where a person with parental responsibility requests that he be joined under paragraph (2)(a), the court shall grant his request.

(5) In proceedings to which this Part applies the court may direct-
- (a) that a person who would not otherwise be a respondent under these rules be joined as a party to the proceedings, or
- (b) that a party to the proceedings cease to be a party.

Service

4.8—(1) Subject to the requirement in rule 4.6(1)(b) of personal service, where service of a document is required under this Part (and not by a provision to which section 105(8) (service of notice or other document under the Act) applies) it may be effected-
- (a) if the person to be served is not known by the person serving to be acting by solicitor-
  - (i) by delivering it to him personally, or
  - (ii) by delivering it at, or by sending it by first-class post to, his residence or his last known residence, or
- (b) if the person to be served is known by the person serving to be acting by solicitor-
  - (i) by delivering the document at, or sending it by first-class post to, the solicitor's address for service,
  - (ii) where the solicitor's address for service includes a numbered box at a document exchange, by leaving the document at that document exchange or at a document exchange which transmits documents on every business day to that document exchange, or
  - (iii) by sending a legible copy of the document by facsimile transmission to the solicitor's office.

(2) In this rule 'first-class post' means first-class post which has been pre-paid or in respect of which pre-payment is not required.

(3) Where a child who is a party to proceedings to which this Part applies is required by these rules or other rules of court to serve a document, service shall be effected by-
- (a) the solicitor acting for the child, or
- (b) where there is no such solicitor, the guardian ad litem, or
- (c) where there is neither such a solicitor nor a guardian ad litem, the court.

(4) Service of any document on a child shall, subject to any direction of the court, be effected by service on-
- (a) the solicitor acting for the child, or
- (b) where there is no such solicitor, the guardian ad litem, or
- (c) where there is neither such a solicitor nor a guardian ad litem with leave of the court, the child.

(5) Where the court refuses leave under paragraph (4)(c) it shall give a direction under paragraph (8).

(6) A document shall, unless the contrary is proved be deemed to have been served-
- (a) in the case of service by first-class post, on the second business day after posting, and
- (b) in the case of service in accordance with paragraph (1)(b)(ii). on the second business day after the day on which it is left at the document exchange.

(7) At or before the first directions appointment in, or hearing of, proceedings to which this Part applies the applicant shall file a statement that service of-
- (a) a copy of the application has been effected on each respondent, and
- (b) notice of the proceedings has been effected under rule 4.4(3);

and the statement shall indicate-
- (i) the manner, date, time and place of service, or
- (ii) where service was effected by post, the date, time and place of posting.

(8) In proceedings to which this Part applies, the court may direct that a requirement of these rules or other rules of court to serve a document shall not apply or shall be effected in such manner as the court directs.

Answer to application

4.9—(1) Within 14 days of service of an application for a section 8 order, each respondent shall file, and serve on the parties, an answer to the application in Form CHA10A.

(2) Within 14 days after service of an application under Schedule 1, each respondent shall file, and serve on the parties, an answer to the application in Form CHA13A.

(3) Following service of an application to which this Part applies, other than an application under rule 4.3 or for a section 8 order, a

respondent may, subject to paragraph (4), file a written answer, which shall be served on the other parties.

(4) An answer under paragraph (3) shall, except in the case of an application under section 25, 31, 34, 38, 43, 44, 45, 46, 48 or 50, be filed, and served, not less than 2 days before the date fixed for the hearing of the application.

Appointment of guardian ad litem

4.10—(1) As soon as practicable after the commencement of specified proceedings, or the transfer of such proceedings to the court, the court shall appoint a guardian ad litem, unless-

(a) such an appointment has already been made by the court which made the transfer and is subsisting, or

(b) the court considers that such an appointment is not necessary to safeguard the interests of the child.

(2) At any stage in specified proceedings a party may apply, without notice to the other parties unless the court directs otherwise, for the appointment of a guardian ad litem.

(3) The court shall grant an application under paragraph (2) unless it considers such an appointment not to be necessary to safeguard the interests of the child, in which case it shall give its reasons; and a note of such reasons shall be taken by the proper officer.

(4) At any stage in specified proceedings the court may, of its own motion, appoint a guardian ad litem.

(5) The proper officer shall, as soon as practicable, notify the parties and any welfare officer of an appointment under this rule or, as the case may be, of a decision not to make such an appointment.

(6) Upon the appointment of a guardian ad litem the proper officer shall, as soon as practicable, notify him of the appointment and serve on him copies of the application and of documents filed under rule 4.17(1).

(7) A guardian ad litem appointed from a panel established by regulations made under section 41(7) shall not-

(a) be a member, officer or servant of a local authority which, or an authorised person (within the meaning of section 31(9)) who is a party to the proceedings unless he is employed by such an authority solely as a member of a panel of guardians ad litem and reporting officers;

(b) be, or have been, a member, officer or servant of a local authority or voluntary organisation (within the meaning of section 105(1)) who has been directly concerned in that capacity in arrangements relating to the care, accommodation or welfare of the child during the five years prior to the commencement of the proceedings;

(c) be a serving probation officer (except that a probation officer who has not in that capacity been previously concerned with the child or his family and who is employed part-time may, when not engaged in his duties as a probation officer, act as a guardian ad litem).

(8) When appointing a guardian ad litem the court shall consider the appointment of anyone who has previously acted as guardian ad litem of the same child.

(9) The appointment of a guardian ad litem under this rule shall continue for such time as is specified in the appointment or until terminated by the court.

(10) When terminating an appointment in accordance with paragraph (9), the court shall give its reasons in writing for so doing.

(11) Where the court appoints a guardian ad litem in accordance with this rule or refuses to make such an appointment, the court or the proper officer shall record the appointment or refusal in Form CHA30.

Powers and duties of guardian ad litem

4.11—(1) In carrying out his duty under section 41(2), the guardian ad litem shall have regard to the principle set out in section 1(2) and the matters set out in section 1(3) (a) to (f) as if for the word 'court' in that section there were substituted the words 'guardian ad litem'.

(2) The guardian ad litem shall–
- (a) appoint a solicitor to represent the child unless such a solicitor has already been appointed, and
- (b) give such advice to the child as is appropriate having regard to his understanding and, subject to rule 4.12(1)(a), instruct the solicitor representing the child on all matters relevant to the interests of the child, including possibilities for appeal, arising in the course of the proceedings.

(2A) Where the guardian ad litem is the Official Solicitor, paragraph 2(a) shall not require him to appoint a solicitor for the child if he intends to act as the child's solicitor in the proceedings, unless–
- (a) the child wishes to instruct a solicitor direct, and
- (b) the official solicitor or the court considers that he is of sufficient understanding to do so. [1991]

(3) Where it appears to the guardian ad litem that the child–
- (a) is instructing his solicitor direct, or
- (b) intends to, and is capable of, conducting the proceedings on his own behalf, he shall so inform the court and thereafter–
  - (i) shall perform all of his duties set out in this rule, other than duties under paragraph (2)(a) and such other duties as the court may direct,
  - (ii) shall take such part in the proceedings as the court may direct, and
  - (iii) may, with leave of the court, have legal representation in his conduct of those duties.

(4) The guardian ad litem shall, unless excused by the court, attend all directions appointments in and hearings of the proceedings and shall advise the court on the following matters–

    (a)   whether the child is of sufficient understanding for any purpose including the child's refusal to submit to a medical or psychiatric examination or other assessment that the court has power to require, direct or order,

    (b)   the wishes of the child in respect of any matter relevant to the proceedings, including his attendance at court;

    (c)   the appropriate forum for the proceedings;

    (d)   the appropriate timing of the proceedings or any part of them;

    (e)   the options available to it in respect of the child and the suitability of each such option including what order should be made in determining the application;

    (f)   any other matter concerning which the court seeks his advice or concerning which he considers that the court should be informed.

(5) The advice given under paragraph (4) may, subject to any order of the court, be given orally or in writing; and if the advice be given orally, a note of it shall be taken by the court or the proper officer.

(6) The guardian ad litem shall, where practicable, notify any person whose joinder as a party to those proceedings would be likely, in the guardian ad litem's opinion, to safeguard the interests of the child, of that person's right to apply to be joined under rule 4.7(2) and shall inform the court–

    (a)   of any such notification given,

    (b)   of anyone whom he attempted to notify under this paragraph but was unable to contact, and

    (c)   of anyone whom he believes may wish to be joined to the proceedings.

(7) The guardian ad litem shall, unless the court otherwise directs, not less than 7 days before the date fixed for the final hearing of the proceedings, file a written report advising on the interests of the child; and the proper officer shall, as soon as practicable, serve a copy of the report on the parties.

(8) The guardian ad litem shall serve and accept service of documents on behalf of the child in accordance with rule 4.8(3)(b) and (4)(b) and, where the child has not himself been served, and has sufficient understanding, advise the child of the contents of any document so served.

(9) The guardian ad litem shall make such investigations as may be necessary for him to carry out his duties and shall, in particular–

    (a)   contact or seek to interview such persons as he thinks appropriate or as the court directs,

    (b)   if he inspects records of the kinds referred to in section 42, bring to the attention of the court and such other persons as the court may direct all such records and documents which may, in his opinion, assist in the proper determination of the proceedings, and

(c)   obtain such professional assistance as is available to him which he thinks appropriate or which the court directs him to obtain.

(10) In addition to his duties under other paragraphs of this rule, the guardian ad litem shall provide to the court such other assistance as it may require.

(11) A party may question the guardian ad litem about oral or written advice tendered by him to the court under this rule.

Solicitor for child

4.12—(1) A solicitor appointed under section 41(3) or in accordance with rule 4.11(2)(a) shall represent the child-

(a)   in accordance with instructions received from the guardian ad litem (unless the solicitor considers, having taken into account the views of the guardian ad litem and any direction of the court under rule 4.11(3), that the child wishes to give instructions which conflict with those of the guardian ad litem and that he is able, having regard to his understanding, to give such instructions on his own behalf in which case he shall conduct the proceedings in accordance with instructions received from the child), or

(b)   where no guardian ad litem has been appointed for the child and the condition in section 41(4)(b) is satisfied, in accordance with instructions received from the child, or

(c)   in default of instructions under (a) or (b), in furtherance of the best interests of the child.

(2) A solicitor appointed under section 41(3) or in accordance with rule 4.11(2)(a) shall serve and accept service of documents on behalf of the child in accordance with rule 4.8(3)(a) and (4)(a) and, where the child has not himself been served and has sufficient understanding, advise the child of the contents of any document so served.

(3) Where the child wishes an appointment of a solicitor under section 41(3) or in accordance with rule 4.11(2)(a) to be terminated, he may apply to the court for an order terminating the appointment; and the solicitor and the guardian ad litem shall be given an opportunity to make representations.

(4) Where the guardian ad litem wishes an appointment of a solicitor under section 41(3) to be terminated, he may apply to the court for an order terminating the appointment; and the solicitor and, if he is of sufficient understanding, the child, shall be given an opportunity to make representations.

(5) When terminating an appointment in accordance with paragraph (3) or (4), the court shall give its reasons for so doing, a note of which shall be taken by the court or the proper officer.

(6) Where the court appoints a solicitor under section 41(3) or refuses to make such an appointment, the court or the proper officer shall record the appointment or refusal in Form CHA31.

Appendix 2

Welfare officer

4.13—(1) The welfare officer shall, unless excused by the court, attend a hearing if the proper officer gives him notice that his report will be given or considered at that hearing; and any party may question the welfare officer about his report at such a hearing.

(2) A welfare officer shall file a copy of any written report at or by such time as the court directs or, in the absence of a direction, at least 5 days before a hearing of which he is given notice under paragraph (1); and the proper officer shall, as soon as practicable, serve a copy of the report on the parties and the guardian ad litem.

Directions

4.14—(1) In this rule, 'party' includes the guardian ad litem and, where a request or a direction concerns a report under section 7, the welfare officer.

(2) In proceedings to which this Part applies the court may, subject to paragraph (3), give, vary or revoke directions for the conduct of the proceedings, including–
  (a) the timetable for the proceedings;
  (b) varying the time within which or by which an act is required, by these rules or by other rules or court, to be done;
  (c) the attendance of the child;
  (d) the appointment of a guardian ad litem, whether under section 41 or otherwise, or of a solicitor under section 41(3);
  (e) the service of documents;
  (f) the submission of evidence including experts' reports;
  (g) the preparation of welfare reports under section 7;
  (h) the transfer of the proceedings to another court;
  (i) consolidation with other proceedings.

(3) Directions under paragraph (2) may be given, varied or revoked either–
  (a) of the court's own motion having given the parties notice of its intention to do so, and an opportunity to attend and be heard or to make written representations,
  (b) on the written request of a party specifying the direction which is sought, filed and served on the other parties, or
  (c) on the written request of a party specifying the direction which is sought, to which the other parties consent and which they or their representatives have signed.

(4) In an urgent case the request under paragraph (3)(b) may, with the leave of the court, be made–
  (a) orally, or
  (b) without notice to the parties, or
  (c) both as in sub-paragraph (a) and as in sub-paragraph (b).

(5) On receipt of a written request under paragraph (3)(b) the proper

officer shall fix a date for the hearing of the request and give not less
than 2 days' notice to the parties of the date so fixed.

(6) On considering a request under paragraph (3)(c) the court shall
either–
- (a) grant the request, whereupon the proper officer shall inform
the parties of the decision, or
- (b) direct that a date be fixed for the hearing of the request,
whereupon the proper officer shall fix such a date and give not
less than 2 days' notice to the parties of the date so fixed.

(7) A party may apply for an order to be made under section 11(3)
or, if he is entitled to apply for such an order, under section 38(1) in
accordance with paragraph (3)(b) or (c).

(8) Where a court is considering making, of its own motion, a section
8 order, or an order under section 31, 34 or 38, the power to give directions
under paragraph (2) shall apply.

(9) Directions of a court which are still in force immediately prior
to the transfer of proceedings to which this Part applies to another
court shall continue to apply following the transfer, subject to any
changes of terminology which are required to apply those directions
to the court to which the proceedings are transferred, unless varied or
discharged by directions under paragraph (2).

(10) The court or the proper officer shall take a note of the giving,
variation or revocation of a direction under this rule and serve, as soon
as practicable, a copy of the note on any party who was not present
at the giving, variation or revocation.

Timing of proceedings

4.15—(1) Where these rules or other rules of court provide a period
of time within which or by which a certain act is to be performed in
the course of proceedings to which this Part applies, that period may
not be extended otherwise than by direction of the court under rule
4.14.

(2) At the–
- (a) transfer to a court of proceedings to which this Part applies,
- (b) postponement or adjournment of any hearing or directions
appointment in the course of proceedings to which this Part
applies, or
- (c) conclusion of any such hearing or directions appointment other
than one at which the proceedings are determined, or so soon
thereafter as is practicable,
the court or the proper officer shall–
- (i) fix a date upon which the proceedings shall come before
the court again for such purposes as the court directs, which
date shall, where paragraph (a) applies, be as soon as
possible after the transfer, and
- (ii) give notice to the parties, the guardian ad litem or the
welfare officer of the date so fixed.

Appendix 2

Attendance at directions appointment and hearing

4.16—(1) Subject to paragraph (2), a party shall attend a directions appointment of which he has been given notice in accordance with rule 4.14(5) unless the court otherwise directs.

(2) Proceedings or any part of them shall take place in the absence of any party, including the child, if–
  (a) the court considers it in the interests of the child, having regard to the matters to be discussed or the evidence likely to be given, and
  (b) the party is represented by a guardian ad litem or solicitor;
and when considering the interests of the child under sub-paragraph (a) the court shall give the guardian ad litem, the solicitor for the child and if he is of sufficient understanding, the child an opportunity to make representations.

(3) Subject to paragraph (4), where at the time and place appointed for a hearing or directions appointment the applicant appears but one or more of the respondents do not, the court may proceed with the hearing or appointment.

(4) The court shall not begin to hear an application in the absence of a respondent unless–
  (a) it is proved to the satisfaction of the court that he received reasonable notice of the date of the hearing; or
  (a) the court is satisfied that the circumstances of the case justify proceeding with the hearing.

(5) Where, at the time and place appointed for a hearing or directions appointment one or more of the respondents appear but the applicant does not, the court may refuse the application or, if sufficient evidence has previously been received, proceed in the absence of the applicant.

(6) Where at the time and place appointed for a hearing or directions appointment neither the applicant nor any respondent appears, the court may refuse the application.

(7) Unless the court otherwise directs, a hearing of, or directions appointment in, proceedings to which this Part applies shall be in chambers.

Documentary evidence

4.17—(1) Subject to paragraphs (4) and (5), in proceedings to which this Part applies a party shall file and serve on the parties, any welfare officer and any guardian ad litem of whose appointment he has been given notice under rule 4.10(5)-
  (a) written statements of the substance of the oral evidence which the party intends to adduce at a hearing of, or a directions appointment in, those proceedings, which shall–
    (i) be dated,
    (ii) be signed by the person making the statement, and
    (iii) contain a declaration that the maker of the statement believes it to be true and understands that it may be placed before the court; and

(b) copies of any documents, including experts' reports, upon which the party intends to rely at a hearing of, or a directions appointment in, those proceedings,

at or by such time as the court directs or, in the absence of a direction, before the hearing or appointment.

(2) A party may, subject to any direction of the court about the timing of statements under this rule, file and serve on the parties a statement which is supplementary to a statement served under paragraph (1).

(3) At a hearing or a directions appointment a party may not, without the leave of the court-

(a) adduce evidence, or

(b) seek to rely on a document,

in respect of which he has failed to comply with the requirements of paragraph (1).

(4) In proceedings for a section 8 order a party shall-

(a) neither file nor serve any document other than as required or authorised by these rules, and

(b) in completing a form prescribed by these rules, neither give information, nor make a statement, which is not required or authorised by that form,

without the leave of the court.

(5) In proceedings for a section 8 order no statement or copy may be filed under paragraph (1) until such time as the court directs.

Expert evidence - examination of child

4.18—(1) No person may, without the leave of the court, cause the child to be medically or psychiatrically examined, or otherwise assessed, for the purpose of the preparation of expert evidence for use in the proceedings.

(2) An application for leave under paragraph (1) shall, unless the court otherwise directs, be served on all parties to the proceedings and on the guardian ad litem.

(3) Where the leave of the court has not been given under paragraph (1), no evidence arising out of an examination or assessment to which that paragraph applies may be adduced without the leave of the court.

Amendment

4.19—(1) Subject to rule 4.17(2), a document which has been filed or served in proceedings to which this Part applies, may not be amended without the leave of the court which shall, unless the court otherwise directs, be requested in writing.

(2) On considering a request for leave to amend a document the court shall either-

(a) grant the request, whereupon the proper officer shall inform the person making the request of that decision, or

(b) invite the parties or any of them to make representations, within a specified period, as to whether such an order should be made.

(3) A person amending a document shall file it and serve it on those persons on whom it was served prior to amendment and the amendments shall be identified.

Oral evidence

4.20 The court or the proper officer shall keep a note of the substance of the oral evidence given at a hearing of, or directions appointment in, proceedings to which this Part applies.

Hearing

4.21—(1) The court may give directions as to the order of speeches and evidence at a hearing, or directions appointment, in the course of proceedings to which this Part applies.

(2) Subject to directions under paragraph (1), at a hearing of, or directions appointment in, proceedings to which this Part applies, the parties and the guardian ad litem shall adduce their evidence in the following order–
   (a) the applicant,
   (b) any party with parental responsibility for the child,
   (c) other respondents,
   (d) the guardian ad litem,
   (e) the child, if he is a party to the proceedings and there is no guardian ad litem.

(3) After the final hearing of proceedings to which this Part applies, the court shall deliver its judgment as soon as is practicable.

(4) When making an order or when refusing an application, the court shall state any findings of fact and the reasons for the court's decision.

(5) An order made in proceedings to which this Part applies shall be recorded, by the court or the proper officer, either in the appropriate form in Appendix 1 to these rules or, where there is no such form, in writing.

(6) Subject to paragraph (7), a copy of an order made in accordance with paragraph (5) shall, as soon as practicable after it has been made, be served by the proper officer on the parties to the proceedings in which it was made on any person with whom the child is living.

(7) Within 48 hours after the making ex parte of–
   (a) a prohibited steps order or specific issue order under section 8, or
   (b) an order under section 44, 48(4), 48(9) or 50,
the applicant shall serve a copy of the order in the appropriate form in Appendix 1 to these Rules on–
      (i)   each party,
      (ii) any person who has actual care of the child or who had such care immediately prior to the making of the order, and
      (iii) in the case of an order referred to in sub-paragraph (b), the local authority in whose area the child lives or is found.

(8) At a hearing of, or directions appointment in, an application

which takes place outside the hours during which the court office is normally open, the court or the proper officer shall take a note of the substance of the proceedings.

Appeals

4.22—(1) Where an appeal lies-
- (a) to the High Court under section 94, or
- (b) from any decision of a district judge to the judge of the court in which the decision was made,

it shall be made in accordance with the following provisions; and references to 'the court below' are references to the court from which, or person from whom, the appeal lies.

(2) The appellant shall file and serve on the parties to the proceedings in the court below, and on any guardian ad litem,
- (a) notice of the appeal in writing, setting out the grounds upon which he relies;
- (b) a certified copy of the summons or application and of the order appealed against, and of any order staying its execution;
- (c) a copy of any notes of the evidence;
- (d) a copy of any reasons given for the decision.

(3) The notice of appeal shall be filed and served in accordance with paragraph (2)(a)-
- (a) within 14 days after the determination against which the appeal is brought, or
- (b) in the case of an appeal against an order under section 38(1), within 7 days after the making of the order, or
- (c) with the leave of the court to which, or judge to whom, the appeal is to be brought, within such other time as that court or judge may direct.

(4) The documents mentioned in paragraph (2)(b) to (d) shall, subject to any direction of the court to which, or judge to whom, the appeal is to be brought, be filed and served as soon as practicable after the filing and service of the notice of appeal under paragraph (2)(a).

(5) Subject to paragraph (6), a respondent who wishes-
- (a) to contend on the appeal that the decision of the court below should be varied, either in any event or in the event of the appeal being allowed in whole or in part, or
- (b) to contend that the decision of the court below should be affirmed on grounds other than those relied upon by that court, or
- (c) to contend by way of cross-appeal that the decision of the court below was wrong in whole or in part,

shall, within 14 days of receipt of notice of the appeal, file and serve on all other parties to the appeal a notice in writing, setting out the grounds upon which he relies.

(6) No notice under paragraph (5) may be filed or served in an appeal against an order under section 38.

(7) In the case of an appeal mentioned in paragraph (1)(a), an application to–
  (a) withdraw the appeal,
  (b) have the appeal dismissed with the consent of all the parties, or
  (c) amend the grounds of appeal,
may be heard by a district judge.

(8) An appeal of the kind mentioned in paragraph (1)(a) shall, unless the President otherwise directs, be heard and determined by a single judge.

Confidentiality of documents
  4.23—(1) Notwithstanding any rule of court to the contrary, no document, other than a record of an order, held by the court and relating to proceedings to which this Part applies shall be disclosed, other than to–
  (a) a party,
  (b) the legal representative of a party,
  (c) the guardian ad litem,
  (d) the Legal Aid Board, or
  (e) a welfare officer,
without leave of the judge or district judge.

(2) Nothing in this rule shall prevent the notification by the court or the proper officer of a direction under section 37(1) to the authority concerned.

Notification of consent
  4.24 Consent for the purposes of–
  (a) section 16(3),
  (b) section 33(7), or
  (c) paragraph 19(3)(c) or (d) of Schedule 2,
shall be given either–
      (i) orally in court, or
      (ii) in writing to the court signed by the person giving his consent.

Secure accommodation – evidence
  4.25 In proceedings under section 25, the court shall, if practicable, arrange for copies of all written reports before it to be made available before the hearing to–
  (a) the applicant;
  (b) the parent or guardian of the child;
  (c) any legal representative of the child;
  (d) the guardian ad litem; and
  (e) the child, unless the court otherwise directs;
and copies of such reports may, if the court considers it desirable, be shown to any person who is entitled to notice of the proceedings in accordance with these rules.

254

Investigation under section 37

4.26—(1) This rule applies where a direction is given to an appropriate authority by the High Court or a county court under section 37(1).

(2) On giving a direction the court shall adjourn the proceedings and the court or the proper officer shall record the direction in writing.

(3) A copy of the direction recorded under paragraph (2) shall, as soon as practicable after the direction is given, be served by the proper officer on the parties to the proceedings in which the direction is given and, where the appropriate authority is not a party, on that authority.

(4) When serving the copy of the direction on the appropriate authority the proper officer shall also serve copies of such of the documentary evidence which has been, or is to be, adduced in the proceedings as the court may direct.

(5) Where a local authority informs the court of any of the matters set out in section 37(3)(a) to (c) it shall do so in writing.

Direction to local education authority to apply for education supervision order

4.27—(1) For the purposes of section 40(3) and (4) of the Education Act 1944(**a**) a direction by the High Court or a county court to a local education authority to apply for an education supervision order shall be given in writing.

(2) Where following such a direction, a local education authority informs the court that they have decided not to apply for an education supervision order, they shall do so in writing.

Transitional provision

4.28 Nothing in any provision of this Part of these rules shall affect any proceedings which are pending (within the meaning of paragraph 1 of Schedule 14 to the Act of 1989) immediately before these rules come into force.

PART V

* * * * *

Orders for use of secure accommodation

5.5 No order shall be made with the effect of placing or keeping a minor in secure accommodation, within the meaning of section 25(1) of the Act of 1989 unless—
  (a) the minor has been made a party to the summons, and
  (b) the minor is being represented either—
      (i) where the minor wishes to instruct a solicitor on his own and is capable of doing so, by such a solicitor, or
      (ii) in any other circumstances, by a guardian ad litem, for

(**a**) 1944 c 31 (7 & Geo 6); relevant amendments are made by paragraphs 8 to 10 of Schedule 13 to the Children Act 1989.

which purpose rule 4.10 shall apply as it applies to specified proceedings. [1991]

Notice to provider of refuge

5.6 Where a child is staying in a refuge which is certified under section 51(1) or 51(2) of the Act of 1989, the person who is providing that refuge shall be given notice of any application under this Part of these rules in respect of that child. [1991]

* * * * *

PART VII
ENFORCEMENT OF ORDERS
Enforcement of order for payment of money, etc

7.1—(1) Before any process is issued for the enforcement of an order made in family proceedings for the payment of money to any person, an affidavit shall be filed verifying the amount due under the order and showing how that amount is arrived at.

In a case to which CCR Order 25 rule 11 (which deals with the enforcement of a High Court judgment in the county court) applies, the information required to be given in an affidavit under this paragraph may be given in the affidavit filed pursuant to that rule.

(2) Except with the leave of the district judge, no writ of fieri facias or warrant of execution shall be issued to enforce payment of any sum due under an order for ancillary relief or an order made under the provisions of section 27 of the Act of 1973(a) where an application for a variation order is pending.

(3) Where a warrant of execution has been issued to enforce an order made in family proceedings pending in the principal registry which are treated as pending in a divorce county court, the goods and chattels against which the warrant has been issued shall, wherever they are situate, be treated for the purposes of section 103 of the County Courts Act 1984(b) as being out of the jurisdiction of the principal registry.

(4) The Attachment of Earnings Act 1971(c) and CCR Order 27 (which deals with attachment of earnings) shall apply to the enforcement of an order made in family proceedings in the principal registry which are treated as pending in a divorce county court as if the order were an order made by such a court.

(5) Where an application under CCR Order 25, rule 3 (which deals

(a) Section 27 was amended by the Domicile and Matrimonial Proceedings Act 1973 (c 45), section 6(1), the Domestic Proceedings and Magistrates' Courts Act 1978 (c 22), sections 63 and 89(2) and Schedule 3, the Matrimonial and Family Proceedings Act 1984 (c 42) sections 41 and 46(1) and Schedule 1. paragraph 12 and the Family Law Reform Act 1987 (c 42). Schedule 2, paragraph 52.
(b) 1984 c 28.
(c) 1971 c 32.

with the oral examination of a judgment debtor) relates to an order made by a divorce county court-

  (a) the application shall be made to such divorce county court as in the opinion of the applicant is nearest to the place where the debtor resides or carries on business, and

  (b) there shall be filed with the application the affidavit required by paragraph (1) of this rule and, except where the application is made to the court in which the order sought to be enforced was made, a copy of the order shall be exhibited to the affidavit:

and accordingly paragraph (2) of the said rule 3 shall not apply.

Committal and injunction

7.2—(1) Subject to RSC Order 52, rule 6 (which, except in certain cases, requires an application for an order of committal to be heard in open court) an application for an order of committal in family proceedings pending in the High Court shall be made by summons.

(2) Where no judge is conveniently available to hear the application, then, without prejudice to CCR Order 29, rule 3(2) (which in certain circumstances gives jurisdiction to a district judge) an application for-

  (a) the discharge of any person committed, or

  (b) the discharge by consent of an injunction granted by a judge,

may be made to the district judge who may, if satisfied of the urgency of the matter and that it is expedient to do so, make any order on the application which a judge could have made.

(3) Where an order or warrant for the committal of any person to prison has been made or issued in family proceedings pending in the principal registry which are treated as pending in a divorce county court, that person shall, wherever he may be, be treated for the purposes of section 122 of the County Courts Act 1984 as being out of the jurisdiction of the principal registry; but if the committal is for failure to comply with the terms of an injunction, the order or warrant may, if a judge so directs, be executed by the tipstaff within any county court district.

(4) For the purposes of section 118 of the County Courts Act 1984 in its application to the hearing of family proceedings at the Royal Courts of Justice, the tipstaff shall be deemed to be an officer of the court.

* * * * *

PART IX

* * * * *

Separate representation of children

9.5—(1) Without prejudice to rule 2.57, if in any family proceedings it appears to the court that any child ought to be separately represented, the court may appoint-

  (a) the Official Solicitor, or

  (b) some other proper person,

(provided, in either case, that he consents) to be the guardian ad litem of the child, with authority to take part in the proceedings on the child's behalf.

(2) An order under paragraph (1) may be made by the court of its own motion or on the application of a party to the proceedings or of the proposed guardian ad litem.

(3) The court may at any time direct that an application be made by a party for an order under paragraph (1) and may stay the proceedings until the application has been made.

(4) Unless otherwise directed, on making an application for an order under paragraph (1) the applicant shall-
  (a)   unless he is the proposed guardian ad litem, file a written consent by the proposed guardian to act as such;
  (b)   unless the proposed guardian ad litem is the Official Solicitor, file a certificate by a solicitor that the proposed guardian has no interest in the proceedings adverse to that of the child and that he is a proper person to be a guardian.

(5) Unless otherwise directed, a person appointed under this rule or rule 2.57 to be the guardian ad litem of a child in any family proceedings shall be treated as a party for the purpose of any provision of these rules requiring a document to be served on or notice to be given to a party to the proceedings.

*   *   *   *   *

PART X
*   *   *   *   *

Disclosure of addresses

10.21—(1) Nothing in these rules shall be construed as requiring any party to reveal the address of their private residence (or that of any child) save by order of the court.

(2) Where a party declines to reveal an address in reliance upon paragraph (1) above, he shall give notice of that address to the court in Form CHA59 and that address shall not be revealed to any person save by order of the court.

*   *   *   *   *

APPENDIX 3
NOTICES AND RESPONDENTS

(i) Provision under which proceedings brought	(ii) Minimum number of days prior to hearing or directions appointment for service under rule 4.4(1)(b)	(iii) Persons to whom notice is to be given	(iv) Respondents
All applications	See separate entries below	Subject to separate entries below– local authority providing accommodation for the child; persons who are caring for the child at the time when the proceedings are commenced; in the case of proceedings brought in respect of a child who is alleged to be staying in a refuge which is certificated under section 51(1) or (2), the person who is providing the refuge.	Subject to separate entries below– every person whom the applicant believes to have parental responsibility for the child: where the child is the subject of a care order, every person whom the applicant believes to have had parental responsibility immediately prior to the making of the care order; in the case of an application to extend, vary or discharge an order, the parties to the proceedings leading to the order which it is sought to have extended, varied or discharged; in the case of specified, proceedings, the child.

Appendix 2

(i) Provision under which proceedings brought	(ii) Minimum number of days prior to hearing or directions appointment for service under rule 4.4(1)(b)	(iii) Persons to whom notice is to be given	(iv) Respondents
Section 8.	21 days.	As for 'all applications' above, and: in the case of an application for a section 8 order, every person whom the applicant believes- (i) to be named in a court order with respect to the same child, which has not ceased to have effect. (ii) to be a party to pending proeeedings in respect of the same child, or (iii) to be a person with whom the child has lived for at least 3 years prior to the application, unless, in a case to which (i) or (ii) applies, the applicant believes that the court order or pending proceedings are not relevant to the application.	As for 'all applications' above.

(i) Provision under which proceedings brought	(ii) Minimum number of days prior to hearing or directions appointment for service under rule 4.4(1)(b)	(iii) Persons to whom notice is to be given	(iv) Respondents
Section 4(1)(a), 4(3), 5(1), 6(7), 13(1), 16(6), 33(7), Schedule 1, paragraph 19(1) of Schedule 2, or paragraph 11(3) or 16(5) of Schedule 14.	14 days.	As for 'all applications above, and: in the case of an application under paragraph 19(1) of Schedule 2, the parties to the proceedings leading to the care order; in the case of an application under section 5(1), the father of the child if he does not have parental responsibility.	'As for all applications above, and: in the case of proceedings under Schedule 1, those persons whom the applicant believes to be interested in or affected by the proceedings; in the case of an application under paragraph 11(3)(b) or 16(5) of Schedule 14, any person, other than the child, named in the order or directions which it is sought to discharge or vary.
Section 36(1), 39(1), 39(2), 39(3), 39(4), 43(1), or paragraph 6(3), 15(2) or 17(1) of Schedule 3.	7 days.	As for 'all applications' above, and: in the case of an application for an order under section 43(1)– (i) every person whom the applicant believes to be a parent of the child.	As for 'all applications' above and: in the case of an application under section 39(2) or (3), the supervisor; in the case of proceedings under paragraph 17(1) of Schedule 3, the local education authority concerned;

Appendix 2

(i) Provision under which proceedings brought	(ii) Minimum number of days prior to hearing or directions appointment for service under rule 4.4(1)(b)	(iii) Persons to whom notice is to be given	(iv) Respondents
		(ii) every person whom the applicant believes to be caring for the child, (iii) every person in whose favour a contact order is in force with respect to the child, and (iv) every person who is allowed to have contact with the child by virtue of an order under section 34.	in the case of proceedings under section 36 or paragraph 15(2) or 17(1) of Schedule 3, the child.

Section 31, 34(2), 34(3), 34(4), 34(9) or 38(8)(b).	3 days.	As for 'all applications' above, and:
		
		in the case of an application under section 31–
		
		    (i) every person whom the applicant believes to be a party to pending relevant proceedings in respect of the same child, and
		
		    (ii) every person whom the applicant believes to be a parant without parental responsibility for the child.
			As for 'all applications' above, and:
			
			in the case of an application under section 34, the person whose contact with the child is the subject of the application.

(i) Provision under which proceedings brought	(ii) Minimum number of days prior to hearing or directions appointment for service under rule 4.4(1)(b)	(iii) Persons to whom notice is to be given	(iv) Respondents
Section 43(12).	2 days.	Those of the persons referred to in section 43(11)(a) to (e) who were not party to the application for the order which it is sought to have varied or discharged.	As for 'all applications' above.
Section 25, 44(1), 44(9)(b), 45(4), 45(8), 46(7), 48(9), 50(1) or 102(1). [1991]	1 day.	Excpet for applications under section 102(1), as for 'all applications' above, and: in the case of an application under section 44(1), every person whom the applicant believes to be a parent of the child; in the case of an application under section 44(9)(b)– (i) the local authority in whose area the child is living, and (ii) any person whom the applicant believes to be affected by the direction which it is sought to have varied.	As for 'all applications' above, and: in the case of an application under section 44(9)(b) (i) the parties to the application for the order in respect of which it is sought to vary the directions; (ii) any person who was caring for the child prior to the making of the order, and (iii) any person whose contact with the child is affected by the direction which it is sought to have vaned;

Appendix 2

(i) Provision under which proceedings brought	(ii) Minimum number of days prior to hearing or directions appointment for service under rule 4.4(1)(b)	(iii) Persons to whom notice is to be given	(iv) Respondents
		in the case of an application under section 102(1), the person referred to in section 102(1) and any person preventing or likely to prevent such a person from exercising powers under enactments mentioned in subsection (b) of that section. [1991]	in the case of an application under section 50, the person whom the applicant alleges to have effected or to have been or to be responsible for the taking or keeping of the child.

APPENDIX 3

The Children (Allocation of Proceedings) Order 1991
(SI 1991 No 1677)

The Lord Chancellor, in exercise of the powers conferred on him by section 92(9) and (10) of, and Part I of Schedule 11 to, the Children Act 1989(a), and of all other powers enabling him in that behalf, hereby makes the following Order:

Citation, commencement and interpretation

1.—(1) This Order may be cited as the Children (Allocation of Proceedings) Order 1991 and shall come into force on 14th October 1991.

(2) In this Order, unless the context otherwise requires–
'child'–
    (a)   means, subject to sub-paragraph (b), a person under the age of 18 with respect to whom proceedings are brought, and
    (b)   where the proceedings are under Schedule 1, also includes a person who has reached the age of 18;
'London commission area' has the meaning assigned to it by section 2(1) of the Justices of the Peace Act 1979(b);
'petty sessions area' has the meaning assigned to it by section 4 of the Justices of the Peace Act 1979(c); and
'the Act' means the Children Act 1989, and a section, Part or Schedule referred to by number alone means the section, Part or Schedule so numbered in that Act.

Classes of county court

2. For the purposes of this Order there shall be the following classes of county court:
    (a)   divorce county courts, being those courts designated for the time

(a) 1989 c 41.
(b) 1979 c 55.
(c) Section 4 was amended by the Local Government Act 1985 (c 51), section 12.

being as divorce county courts by an order under section 33 of the Matrimonial and Family Proceedings Act 1984(a);
  (b) family hearing centres, being those courts set out in Schedule 1 to this Order;
  (c) care centres, being those courts set out in column (ii) of Schedule 2 to this Order.

COMMENCEMENT OF PROCEEDINGS

Proceedings to be commenced in magistrates' court

3.—(1) Subject to paragraphs (2) and (3) and to article 4, proceedings under any of the following provisions shall be commenced in a magistrates' court:
  (a) section 25 (use of accommodation for restricting liberty);
  (b) section 31 (care and supervision orders);
  (c) section 33(7) (leave to change name of or remove from United Kingdom child in care);
  (d) section 34 (parental contact);
  (e) section 36 (education supervision orders);
  (f) section 43 (child assessment orders);
  (g) section 44 (emergency protection orders);
  (h) section 45 (duration of emergency protection orders etc.);
  (i) section 46(7) (application for emergency protection order by police officer);
  (j) section 48 (powers to assist discovery of children etc.);
  (k) section 50 (recovery orders);
  (l) section 75 (protection of children in an emergency);
  (m) section 77(6) (appeal against steps taken under section 77(1));
  (n) section 102 (powers of constable to assist etc.);
  (o) paragraph 19 of Schedule 2 (approval of arrangements to assist child to live abroad);
  (p) paragraph 23 of Schedule 2 (contribution orders);
  (q) paragraph 8 of Schedule 8 (certain appeals);
  (r) section 21 of the Adoption Act 1976(b).

(2) Notwithstanding paragraph (1) and subject to paragraph (3), proceedings of a kind set out in sub-paragraph (b), (e), (f), (g), (i) or (j) of paragraph (1), and which arise out of an investigation directed,

(a) 1984 c 42.
(b) 1976 c 36; a new section 21 was substituted by paragraph 9 of Schedule 10 to the Children Act 1989 (c 41).

by the High Court or a county court, under section 37(1), shall be commenced-

(a) in the court which directs the investigation, where that court is the High Court or a care centre, or

(b) in such care centre as the court which directs the investigation may order.

(3) Notwithstanding paragraphs (1) and (2), proceedings of a kind set out in sub-paragraph (a) to (k), (n) or (o) of paragraph (1) shall be made to a court in which are pending other proceedings, in respect of the same child, which are also of a kind set out in those sub-paragraphs.

Application to extend, vary or discharge order

4.—(1) Subject to paragraphs (2) and (3), proceedings under the Act, or under the Adoption Act 1976-

(a) to extend, vary or discharge an order, or

(b) the determination of which may have the effect of varying or discharging an order,

shall be made to the court which made the order.

(2) Notwithstanding paragraph (1), an application for an order under section 8 which would have the effect of varying or discharging an order made, by a county court, in accordance with section 10(1)(b) shall be made to a divorce county court.

(3) Notwithstanding paragraph (1), an application to extend, vary or discharge an order made, by a county court, under section 38, or for an order which would have the effect of extending, varying or discharging such an order, shall be made to a care centre.

(4) A court may transfer proceedings made in accordance with paragraph (1) to any other court in accordance with the provisions of articles 5 to 13.

TRANSFER OF PROCEEDINGS

Disapplication of enactments about transfer

5. Sections 38 and 39 of the Matrimonial and Family Proceedings Act 1984(a) shall not apply to proceedings under the Act or under the Adoption Act 1976.

Transfer from one magistrates' court to another

6. A magistrates' court (the 'transferring court') shall transfer proceedings under the Act or under the Adoption Act 1976 to another magistrates' court (the 'receiving court') where-

(a) 1984 c 42.

    (a) having regard to the principle set out in section 1(2), the transferring court considers that the transfer is in the interests of the child–

        (i) because it is likely significantly to accelerate the determination of the proceedings,

      (ii) because it would be appropriate for those proceedings to be heard together with other family proceedings which are pending in the receiving court, or

     (iii) for some other reason, and

    (b) the receiving court, by its justices' clerk (as defined by rule 1(2) of the Family Proceedings Courts (Children Act 1989) Rules 1991(**a**)), consents to the transfer.

Transfer from magistrates' court to county court by magistrates' court

7.—(1) Subject to paragraphs (2), (3) and (4) and to articles 15 to 18, a magistrates' court may, upon application by a party or of its own motion, transfer to a county court proceedings of any of the kinds mentioned in article 3(1) where it considers it in the interests of the child to do so having regard, first, to the principle set out in section 1(2) and, secondly, to the following questions:

    (a) whether the proceedings are exceptionally grave, important or complex, in particular–

        (i) because of complicated or conflicting evidence about the risks involved to the child's physical or moral well-being or about other matters relating to the welfare of the child;

      (ii) because of the number of parties;

     (iii) because of a conflict with the law of another jurisdiction;

     (iv) because of some novel and difficult point of law; or

     (v) because of some question of general public interest;

    (b) whether it would be appropriate for those proceedings to be heard together with other family proceedings which are pending in another court; and

    (c) whether transfer is likely significantly to accelerate the determination of the proceedings, where–

        (i) no other method of doing so, including transfer to another magistrates' court, is appropriate, and

      (ii) delay would seriously prejudice the interests of the child who is the subject of the proceedings.

(2) Notwithstanding paragraph (1), proceedings of the kind mentioned in sub-paragraph (g) to (j), (l), (m), (p) or (q) of article 3(1) shall not be transferred from a magistrates' court.

(3) Notwithstanding paragraph (1), proceedings of the kind mentioned in sub-paragraph (a) or (n) of article 3(1) shall only be transferred from a magistrates' court to a county court in order to be heard together

(**a**) SI 1991/1395.

with other family proceedings which arise out of the same circumstances as gave rise to the proceedings to be transferred and which are pending in another court.

(4) Notwithstanding paragraphs (1) and (3), proceedings of the kind mentioned in article 3(1)(a) shall not be transferred from a magistrates' court which is not a family proceedings court within the meaning of section 92(1).

8. Subject to articles 15 to 18, a magistrates' court may transfer to a county court proceedings under the Act or under the Adoption Act 1976, being proceedings to which article 7 does not apply, where, having regard to the principle set out in section 1(2), it considers that in the interests of the child the proceedings can be dealt with more appropriately in that county court.

Transfer from magistrates' court following refusal of magistrates' court to transfer

9.—(1) Where a magistrates' court refuses to transfer proceedings under article 7, a party to those proceedings may apply to the care centre listed in column (ii) of Schedule 2 to this Order against the entry in column (i) for the petty sessions area or London commission area in which the magistrates' court is situated for an order under paragraph (2).

(2) Upon hearing an application under paragraph (1) the court may transfer the proceedings to itself where, having regard to the principle set out in section 1(2) and the questions set out in article 7(1)(a) to (c), it considers it in the interests of the child to do so.

(3) Upon hearing an application under paragraph (1) the court may transfer the proceedings to the High Court where, having regard to the principle set out in section 1(2), it considers-
  (a) that the proceedings are appropriate for determination in the High Court, and
  (b) that such determination would be in the interests of the child.

Transfer from one county court to another

10. Subject to articles 15 to 17, a county court (the 'transferring court') shall transfer proceedings under the Act or under the Adoption Act 1976 to another county court (the 'receiving court') where-
  (a) the transferring court, having regard to the principle set out in section 1(2), considers the transfer to be in the interests of the child, and
  (b) the receiving court is-
      (i) of the same class or classes, within the meaning of article 2, as the transferring court, or

269

Appendix 3

(ii) to be presided over by a judge or district judge who is specified by directions under section 9 of the Courts and Legal Services Act 1990(a) for the same purposes as the judge or district judge presiding over the transferring court.

Transfer from county court to magistrates' court by county court

11. A county court may transfer to a magistrates' court before trial proceedings which were transferred under article 7(1) where the county court, having regard to the principle set out in section 1(2) and the interests of the child, considers that the criterion cited by the magistrates' court as the reason for transfer–
  (a) in the case of the criterion in article 7(1)(a), does not apply,
  (b) in the case of the criterion in article 7(1)(b), no longer applies, because the proceedings with which the transferred proceedings were to be heard have been determined,
  (c) in the case of the criterion in article 7(1)(c), no longer applies.

Transfer from county court to High Court by county court

12. A county court may transfer proceedings under the Act or the Adoption Act 1976 to the High Court where, having regard to the principle set out in section 1(2), it considers–
  (a) that the proceedings are appropriate for determination in the High Court, and
  (b) that such determination would be in the interests of the child.

Transfer from High Court to county court

13. Subject to articles 15, 16 and 18, the High Court may transfer to a county court proceedings under the Act or the Adoption Act 1976 where, having regard to the principle set out in section 1(2), it considers that the proceedings are appropriate for determination in such a court and that such determination would be in the interests of the child.

ALLOCATION OF PROCEEDINGS TO PARTICULAR COUNTY COURTS

Commencement

14. Subject to articles 18, 19 and 20 and to rule 2.40 of the Family Proceedings Rules 1991(b) (Application under Part I or II of the Children Act 1989 where matrimonial cause is pending), an application under the Act or under the Adoption Act 1976 which is to be commenced in a county court shall be commenced in a divorce county court.

(a) 1990 c 41.
(b) SI 1991/1247.

270

Proceedings under Part I or II or Schedule 1

15.—(1) Subject to paragraph (3), where an application under Part I or II or Schedule 1 is to be transferred from a magistrates' court to a county court, it shall be transferred to a divorce county court.

(2) Subject to paragraph (3), where an application under Part I or II or Schedule 1, other than an application for an order under section 8, is to be transferred from the High Court to a county court, it shall be transferred to a divorce county court.

(3) Where an application under Part I or II or Schedule 1, other than an application for an order under section 8, is to be transferred to a county court for the purpose of consolidation with other proceedings, it shall be transferred to the court in which those other proceedings are pending.

Orders under section 8 of the Children Act 1989

16.—(1) An application for an order under section 8 in a divorce county court, which is not also a family hearing centre, shall, if the court is notified that the application will be opposed, be transferred for trial to a family hearing centre.

(2) Subject to paragraph (3), where an application for an order under section 8 is to be transferred from the High Court to a county court it shall be transferred to a family hearing centre.

(3) Where an application for an order under section 8 is to be transferred to a county court for the purpose of consolidation with other proceedings, it may be transferred to the court in which those other proceedings are pending whether or not it is a family hearing centre; but paragraph (1) shall apply to the application following the transfer.

Application for adoption or freeing for adoption

17.—(1) Subject to article 22, proceedings in a divorce county court, which is not also a family hearing centre, under section 12 or 18 of the Adoption Act 1976(a) shall, if the court is notified that the proceedings will be opposed, be transferred for trial to a family hearing centre.

(2) Where proceedings under the Adoption Act 1976 are to be transferred from a magistrates' court to a county court, they shall be transferred to a divorce county court.

Applications under Part III, IV or V

18.—(1) An application under Part III, IV or V, if it is to be commenced in a county court, shall be commenced in a care centre.

(a) 1976 c 36.

(2) An application under Part III, IV or V which is to be transferred from the High Court to a county court shall be transferred to a care centre.

(3) An application under Part III, IV or V which is to be transferred from a magistrates' court to a county court shall be transferred to the care centre listed against the entry in column (i) of Schedule 2 to this Order for the petty sessions area or London commission area in which the relevant magistrates' court is situated.

Principal Registry of the Family Division

19. The principal registry of the Family Division of the High Court shall be treated, for the purposes of this Order, as if it were a divorce county court, a family hearing centre and a care centre listed against every entry in column (i) of Schedule 2 to this Order (in addition to the entries against which it is actually listed).

Lambeth and Woolwich County Courts

20. Notwithstanding articles 14,16 and 17, an application for an order under section 8 or under the Adoption Act 1976 may be commenced and tried in Lambeth County Court or in Woolwich County Court.

MISCELLANEOUS

Contravention of provision of this Order

21. Where proceedings are commenced or transferred in contravention of a provision of this Order, the contravention shall not have the effect of making the proceedings invalid; and no appeal shall lie against the determination of proceedings on the basis of such contravention alone.

Transitional provision – proceedings under Adoption Act 1976

22. Proceedings under the Adoption Act 1976 which are commenced in a county court prior to the coming into force of this Order may, notwithstanding article 17(1), remain in that court for trial.

20th June 1991 *Mackay of Clashfern, C*

SCHEDULE I
Article 2
FAMILY HEARING CENTRES

Midland and Oxford Circuit
Birmingham County Court
Coventry County Court
Derby County Court
Leicester County Court
Lincoln County Court
Mansfield County Court
Northampton County Court
Nottingham County Court
Oxford County Court
Peterborough County Court
Stafford County Court
Stoke-on-Trent County Court
Telford County Court
Walsall County Court
Wolverhampton County Court
Worcester County Court

Northern Circuit
Blackburn County Court
Bolton County Court
Carlisle County Court
Lancaster County Court
Liverpool County Court
Manchester County Court
Stockport County Court

North Eastern Circuit
Barnsley County Court
Bradford County Court
Darlington County Court
Dewsbury County Court
Doncaster County Court
Durham County Court
Halifax County Court
Harrogate County Court
Huddersfield County Court
Keighley County Court
Kingston-upon-Hull County Court
Leeds County Court
Newcastle-upon-Tyne County
    Court
Pontefract County Court
Rotherham County Court
Scarborough County Court

Sheffield County Court
Skipton County Court
Sunderland County Court
Teesside County Court
Wakefield County Court
York County Court

South Eastern Circuit
Brighton County Court
Bow County Court
Brentford County Court
Bromley County Court
Cambridge County Court
Canterbury County Court
Chelmsford County Court
Chichester County Court
Colchester and Clacton County
    Court
Croydon County Court
Edmonton County Court
Guildford County Court
Hitchin County Court
Ilford County Court
Ipswich County Court
Kingston-upon-Thames County
    Court
Luton County Court
Maidstone County Court
Medway County Court
Milton Keynes County Court
Norwich County Court
Reading County Court
Romford County Court
Slough County Court
Southend County Court
Wandsworth County Court
Watford County Court
Willesden County Court

Wales and Chester Circuit
Aberystwyth County Court
Caernarfon County Court
Cardiff County Court
Carmarthen County Court
Chester County Court

273

Appendix 3

Wales and Chester Circuit—cont
Crewe County Court
Haverfordwest County Court
Llangefni County Court
Macclesfeld County Court
Merthyr Tydfil County Court
Newport (Gwent) County Court
Rhyl County Court
Swansea County Court
Warrington County Court
Welshpool and Newtown County
   Court
Wrexham County Court

Western Circuit
Basingstoke County Court
Bournemouth County Court
Bristol County Court
Exeter County Court
Gloucester County Court
Plymouth County Court
Portsmouth County Court
Southampton County Court
Swindon County Court
Taunton County Court
Truro County Court

SCHEDULE 2   Article 2
CARE CENTRES

(i) Petty Sessions Areas	(ii) Care Centres
	Midland and Oxford Circuit
Abingdon	Oxford County Court
Aldridge and Brownhills	Wolverhampton County Court
Alfreton and Belper	Derby County Court
Ashby-De-La-Zouche	Leicester County Court
Atherstone and Coleshill	Coventry County Court
Barton-on-Humber	Lincoln County Court
Bewdley and Stourport	Worcester County Court
Bicester	Oxford County Court
Birmingham	Birmingham County Court
Boston	Lincoln County Court
Bourne and Stamford	Lincoln County Court
Bridgnorth	Telford County Court
Brigg	Lincoln County Court
Bromsgrove	Worcester County Court
Burton-upon-Trent	Stoke-on-Trent County Court
Caistor	Lincoln County Court
Cannock	Wolverhampton County Court
Cambridge	Peterborough County Court
Cheadle	Stoke-on-Trent County Court
Chesterfield	Derby County Court
City of Hereford	Worcester County Court
Congleton	Stoke-on-Trent County Court
Corby	Northampton County Court
Coventry	Coventry County Court
Crewe and Nantwich	Stoke-on-Trent County Court
Daventry	Northampton County Court
Derby and South Derbyshire	Derby County Court
Didcot and Wantage	Oxford County Court
Drayton	Telford County Court
Dudley	Wolverhampton County Court
East Retford	Nottingham County Court
East Oxfordshire	Oxford County Court
Eccleshall	Stoke-on-Trent County Court
Elloes	Lincoln County Court
Ely	Peterborough County Court
Epworth and Goole	Lincoln County Court
Gainsborough	Lincoln County Court
Glossop	Derby County Court
Grantham	Lincoln County Court

(i) Petty Sessions Areas	(ii) Care Centres
Grimsby and Cleethorpes	Lincoln County Court
Halesowen	Wolverhampton County Court
Henley	Oxford County Court
High Peak	Derby County Court
Huntingdon	Peterborough County Court
Ilkeston	Derby County Court
Kettering	Northampton County Court
Kidderminster	Worcester County Court
Leek	Stoke-on-Trent County Court
Leicester (City)	Leicester County Court
Leicester (County)	Leicester County Court
Lichfield	Stoke-on-Trent County Court
Lincoln District	Lincoln County Court
Loughborough	Leicester County Court
Louth	Lincoln County Court
Ludlow	Telford County Court
Lutterworth	Leicester County Court
Malvern Hills	Worcester County Court
Mansfield	Nottingham County Court
Market Bosworth	Leicester County Court
Market Harborough	Leicester County Court
Market Rasen	Lincoln County Court
Melton and Belvoir	Leicester County Court
Mid-Warwickshire	Coventry County Court
Mid-Worcestershire	Worcester County Court
Newark and Southwell	Nottingham County Court
Newcastle-under-Lyme	Stoke-on-Trent County Court
Newmarket	Peterborough County Court or Ipswich County Court
Northampton	Northampton County Court
North Herefordshire	Worcester County Court
North Oxfordshire and Chipping Norton	Oxford County Court
North Witchford	Peterborough County Court
Nottingham	Nottingham County Court
Nuneaton	Coventry County Court
Oswestry	Telford County Court
Oxford	Oxford County Court
Peterborough	Peterborough County Court
Pirehill North	Stoke-on-Trent County Court
Redditch	Worcester County Court
Rugby	Coventry County Court
Rugeley	Wolverhampton County Court
Rutland	Leicester County Court

(i) *Petty Sessions Areas*	*(ii)* *Care Centres*
Scunthorpe	Lincoln County Court
Seisdon	Wolverhampton County Court
Sleaford	Lincoln County Court
Shrewsbury	Telford County Court
Solihull	Birmingham County Court
South Herefordshire	Worcester County Court
South Warwickshire	Coventry County Court
Spilsby and Skegness	Lincoln County Court
Stoke-on-Trent	Stoke-on-Trent County Court
Stone	Stoke-on-Trent County Court
Stourbridge	Wolverhampton County Court
Sutton Coldfield	Birmingham County Court
Tamworth	Stoke-on-Trent County Court
Telford	Telford County Court
Toseland	Peterborough County Court
Towcester	Northampton County Court
Uttoxeter	Stoke-on-Trent County Court
Vale of Evesham	Worcester County Court
Warley	Wolverhampton County Court
Walsall	Wolverhampton County Court
Wellingborough	Northampton County Court
West Bromwich	Wolverhampton County Court
West Derbyshire	Derby County Court
Wisbech	Peterborough County Court
Witney	Oxford County Court
Wolds	Lincoln County Court
Wolverhampton	Wolverhampton County Court
Woodstock	Oxford County Court
Worcester City	Worcester County Court
Worksop	Nottingham County Court

Northern Circuit

Appleby	Carlisle County Court
Ashton-under-Lyne	Manchester County Court
Barrow with Bootle	Lancaster County Court
Blackburn	Blackburn County Court
Blackpool	Lancaster County Court
Bolton	Manchester County Court
Burnley	Blackburn County Court
Bury	Manchester County Court
Carlisle	Carlisle County Court
Chorley	Blackburn County Court
Darwen	Blackburn County Court

Appendix 3

(i) Petty Sessions Areas	(ii) Care Centres
Eccles	Manchester County Court
Fylde	Lancaster County Court
Hyndburn	Blackburn County Court
Kendal and Lonsdale	Lancaster County Court
Keswick	Carlisle County Court
Knowsley	Liverpool County Court
Lancaster	Lancaster County Court
Leigh	Manchester County Court
Liverpool	Liverpool County Court
Manchester	Manchester County Court
Middleton and Heywood	Manchester County Court
North Lonsdale	Lancaster County Court
North Sefton	Liverpool County Court
Oldham	Manchester County Court
Ormskirk	Liverpool County Court
Pendle	Blackburn County Court
Penrith and Alston	Carlisle County Court
Preston	Blackburn County Court
Ribble Valley	Blackburn County Court
Rochdale	Manchester County Court
Rossendale	Blackburn County Court
St Helens	Liverpool County Court
Salford	Manchester County Court
South Lakes	Lancaster County Court
South Ribble	Blackburn County Court
South Sefton	Liverpool County Court
South Tameside	Manchester County Court
Stockport	Manchester County Court
Trafford	Manchester County Court
West Allerdale	Carlisle County Court
Whitehaven	Carlisle County Court
Wigan	Liverpool County Court
Wigton	Carlisle County Court
Wirral	Liverpool County Court
Wyre	Lancaster County Court

North Eastern Circuit

Bainton Beacon	Kingston-upon-Hull County Court
Barnsley	Sheffield County Court
Batley and Dewsbury	Leeds County Court
Berwick-upon-Tweed	Newcastle-upon-Tyne County Court
Beverley	Kingston-upon-Hull County Court
Blyth Valley	Newcastle-upon-Tyne County Court

(i) Petty Sessions Areas	(ii) Care Centres
Bradford	Leeds County Court
Brighouse	Leeds County Court
Calder	Leeds County Court
Chester-le-Street	Newcastle-upon-Tyne County Court
Claro	York County Court
Coquetdale	Newcastle-upon-Tyne County Court
Darlington	Teesside County Court
Derwentside	Newcastle-upon-Tyne County Court
Dickering	Kingston-upon-Hull County Court
Doncaster	Sheffield County Court
Durham	Newcastle-upon-Tyne County Court
Easington	Sunderland County Court
Easingwold	York County Court
Gateshead	Newcastle-upon-Tyne County Court
Hartlepool	Teesside County Court
Holme Beacon	Kingston-upon-Hull County Court
Houghton-le-Spring	Sunderland County Court
Howdenshire	Kingston-upon-Hull County Court
Huddersfield	Leeds County Court
Keighley	Leeds County Court
Kingston-upon-Hull	Kingston-upon-Hull County Court
Langbaurgh East	Teesside County Court
Leeds	Leeds County Court
Middle Holderness	Kingston-upon-Hull County Court
Morley	Leeds County Court
Morpeth Ward	Newcastle-upon-Tyne County Court
Newcastle-upon-Tyne	Newcastle-upon-Tyne County Court
Northallerton	Teesside County Court
NortBuzardh Holderness	Kingston-upon-Hull County Court
North Tyneside	Newcastle-upon-Tyne County Court
Pontefract	Leeds County Court
Pudsey and Otley	Leeds County Court
Richmond	Teesside County Court
Ripon Liberty	York County Court
Rotherham	Sheffield County Court
Ryedale	York County Court
Scarborough	York County Court
Sedgefield	Newcastle-upon-Tyne County Court
Selby	York County Court
Sheffield	Sheffield County Court
Skyrack and Wetherby	Leeds County Court
South Holderness	Kingston-upon-Hull County Court
South Hunsley Beacon	Kingston-upon-Hull County Court
South Tyneside	Sunderland County Court

(i) *Petty Sessions Areas*	(ii) *Care Centres*
Staincliffe	Leeds County Court
Sunderland	Sunderland County Court
Teesdale and Wear Valley	Newcastle-upon-Tyne County Court
Teesside	Teesside County Court
Todmorden	Leeds County Court
Tynedale	Newcastle-upon-Tyne Court
Wakefield	Leeds County Court
Wansbeck	Newcastle-upon-Tyne County Court
Whitby Strand	Teesside County Court
Wilton Beacon	Kingston-upon-Hull County Court
York	York County Court
	South Eastern Circuit
Ampthill	Luton County Court
Arundel	Brighton County Court
Ashford and Tenterden	Medway County Court
Aylesbury	Milton Keynes County Court
Barnet	Principal Registry of the Family Division
Barking and Dagenham	Principal Registry of the Family Division
Basildon	Chelmsford County Court
Battle and Rye	Brighton County Court
Beccles	Ipswich County Court
Bedford	Luton County Court
Bexhill	Brighton County Court
Bexley	Principal Registry of the Family Division
Biggleswade	Luton County Court
Bishop's Stortford	Watford County Court
Brent	Principal Registry of the Family Division
Brentwood	Chelmsford County Court
Brighton	Brighton County Court
Bromley	Principal Registry of the Family Division
Buckingham	Milton Keynes County Court
Burnham	Milton Keynes County Court
Cambridge	Peterborough County Court
Canterbury and St Augustine	Medway County Court
Chelmsford	Chelmsford County Court
Chertsey	Guildford County Court

(i) Petty Sessions Areas	(ii) Care Centres
Cheshunt	Watford County Court
Chichester and District	Brighton County Court
Chiltern	Milton Keynes County Court
Colchester	Chelmsford County Court
Crawley	Brighton County Court
Cromer	Norwich County Court
Crowborough	Brighton County Court
Croydon	Principal Registry of the Family Division
Dacorum	Watford County Court
Dartford	Medway County Court
Diss	Norwich County Court
Dorking	Guildford County Court
Dover and East Kent	Medway County Court
Downham Market	Norwich County Court
Dunmow	Chelmsford County Court
Dunstable	Luton County Court
Ealing	Principal Registry of the Family Division
Eastbourne	Brighton County Court
East Dereham	Norwich County Court
Ely	Peterborough County Court
Enfield	Principal Registry of the Family Division
Epping and Ongar	Chelmsford County Court
Epsom	Guildford County Court
Esher and Walton	Guildford County Court
Fakenham	Norwich County Court
Farnham	Guildford County Court
Faversham and Sittingbourne	Medway County Court
Felixstowe	Ipswich County Court
Folkestone and Hythe	Medway County Court
The Forest	Reading County Court
Freshwell and South Hinckford	Chelmsford County Court
Godstone	Guildford County Court
Guildford	Guildford County Court
Gravesham	Medway County Court
Great Yarmouth	Norwich County Court
Hailsham	Brighton County Court
Halstead and Hedingham	Chelmsford County Court
Harlow	Chelmsford County Court

(i) Petty Sessions Areas	(ii) Care Centres
Harrow Gore	Principal Registry of the Family Division
Haringey	Principal Registry of the Family Division
Harwich	Chelmsford County Court
Hastings	Brighton County Court
Havering	Principal Registry of the Family Division
Hertford and Ware	Watford County Court
Hillingdon	Principal Registry of the Family Division
Horsham	Brighton County Court
Hounslow	Principal Registry of the Family Division
Hove	Brighton County Court
Hunstanton	Norwich County Court
Huntingdon	Peterborough County Court
Ipswich	Ipswich County Court
King's Lynn	Norwich County Court
Kingston-upon-Thames	Principal Registry of the Family Division
Leighton Buzzard	Luton County Court
Lewes	Brighton County Court
Lowestoft	Ipswich County Court
Luton	Luton County Court
Maidenhead	Reading County Court
Maidstone	Medway County Court
Maldon and Witham	Chelmsford County Court
Margate	Medway County Court
Medway	Medway County Court
Merton	Principal Registry of the Family Division
Mid-Hertfordshire	Watford County Court
Mid-Sussex	Brighton County Court
Mildenhall	Ipswich County Court
Milton Keynes	Milton Keynes County Court
Newham	Principal Registry of the Family Division
Newmarket	Ipswich County Court or Peterborough County Court
North Hertfordshire	Watford County Court
North Walsham	Norwich County Court
North Witchford	Peterborough County Court
Norwich	Norwich County Court

(i) *Petty Sessions Areas*	(ii) *Care Centres*
Peterborough	Peterborough County Court
Ramsgate	Medway County Court
Reading and Sonning	Reading County Court
Redbridge	Principal Registry of the Family Division
Reigate	Guildford County Court
Richmond-upon-Thames	Principal Registry of the Family Division
Risbridge	Ipswich County Court
Rochford and Southend-on-Sea	Chelmsford County Court
Saffron Walden	Chelmsford County Court
St Albans	Watford County Court
St Edmundsbury	Ipswich County Court
Saxmundham	Ipswich County Court
Sevenoaks	Medway County Court
Slough	Reading County Court
South Mimms	Watford County Court
Staines and Sunbury	Guildford County Court
Stevenage	Watford County Court
Steyning	Brighton County Court
Stow	Ipswich County Court
Sudbury and Cosford	Ipswich County Court
Sutton	Principal Registry of the Family Division
Swaffham	Norwich County Court
Tendring	Chelmsford County Court
Thetford	Norwich County Court
Thurrock	Chelmsford County Court
Tonbridge and Malling	Medway County Court
Toseland	Peterborough County Court
Tunbridge Wells and Cranbrook	Medway County Court
Waltham Forest	Principal Registry of the Family Division
Watford	Watford County Court
West Berkshire	Reading County Court
Windsor	Reading County Court
Wisbech	Peterborough County Court
Woking	Guildford County Court
Woodbridge	Ipswich County Court
Worthing	Brighton County Court
Wycombe	Milton Keynes County Court
Wymondham	Norwich County Court

Appendix 3

(i) *Petty Sessions Areas*	(ii) *Care Centres*
	Wales and Chester Circuit
Ardudwy-is-Artro	Caernarfon/Llangefni County Court
Ardudwy-uwch-Artro	Caernarfon/Llangefni County Court
Bangor	Caernarfon/Llangefni County Court
Bedwellty	Newport (Gwent) County Court
Berwyn	Rhyl County Court
Brecon	Merthyr Tydfil County Court
Caernarfon and Gwyrfai	Caernarfon/Llangefni County Court
Cardiff	Cardiff County Court
Carmarthen North	Swansea County Court
Carmarthen South	Swansea County Court
Ceredigion Ganol	Swansea County Court
Chester	Chester County Court
Cleddau	Swansea County Court
Colwyn	Rhyl County Court
Congleton	Stoke-on-Trent County Court
Conwy and Llandudno	Caernarfon/Llangefni County Court
Crewe and Nantwich	Stoke-on-Trent County Court
Cynon Valley	Merthyr Tydfil County Court
De Ceredigion	Swansea County Court
Dinefwr	Swansea County Court
Dyffryn Clwyd	Rhyl County Court
East Gwent	Newport (Gwent) County Court
Eifionydd	Caernarfon/Llangefni County Court
Ellesmere Port and Neston	Chester County Court
Estimaner	Caernarfon/Llangefni County Court
Flint	Rhyl County Court
Gogledd Ceredigion	Swansea County Court
Gogledd Preseli	Swansea County Court
Halton	Warrington County Court
Hawarden	Rhyl County Court
Llandrindod Wells	Merthyr Tydfil County Court
Llanelli	Swansea County Court
Lliw Valley	Swansea County Court
Lower Rhymney Valley	Cardiff County Court
Macclesfield	Warrington County Court
Machynlleth	Merthyr Tydfil County Court
Merthyr Tydfil	Merthyr Tydfil County Court
Miskin	Merthyr Tydfil County Court
Mold	Rhyl County Court
Nant Conwy	Caernarfon/Llangefni County Court
Neath	Swansea County Court
Newcastle and Ogmore	Cardiff County Court

Children (Allocation of Proceedings) Order 1991

(i) Petty Sessions Areas	(ii) Care Centres
Newport	Newport (Gwent) County Court
Newton	Merthyr Tydfil County Court
North Anglesey	Caernarfon/Llangefni County Court
Penllyn	Caernarfon/Llangefni County Court
Port Talbot	Swansea County Court
Pwllheli	Caernarfon/Llangefni County Court
Rhuddlan	Rhyl County Court
South Anglesey	Caernarfon/Llangefni County Court
South Pembrokeshire	Swansea County Court
Swansea	Swansea County Court
Talybont	Caernarfon/Llangefni County Court
Upper Rhymney Valley	Merthyr Tydfil County Court
Vale of Glamorgan	Cardiff County Court
Vale Royal	Chester County Court
Warrington	Warrington County Court
Welshpool	Merthyr Tydfil County Court
Wrexham Maelor	Rhyl County Court
Ystradgynlais	Swansea County Court

Western Circuit

Alton	Portsmouth County Court
Andover	Portsmouth County Court
Axminster	Taunton County Court
Barnstaple	Taunton County Court
Basingstoke	Portsmouth County Court
Bath and Wansdyke	Bristol County Court
Bideford and Great Torrington	Taunton County Court
Blandford and Sturminster	Bournemouth County Court
Bodmin	Truro County Court
Bournemouth	Bournemouth County Court
Bristol	Bristol County Court
Bridport	Bournemouth County Court
Cheltenham	Bristol County Court
Christchurch	Bournemouth County Court
Cirencester, Fairford and Tetbury	Bristol County Court
Cullompton	Taunton County Court
Dorchester	Bournemouth County Court
Droxford	Portsmouth County Court
Dunheved and Stratton	Truro County Court
Eastleigh	Portsmouth County Court
East Penwith	Truro County Court

(i) Petty Sessions Areas	(ii) Care Centres
East Powder	Truro County Court
Exeter	Plymouth County Court
Exmouth	Plymouth County Court
Falmouth and Kerrier	Truro County Court
Fareham	Portsmouth County Court
Forest of Dean	Bristol County Court
Gloucester	Bristol County Court
Gosport	Portsmouth County Court
Havant	Portsmouth County Court
Honiton	Taunton County Court
Hythe	Bournemouth County Court
Isle of Wight	Portsmouth County Court
Isles of Scilly	Truro County Court
Kennet	Bristol County Court
Kingsbridge	Plymouth County Court
Long Ashton	Bristol County Court
Lymington	Bournemouth County Court
Mendip	Taunton County Court
North Avon	Bristol County Court
North Cotswold	Bristol County Court
North Wiltshire	Bristol County Court
Odiham	Portsmouth County Court
Okehampton	Plymouth County Court
Penwith	Truro County Court
Petersfield	Portsmouth County Court
Plymouth	Plymouth County Court
Plympton	Plymouth County Court
Portsmouth	Portsmouth County Court
Poole	Bournemouth County Court
Pydar	Truro County Court
Ringwood	Bournemouth County Court
Romsey	Bournemouth County Court
Salisbury	Bournemouth County Court
Sedgemoor	Taunton County Court
Shaftesbury	Bournemouth County Court
Sherborne	Bournemouth County Court
Southampton	Portsmouth County Court
South East Cornwall	Plymouth County Court
South Gloucestershire	Bristol County Court
South Molton	Taunton County Court
South Somerset	Taunton County Court
Swindon	Bristol County Court
Taunton Deane	Taunton County Court
Tavistock	Plymouth County Court

(i) Petty Sessions Areas	*(ii)* Care Centres
Teignbridge	Plymouth County Court
Tewkesbury	Bristol County Court
Tiverton	Taunton County Court
Torbay	Plymouth County Court
Totnes	Plymouth County Court
Totton and New Forest	Bournemouth County Court
Truro and South Powder	Truro County Court
Wareham and Swanage	Bournemouth County Court
West Somerset	Taunton County Court
Weston-Super-Mare	Bristol County Court
West Wiltshire	Bristol County Court
Weymouth and Portland	Bournemouth County Court
Wimborne	Bournemouth County Court
Winchester	Portsmouth County Court
Wonford	Plymouth County Court

(i) London Commission Area	*(ii)* Care Centre
Inner London Area and City of London	Principal Registry of the Family Division

APPENDIX 4

Maps of locations of family hearing and care centres

The Children Act 1989
Locations of Combined
'Care' and Family
Hearing Centres

Newcastle upon Tyne
Carlisle   Sunderland
                  Middlesborough

Lancaster   York
              Leeds
Blackburn
        Manchester
Liverpool
Llangefni   Warrington   Sheffield
        Rhyl   Chester
Caernarfon   Stoke-on-Trent
                        Nottingham
                     Derby
Telford
Wolverhampton   Leicester
              Birmingham
              Coventry

Kingston-on-Hull

Lincoln

Norwich
Peterborough

Northampton
                              Ipswich
Worcester
        Milton Keynes
Swansea Merthyr   Luton   Chelmsford
         Tydfil
         Newport   Oxford   Watford
Cardiff   (PRFD)
        Bristol   Reading   Medway
                    Guildford
Taunton
                Bournemouth Portsmouth Brighton
        Plymouth
Truro

The Children Act 1989
Locations of Additional
Family Hearing
Centres

APPENDIX 5

The Parental Responsibility Agreement Regulations 1991
(SI 1991 No 1478)

Citation, commencement and interpretation

1.—(1) These Regulations may be cited as the Parental Responsibility Agreement Regulations 1991 and shall come into force on 14th October 1991.

(2) In these Regulations. 'the Principal Registry' means the principal registry of the Family Division of the High Court.

Form of parental responsibility agreement

2. A parental responsibility agreement shall be made in the form set out in the Schedule to these Regulations.

Recording of parental responsibility agreement

3.—(1) A parental responsibility agreement shall be recorded by the filing of the agreement, together with two copies, in the Principal Registry.

(2) Upon the filing of documents under paragraph (1), an officer of the Principal Registry shall seal the copies and send one to the child's mother and one to the child's father.

(3) The record of an agreement under paragraph (1) shall be made available, during office hours, for inspection by any person upon-
   (a) written request to an officer of the Principal Registry, and
   (b) payment of such fee as may be prescribed in an Order under section 41 of the Matrimonial and Family Proceedings Act 1984 (fees in family proceedings).

Parental Responsibility Agreement Regulations 1991

SCHEDULE — FORM OF AGREEMENT Regulation 2

Parental Responsibility Agreement

Section 4(1)(b)   The Children Act 1989   **Date Recorded**

▶ Please use black ink.

▶ The making of this agreement will seriously affect the legal position of both parents.
You should both seek legal advice before completing this form.

▶ If there is more than one child, you should fill in a separate form for each child.

———————————— THE —— CHILDREN —— ACT ————————

This is a parental responsibility agreement between

the child's mother

| Name |
| Address |

and

the child's father

| Name |
| Address |

We agree that the father of the child named below should have parental responsibility for [him] [her] in addition to the mother.

Name	Boy/Girl	Date of birth	Date of 18th birthday

Ending of the agreement

Once a parental responsibility agreement has been made it can only end

● by an order of the court made on application of any person who has parental responsibility for the child

● by an order of the court made on the application of the child with leave of the court

● when the child reaches the age of 18

Signed (mother) [   ] Date [   ]

Signature of witness [   ] Date [   ]

Signed (father) [   ] Date [   ]

Signature of witness [   ] Date [   ]

This agreement will not take effect until this form has been filed with the Principal Registry of the Family Division. Once this form has been completed and signed please take or send it and two copies to:

> **The Principal Registry of the Family Division**
> **Somerset House**
> **Strand**
> **London WC2R 1LP**

———————————— THE —— CHILDREN —— ACT ————————

Index

Index